AFTER THE DEATH OF A CHILD

THE FREE PRESS

New York   London   Toronto   Sydney   Tokyo   Singapore

AFTER THE DEATH OF A CHILD

Living with Loss Through the Years

ANN K. FINKBEINER

THE FREE PRESS
A Division of Simon & Schuster Inc.
1230 Avenue of the Americas
New York, NY 10020

THE FREE PRESS and colophon are trademarks
of Simon & Schuster Inc.

Designed by Carla Bolte

Manufactured in the United States of America
10 9 8 7 6 5 4 3 2 1

Library of Congress Cataloging-in-Publication Data

Finkbeiner, Ann K.
    After the death of a child : living with loss through the years / Ann K. Finkbeiner.
        p.   cm.
    ISBN 0-684-82965-7
    1. Bereavement—Psychological aspects. 2. Grief. 3. Teenagers—
Death—Psychological aspects. 4. Children—Death—Psychological
aspects. 5. Loss (Psychology)   I. Title.
    BF575.G7F55 1996
    155.9'37'085—dc20   96-1358
                                                                      CIP

I want to thank all the parents kind enough to talk to me,
some of whom I could not include in the book.

I want to thank Renee Dudnikov.

I want to thank my husband, Cal Walker.

This book is for T.C. Colley.

CONTENTS

INTRODUCTION

The pain of grief is just as much a part of life as the joy of love;
it is perhaps the price we pay for love.

—Colin Murray Parkes, *Bereavement*

I have a mental picture of myself in my twenties, standing on a hillside talking to a neighbor, with my four-year-old son wandering somewhere behind me. My son was skinny and had yellow hair I didn't cut often enough and glasses that slid down his nose. He had a bad attitude: he seemed to think his character was his own business and none of mine. I thought he was some sort of appendage, but more loosely attached, like a balloon tethered to my ankle. Anywhere I tried to walk, he was so underfoot I fell over him.

Anyway, that day the neighbor was telling me about mutual friends whose child just died. I tried to understand this. What happens when someone's child dies? I had thought about this, of course; all parents do. But I always hit some sort of wall. I was so attached to my son. What could people do when someone so attached to them dies? The neighbor was vague: "They'll never get over it." What does that mean, never get over it? This mental exercise was painful and I gave it up. I remember saying, "I'll bet for those people, everything will be entirely different."

Fourteen years later, my son died. His name was T.C. (for Thomas Carl) Colley and he was eighteen years old, a freshman at the Rhode Island School of Design, a superb art school that unaccountably admitted him with mediocre high school grades, a small portfolio, and the attitude he'd always had. At RISD, T.C. hit full flower in four months. "I bet you don't know what icongraphy is," he told me over the phone. He was not going to be a photojournalist, he said; he was going to be an *artistic* photographer. A few weeks later in another phone call, he said he'd met a girl named Janie from Charleston, South Carolina, and they stayed up all night talking and since then, he said, "we haven't been apart for more than three hours." After the Christmas holidays, he wanted to get right back to school and Janie. So on January 4, 1987, I took him to the Baltimore train station, kissed him good-bye, and told him I was proud of him. "I know," he said. "I am too." Twenty minutes later, a freight train hit the train on which he was a passenger. He was one of sixteen who died, many of the others also students going back to school.

About four years later, I noticed I was better. The pain was mostly controllable, acting normal was only intermittently difficult, and I was increasingly interested in my job, other people, and in life in general. I felt younger, lighter, and smarter. I wondered if this was recovery, though I had recovered nothing except this spark of interest and a sense of equanimity. Anything I would have wanted to recover was gone. I was clear about T.C. being dead; I understood that I would live without him the rest of my life. I disliked being part of a world in which such things happened. I still felt as attached to T.C. as I had before. I had been right: everything was entirely different.

But exactly how it was different, I wasn't sure. The closest I could get to articulating the difference was a series of metaphors. One metaphor was that I was a fish, flopping around on dry land. I yelled, "Hey, you guys, where's the water?" The guys looked at me and said, "What water?" At this point, I thought, if I'm a smart fish, I'll grow lungs and legs.

Another metaphor was that my life was a story I had been writing and now I knew the story was out of my hands. If it was even a story at all, it was not me writing it. The third metaphor was that I had thought that life was a bargain I made: you get an interesting, pretty world, you pay with death. But, I had thought, my own death, not T.C.'s; I've paid a fortune for some dime-store junk.

Separately the metaphors each made a kind of sense, but together they made no sense at all. I knew the metaphors were saying something about how T.C.'s death made everything different, but I didn't understand what.

So I thought I would see what the experts said about the effects of a child's death. I am a science writer by trade; I learn about some field of science, then write it up for the general reader. So I knew how to find and read the psychiatric, psychological, and sociological research on grief. Most grief research concentrated on the year or so following the death of a spouse. Less research was on the death of a child, and only a handful of studies were on the long-term effects of that death. In short, not much research was directly relevant to my question.

The research was not only sparse, it was focused on recovery. Grief researchers have a mild obsession with how people recover; the reason is that grief researchers are usually in the helping professions, and people whose children die often need help. Earlier research said that people recover from grief well within a year, that recovery meant detaching emotional investment from the person who had died, and that failure to detach was pathological. Since the early 1980s, however, grief researchers have been saying they not only don't know what pathological is, they're also not sure what normal is, and they doubt whether recovery even exists.

I don't think recovery exists either, and anyway, that hadn't been exactly what I wanted to know. I wanted to know, when a child dies, what happens afterward to the parent? What are the long-term, large-scale effects? So I did what writers do: interviewed people and got a contract to write a book.

I put an ad in the Baltimore newsletter of a national self-help organization for bereaved parents called The Compassionate Friends, asking parents whose children had died five or more years before to call me if they wished. About thirty called, we met, and I asked them questions. Has your marriage changed? Has your relationship with your other children changed? Do you notice yourself more distant from people or closer to people? Which people? Do you have any guilt or self-blame? Has your feeling about God changed? Do you feel more vulnerable in life? Do you feel the same about your own death? What is most satisfying to you? Do you still feel pain? At any particular times? Do you have a way of making sense of the death? In general, the questions broke down into two categories: the effects of the child's death on your relationships with the outside world and on your internal world.

The parents—rich and poor, old and young, Christian and Jewish, black and white, biological and adoptive, educated and not—talked articulately, thoughtfully, and honestly. I could hardly do better than to get out of the way and let them talk. But I think a reader wants some context, wants to know what experts think and what the author makes of all of it. So this book is a series of profiles, alternating with a series of essays. But essays on what?

Many of the questions I asked got single-word, uninterested answers. For instance: has your child's death affected your feeling of your own competence in life? Researchers say that bereaved parents feel incompetent because they couldn't keep their children alive, and I thought that sounded reasonable. But no one got interested in the question. Some felt a little more competent, some a little less, most said no change: no big deal. What *was* a big deal, however, was guilt. I heard about guilt not only when I asked about guilt, but also when I asked about something else altogether. Guilt was on their minds. So the essays will be on those subjects that parents wanted most to talk about. The researchers are included in the essays as a sort of Greek chorus, a mostly nameless group of experts with a large statistical base who comment on what the main characters are saying.

The reader should be careful about drawing conclusions from these profiles and essays. These parents were not selected scientifically; they selected themselves. So any apparent pattern might rather be the result of something peculiar about Baltimore, or about newsletter readers, or more likely, about people who are willing to share their private experiences with the public. For instance, none of the parents I interviewed had withdrawn from the world, refused pleasure, or stopped functioning, though such parents surely exist. In short, these parents may or may not be representative of all bereaved parents, and this is not science. It is a writer's view of some interesting and ordinary people doing an extraordinary thing.

In the end, I learned two things about the long-term effects of losing a child. One is that a child's death is disorienting. The human mind is wired to find patterns and attach meanings, to associate things that are alike, to generalize from one example to another, in short, to make sense of things. Your mind could no more consciously stop doing this than your heart could consciously stop beating. But children's deaths make no sense, have no precedents, are part of no pattern; their deaths are unnatural and wrong. So parents fight their wiring, change their perspectives, and adjust to a reality that makes little sense.

The other thing I learned is that letting go of a child is impossible. One of my earliest and most persistent reactions to T.C.'s death was surprise. I had no idea whatever how much he had meant to me. All I knew was that I hadn't wanted to think about it. Our children are in our blood; the bond with them doesn't seem to break, and the parents found subtle and apparently unconscious ways of preserving that bond.

Each profile illustrates how a particular parent preserves the bond. And because their ways of preserving the bond happily coincided with the subjects of the essays, each profile also illustrates a particular subject. For instance, one mother's profile accompanies the essay on marriages. This particular mother, whose son died just after she'd separated from his father, preserved the bond by volunteering in a charity that worked to keep families together.

With the exception of the few parents who requested pseudonyms, the parents' names are real. All details of their experiences are real. Their words are nearly verbatim. I left out some things they said when they digressed or repeated; and when they left a subject and came back to it, I quote them out of order. I was careful not to quote them out of context.

The subject of this book is painful, and the interviews were full of pain. And I worry about newly bereaved readers who are desperate to know that the pain will go away and that things will be all right again. The book says that the pain never entirely goes away, and that whether things are all right again depends on what "all right" means. Nevertheless, the book is not depressing. If the parents I interviewed said any one thing, it was on the whole reassuring—not that they've gotten over their children's deaths or that they're better, stronger people for it, but that the amount of their pain is a measure of the amount of their love, that they've learned to live with the pain, and that they hope they do so in a way that does honor to the lives their children should have lived.

Chapter 1

AT FIRST

⚭

Walter Farnandis is a lawyer, now seventy-two years old. Nine years ago, Walter was playing golf when his son, James, was killed in a motorcycle accident. James was eighteen.

"James was a late-in-life child for me, which was a real pleasure," Walter said. "When James came along, I was forty-six, and if he called my office, everything dropped for me to talk to James. His mother left when he was fourteen, and after that time I was a mother and father both to him. He and I became father-son and buddy-buddy and brother-brother and everything else. We were together every day. He was tops, he was the man. I was single, and if I went out on a date, he wanted to know what time I was coming home. He was very solicitous with me, I think that's the word. A drunken garbage-truck driver made a left-hand turn right in front of me." Walter means not "me," but "him," James; the slip is natural.

"Two-thirty in the afternoon," Walter went on, "while I was on the eleventh hole on Pine Ridge. At first, it was total shock. After that, it was like a sickness inside of me, an inward illness. I saw him in the funeral home. I went in there and talked to him—I didn't get an answer—

1

for about an hour, just sat there and talked. Which, since we'd been so close, you know, I felt the need to do and I'm glad I did it."

In the months that followed James's death, Walter said, he made some bad business decisions, including selling a family business at a loss. He also gave up golf, though he didn't necessarily connect this with his playing golf at the time James died. "I sort of lost interest in the game," he said. "I sort of lost interest in everything. I was a basket case."

During those early months, a woman he'd been dating moved in with him. "But of course," he said, "for a year and a half at least, there was no sex. I couldn't have sex when I was sick on the stomach." The relationship didn't last, and Walter went back to living on his own. "There was a tremendous loneliness," he said. "I was used to having James there and his girlfriend, and he always brought his friends home. There was nothing, just an empty house.

"I feel I had an experience in life that no one else has had unless they've lost a child," Walter said. "People lose their spouses, they lose their mother and father. But you realize they may die. The problem with the death I have experienced is, it's so sudden. Bang! It's over, completely, forever. And the difficult realization—that it's final. That's the *difficult* realization. I think you find that out in a month or two after he's dead. I don't think you understand anything until a few months go by. Maybe more than a few months."

Realizing James's death was final took Walter more than a few months. "The first year James died, I'd see a blond-haired boy and I'd say, 'Is that James? Is that James?' I don't do that any more. Now if I see a kid, I think, 'He's as good-looking as James was.' Then I think, 'Naw, he's not that good-looking.'"

After about two years, Walter said, "I sat down and I wrote a complete accounting of what happened that day. I mailed it to The Compassionate Friends and they printed it. So I thought, 'OK, I've done all I can do, and I've put the thing to rest.' And that helped me. That helped. At this point, I look back on it, I'm happy I had him while I did. I could have been without him, very easily. At least I had almost eighteen years—and it was a pleasure."

By now, nine years after James died, Walter said he has come to understand two things. "Number one is that death is final. There's nothing more final in the world than death. There's no second chance. There's no see-him-again. There's no nothing. There's no way of ever bringing him back. It's final. And the other thing is, life does go on. You have to realize there are other things in life. Takes a long time to feel that way."

So Walter did what everyone does, got on with life. He continued his law practice; he has remarried. James had a sister, Walter's daughter, and Walter takes great pleasure in her and her children, his grandchildren. And though he never went back to golf, he now spends a couple of nights a week singing in a karaoke bar. He is an outgoing man who lives with his wife in a carefully kept and decorated house. On the table next to the couch is James's picture.

"Thoughts do come in my mind quite often of the good times," Walter said, "the fun we had, his worrying over me. It's always there, but you don't get into the details of it unless you're not busy and you sit here and look at his picture. And then you may start thinking about it. I think the secret is to keep busy at something you enjoy in life—keep yourself occupied. Of course, that's the secret in *life*. I think the feeling of loss lasts forever. I think that all I do is hide the feeling by being involved in these other things. There's always the loss. The way you make out is, you don't think about it. But it's always there."

Walter's path, seen in broad outlines, is typical. Like everyone else, he doesn't want to spend much time remembering the first months, and when asked, describes it in a few sentences: it was a "total shock," then an "inward illness." After two years, he wrote an article that he considered a turning point, that is, the point at which he could turn away from the problems of grieving back to the problems of living. Walter now lives what anyone would call a normal life. But if "recover" means getting back the life and self he had before James's death, Walter didn't recover. The loss, he says, is "always there" and "the way you make out is, you don't think about it."

What most people feel those first months are shock and, alternately, unbelievable pain. Shock is an emergency shut-down of all your abilities except those that get you out of bed, bathed, dressed, fed, talking, working, and back into bed again. People say that they're on automatic, that they keep going because they don't know what else to do. Shock is probably the body's kindness, the time to realize the facts slowly, to ease into the pain.

Ten years ago, Chris Reed's nineteen-year-old daughter, Mary, combined an overdose of antidepressants with alcohol and killed herself. "I can't put a time frame on it," he said, "but for weeks or months after Mary died, I was still in somewhat of a daze. I remember for a few days after she died, I kept thinking this was all a bad dream. I think this is the body's way of not hitting us full force all at one time, which you probably wouldn't be able to cope with. And so maybe that's why I was in a daze, because reality was gradually, gradually setting in."

With reality comes pain, and the pain, when it comes, is stunning. The pain is actually physical, mostly in your stomach and chest. Your chest feels crushed and you can't seem to catch your breath. I remember feeling pinned like a butterfly, or somehow eviscerated. One woman drew an arc that started at her head and ended at her knees and said, "His death was cut out of *here*." The pain comes in waves—moves in, backs off, then in again. People try describing it with superlatives or metaphors, then give up the attempt. And no one wants to try too hard anyway; they'd much rather talk about how, with time, the waves of pain gradually became less frequent. "Now when I think of him," one woman said, "I don't get that *wrenching*, I don't know the word to use, that *wrenching* feeling."

Sally Lambert's twenty-year-old daughter, Lisa, hanged herself on New Year's Eve. For a long time afterward, Sally said, "I can remember, just to get out of bed in the morning was so difficult. It was just so *painful* to get up. I can remember, within days, being in a shower and I thought, 'My God, this pain is all over my body, from my head to my toes.' You just couldn't understand, it was something you just couldn't understand. Your whole *body* is in pain. Not just here in your heart."

4

Along with the pain goes an odd mental confusion. People feel that they've just been dumped on another planet, that a new world has started but that they're the only ones who know this. One woman, en route from Florida to Maryland where her son had died, said, "I remember being in the airport. It was like six in the morning and I was looking at everybody with suitcases, and I'm thinking, 'Where are these people going? Don't they know my son just died?'"

At the same time, however, the old world is still around and going on as usual, so people aren't sure which world they're in. They are no longer sure how to behave, and are dislocated. Maybe this dislocation is a natural successor to shock. Maybe shock makes people act as though nothing new had happened, and as the shock wears off, they begin to understand how different the new world is. Meanwhile, they feel they are living in two worlds at once, one old and familiar and the other altogether foreign. The result feels like a minor, transient insanity.

Chris Reed, like a lot of people, went right back to work. "Mary died on Monday, we buried her on Friday, the following Monday I went back to work," Chris said, "because I felt like I didn't want to sit home all day in the depth of my grief. But it was difficult with my normal routine functions of life. I had strange feelings after Mary died. I remember for several weeks after she died, whenever I went out in public, I felt like I didn't belong there. I felt like maybe I had come from another world or something. It's difficult to put into words. It's not like I felt I was something peculiar, because on the outside I looked like all these other people. But I just felt that I was out of place among people. I felt almost like I was floating. Does that make sense?"

In fact, nothing in this new world makes sense at all; the minor insanity isn't in the parents, it's in this world. In such insanity, you are dumbstruck and stupid. The first thing you're aware of is that you're either numb or in pain. The next thing is that the child seems gone and doesn't seem to be coming back, and this doesn't seem possible. The death of a child can't be final, the child just can't be so *gone*.

Five years ago, Octavia Pompey's son, Erin, was a basketball player just graduating from high school. He was playing in a summer league championship game when a player from the opposing team picked a fight with him. The game was stopped, the opposing player went home, got a gun, came back to the gym, and shot Erin. Erin was taken to the hospital, where he died.

"I just couldn't believe it," Octavia said. "After we left the hospital and got back home, I just expected him to walk in the door. The last thing he said to me—I remember his last words to me because, out of my three boys, he got so much taller than his brothers. I remember that day, being in the kitchen and he came in behind me and I turned around and then I had to look up, because it seemed like all of a sudden he had shot up. And the last thing he said to me that day was, 'I'm going, Shorty'—because he got so he called me Shorty. And I said, 'OK, score twenty points.' And he said, *'OK!'* And for the longest time, whenever that front door opened, I expected him to walk through the door."

Researchers call expectations like Octavia's and Walter's ("Is that James? Is that James?") "searching behavior," meaning that people continue to search for someone who's died. Searching behavior includes dreaming about the person still being alive; "seeing" the person in the street; and like Octavia, expecting the person who died to walk in the door, or call on the phone, or be where he or she is supposed to be. Searching behavior is normal for a while for any bereaved person, not just for parents.

But parents seem to have extra reason for searching. All along they expected to die before their children, and this expectation runs deep. Parents dying first is the natural order of the world. A world in which you are alive and your child is not feels unnatural. Your child isn't here so you shouldn't be; and so, like Chris, you feel "out of place." You're still here so the child must be too; and so, like Walter and Octavia, you search.

Researchers say searching behavior stops when the bereaved understands the person who died is not coming back. I suspect it continues, but in a different form. Walter understood that he would never see James again, and said so with eloquence—"There's no see-

him-again. It's final."—but nine years later, Walter is still reminded of
James with every blond boy he sees. For myself, I understand T.C. is
not coming back; but eight years later, because he died on his way
back to college, I still feel that maybe he reached his college after all.
I go there once a year on business, and on the way I always feel excited, as though I'll see him again. When I told this to a man whose
son died sixteen years ago, he said, "That's more reasonable for you,
the death is more recent. But I still do it. There was one person that
worked in the library and I swear to God, he looked just like my son,
honest to God. What could you say? You're not going to say anything. I *didn't* say anything."

Perhaps by "searching behavior" researchers mean only the early
confusion about the finality of death, the sense of dislocation in this
new, unnatural world. Perhaps the searching that Walter and I and the
sixteen-year veteran still do is neither confusion nor dislocation, but
longing intense enough to create a mild, temporary hallucination, or
at least a vivid reminder.

Octavia stopped expecting Erin to walk through the front door
but she still, five years later, takes great pleasure in seeing someone
who reminds her of him. "There's still not a day that goes by that I
don't think of Erin," she said, sounding so happy she was almost
singing. "I can walk down the street or ride down the street, and I see
a boy that walks like him or looks like him, or I would go to the
shopping malls and see all these young people hanging out. Because
in my mind, he's still nineteen, he's not twenty-five, which he would
have been, so he would be doing things that nineteen-year-olds
should be."

Along with dislocation and pain and searching come the first
inklings that the child is going to remain dead. I think this realization
of finality—what Walter called "the *difficult* realization"—takes at
least a year to sink in and accounts for the common wisdom at Compassionate Friends, that the second year is worse than the first. Walter
first said he thought it took a month or two, then he said a few
months, then maybe more than a few months. However long it takes,
you come to understand that the child is dead and you can't do a

thing about it. For the rest of your life, the child will be dead. Through dislocation and pain you can more or less continue functioning, but such finality stops you cold.

Octavia just didn't want to live, she said, didn't want to wake up in the morning: "I felt that for a long time. I wished I could just lay down and go to sleep." Octavia said she didn't have the nerve to do anything about those feelings. But, she said, "These thoughts went through my mind, that I'm just going through the motions. I had this pain in my chest that just wouldn't go away. I had this emptiness."

Like Octavia, other parents occasionally considered suicide, though when they talked about this later, they emphasized the reasons they didn't go through with it. Betty Jones's seventeen-year-old son, Bruce, died when a semitrailer truck hit his car. "The initial feeling is, on the outside you put on a nice front and on the inside you're ground-up hamburger meat. I was suicidal for three months or more, had it all planned, but I didn't carry it out. After that, I just wished I had been killed. I wasn't willing to do it to myself any more, but I would have loved to have been hit by a truck. That went on for a number of years. I can tell you right now that what kept me from committing suicide was the fact that if I had, people would have said I loved my son more than my daughter. And I didn't. And that was the only reason I didn't do it—I couldn't let her live thinking I loved her brother more."

I had asked Sally Lambert, whose daughter had hanged herself, if she felt differently about her own death. "Oh yes," she said. "*Yes.* Ten months before Lisa died, I had had surgery for cancer of the colon. So in my mind afterward, I thought there could be a recurrence. And I really didn't care. Or maybe I didn't care that the cancer *didn't* happen. There were plenty of times when I gladly would have slipped off quietly. But no, now I'm not looking to die like I was years back, when I would have said, 'Hey, good.'"

Grief researchers seem not to have studied suicide in bereaved parents. Several studies have found that suicide rates among adults increase in the first years after the death of a parent. Others found suicide rates particularly high in bereaved spouses. Generalizing from parents and spouses to children seems reasonable, and hearing parents talk about suicide at Compassionate Friends meetings is never surprising. But no one seems to have any data about whether bereaved parents are more likely than ordinary parents to commit suicide, let alone why or why not. Maybe bereaved parents consider suicide to get away from the pain. Many of them say, like Octavia and Sally, that they just wanted to slip away or go to sleep or not wake up.

Or maybe, in their dislocation, they think of suicide as a way of going after their children. Maybe the parents think the child is in some place, "death," to which they can go, and if the child must stay there, then the parents could stay there too. I remember thinking that. In any case, for some people, considering suicide forces, or at least clarifies, a decision. As one woman said, "You have two choices: either kill yourself or just keep going on day to day." One psychologist who had been treating bereaved people in private practice for twelve years noticed this woman's thinking in his patients. Early in their grief, he said, his patients didn't so much choose to live; they just didn't choose to die.

Choosing to live comes later. Twenty-seven years ago, Joan Gresser's three-year-old son Steven died of tonsillitis, and ten years later, her eleven-year-old son Teddy drowned. "Even people who lost children wondered why I didn't kill myself, or my husband didn't—why we didn't commit suicide. You *want* to, but you just don't do it. I had pills in my hand and I was convincing myself that all I wanted to do was go to sleep. I didn't want to deal with this any more. I didn't want my mother sitting in the rocking chair downstairs knitting the fucking afghan. That's what she was doing,"—Joan raised her voice in real anger—"an *afghan*. What did I *need* it for? And that moment I said, 'What are you, nuts?' I made a choice—I wasn't aware of the choice at that time, but I did—to live. Even though living at that point for me was just getting around."

"I read so many books in those days," Sally said. "And one of them said, 'You have to make a choice whether you're going to continue to live, or just exist.' I know there was one point, I don't know at what year, when I said, 'I want to live.' In those books—boy, I was reading them all—when it said you need exercise, I got exercise. I guess I meant that I wanted to participate in life. I wanted to enjoy again the good parts of life. Which I wasn't doing."

For Joan, holding her pills in her hand and deciding she wasn't nuts was the same as Sally's saying she wanted to live and Walter's writing about James's death for The Compassionate Friends newsletter. These are specific acts or occurrences or realizations that mark some sort of refocus, some change in outlook, some point at which people turn from grieving back to living. Some people have discrete turning points, some don't; whether or not they have turning points might just be a function of whether or not they remember having them. I don't remember having any such turning point, but I do remember the feeling of trying hard to stay alive. This feeling was mixed: the hypocrisy of trying to stay alive when T.C. was already dead, against the body's desire for survival and the mind's for sanity and joy.

Sally, after talking about the book advising her that the pain will pass, went on to say, "And it does. There's nothing really you have to do about it. Nature takes care of it. You can't stand that pain for that long. Lisa's birthday was July 14, and that's the same day as my husband's, but it was always hers rather than his when she was living and even after she died. So up until last year, that was bad. But last year was Bob's sixty-fifth birthday, and I gave a big surprise party for him, and it was almost like a turning of the leaf. This was *his* birthday."

Brandt Jones is married to Betty, the woman who felt like ground-up hamburger meat but didn't commit suicide so no one would say she loved her son more than her daughter. The accident that killed their son had happened sixteen years before I talked to them. I asked Brandt what he thought it meant to get over his son's death. "I don't know about getting over it," he said. "I don't think you get over it. But I think there comes a point—and I don't know when it happened, a number of years ago—where I said, 'There are other things that I want to do, and if I dwell on this grief, I can't do those things.' It wasn't going anywhere, and the only person that could make it go anywhere was me. It's just a conscious decision to spend my energy doing things I wanted to do." Later, after Brandt retired, the number of things he actually did was impressive: he taught scuba diving, officiated at the Masonic Lodge, presided over a square dancing club, and went on speaking assignments for The Compassionate Friends. These things, he said, "take the focus from grieving continuously. You have something now where you can feel completion. I guess that's the thing. With grief there's no 'The End.' And that's what I'm saying. I swung away to put my energies where I could see something accomplished at the end of the day. I think that's the break point."

For a few parents, the break point was a dream.

Joan, whose sons Teddy and Steven both died: "I always had this recurring nightmare. I was walking up a cliff and I was holding Teddy and Teddy was holding a doll—I'm assuming the doll was Steven. And I was pulling them up the cliff, and this giant black wave would come and the wave would catch the doll, and before the wave would catch Teddy, I would wake up. And I had insomnia so I wouldn't go back to sleep. I remember one night laying in bed. I could hear my husband snoring, and all of a sudden the room became—have you ever had your hearing tested and you're in a sound-proof room, do you know how deadened that sound is? It's *no* sound. I don't know if I was asleep. But I looked over at my husband, his mouth was open but there was no sound. And I had this overwhelming feeling of joy, of peace. And I opened my eyes and Teddy was sitting on my bed and he had on his red jacket, and he had this doll. And he said to me, 'Mommy, I'm happy. I have my doll. I'm OK.' That was the end of it. I never had that dream again. And that was the beginning of my getting on with it."

Loretta Marsh's nineteen-year-old son, Mike, was killed by a drunk driver: "One night, I went to bed, I remember I said, 'God help me, you've got to help me.' And I dreamed that I was in this city, and there were thousands and thousands of people. And I was looking for Mike. And I was hollering, 'Mike, I gotta find you, I gotta find you.' I saw him and he was in a solid white suit and he heard me hollering and he said, 'Mom.' And I walked up to him and I said, 'Mike, you look so pretty.' He said, 'Mom, I am. And I'm all right.' And after

I had that dream, it took like a burden, like a heaviness in my heart, off of me."

These "break points," or turning points, make the process sound simple: one day you're grieving, boom, next day you're home free. And of course, the process isn't simple or sudden at all. The process is more like living through a high fever. People are isolated, preoccupied with their pain, and for a while they lose the ability to care about their own lives, let alone anyone or anything else. I remember truly not caring. I didn't return phone calls, I missed deadlines, I let the house go, I was interested in nothing and nobody. But in time, as Sally said, nature takes care of it; the waves of pain lose intensity a little and come less frequently. Then friends and relatives say the parents are getting over it, and that time heals all wounds. The parents themselves say that as the pain lessens, they begin to have energy for people and things outside themselves.

I suspect when people talk about a new leaf or a break point, they are saying that some event—a newsletter article, a birthday party, a dream—came to symbolize the end of preoccupation and despair, and the beginning, as Joan said, of getting on with it. The process had been going on all along, too gradually to notice, and only with this event did the change become evident. A quantitative change has become qualitative.

Exactly how long after the child's death this change occurs is unclear. Walter wrote his letter two years later; Joan's dream was two years after Teddy's death, twelve years after Steven's; Brandt's son had been dead sixteen years and Brandt made his decision to get on with his life "a number of years ago." Probably the truth is that the change begins after a year or two and becomes obvious a few years after that: Sally was reading those self-help books and deciding "to participate in life" right away, but the "new leaf" of her husband's birthday came five years later. A hospital social worker in pediatric oncology, whose hospital follows up bereaved parents, said she notices a change in these parents after four or five years. I noticed I felt better after about four years. One parent said, "Six, six and half years before I started feeling like myself." A grief researcher found few differences in the general functioning of parents four years or thirteen years after their children's deaths, and concluded that "by four years post-loss, a number of responses to the loss have stabilized." And when I asked another grief researcher, Robert Weiss, a sociologist at the University of Massachusetts in Boston, if I should limit the people I interview to veterans of five-plus years, he said, "That's as good a guess as any."

So sooner or later, most people try actively to get on with the grief process, to find relief from the pain, to understand the child isn't coming back, to become accustomed to living in two worlds, to find some equanimity and peace. "Peace," one woman said, "is the best thing you can wish someone who's lost a child."

And unlike the early part of the process, which time and nature take care of, people now begin taking charge. They go to The Compassionate Friends or to similar self-help groups for the survivors of suicides, and faithfully read those groups' newsletters. "You'd go to Compassionate Friends and talk to people who understood your situation," said Leight Johnson, who still goes fifteen years after Johnny died. "They're the *only* people in the world that really know how you feel; nobody else does. Other people try but they don't."

They get help from everywhere: they see therapists, go to therapy workshops, talk to their priests or ministers or rabbis, talk to their friends and relatives, read books. "I got a lot of consolation from reading books about survivors of bad things," said one woman. "I like reading those books about how people overcome *adversity*. I thought, 'How could I be one of those people?'"

They find models, of one sort or another. They see other grieving parents and imitate or criticize them. Emily Miller went to suicide survivors meetings after her twenty-five-year-old daughter, Sue, committed suicide. "We saw a lot of people there who are going to be zombies forever," she said. "There was one couple whose son had committed suicide. For two or three years they came to meetings and never said a word. Another couple, also two or three years later— there was such *fury*. I remember the woman saying, 'When my time comes and I go to meet him, I'm going to punch him out.' There was a couple whose son's been gone eight years, I mean, they were in

13

worse shape than I was. There are some people that *never* get better. I couldn't bear it. I consciously determined I couldn't live the rest of my life with such pain. I did whatever I could to make myself better. I went to therapy. I went back to work. The busier I kept, the better it was for me. I think people make a choice, a conscious choice or an unconscious choice, whether they will survive."

Ruth Banick, whose nineteen-year-old daughter, Leslie, died in a car accident, had a different kind of model. "My brother-in-law, Winston, was a personal hero of mine. He was just the neatest, neatest man. He was a diabetic and so he had had heart problems and eye problems; he had lost both of his legs. I used to think of him getting up in the morning and putting on artificial legs, putting a nitroglycerin patch on his heart, taking twenty-some pills a day, two insulin shots, being legally blind. But he took care of the house, he helped us care for my father when my father was dying, and I used to think, 'If Winston can get up and put his armor on and reach out to other people, then you can too, Ruth.' Now Winston could have made life for everybody around him miserable, but he chose to go another way. And I *tried* to pick that way too. I could wallow in my self-pity forever, or I could choose to do what I can while I have to live here."

They figure out the management of grief, the thousand tricks for giving grief its due without being overwhelmed, or at least not for long. "It's not that the pain is any less," said Delores Shoda, whose son, Larry, died seven years ago at age twenty-eight of melanoma. "You know it's going to happen again and again. When he first died, they gave me some medicine because all I did was cry. But the medicine put me in a state of just wanting to sit. I said to myself, 'You're not going to get over this if you keep taking medicine. You have to *work* at it.' After Larry died, it was so easy for me to just stay in the bed and pull the covers over my head and just let the world go on. But I made myself get up every morning when my husband went to work, got dressed, put on my makeup, and went over to a Roy Rogers with the morning paper, had a cup of coffee and did the crossword puzzle. I sat there for an hour, hour and a half. Then I'd think, 'Well, you're up and you're dressed. What are you going to do today?' I made myself do that every day for several years, and I still do it sometimes. I guess it's easier as time goes on, not because it goes away but because you yourself learn to do things to help you get through the bad times."

Ruth Banick, after Leslie died in the accident, got herself through the bad times with what she called a mental exercise. "You always have these horrible memories. Because I did go to the morgue to see Leslie. For the longest time I tortured myself with that—that's a horrible image for a parent to remember. Every time that image would come to my mind, I would replace it with this one, where a couple of weeks before Leslie died, she went out on this date and they hadn't dated before, and the young man came to the door. He sat down in the chair, and she walked into the room, and I happened to be looking at him when she came in. To see his face light up like a Christmas tree—she was such a pretty girl—I just remember the look on his face. He said, 'Oh, Leslie, you look so pretty,' and I thought, 'You know, I think she does too.' You pick a better image, and that's the one that I would remember. At first it was hard, but I did that mental game enough until now it comes instantly. Right away, soon as I think of the morgue, I think of this other picture. It takes a lot of practice."

Tom Ford's seventeen-year-old son, David, was killed in a motorcycle accident. Tom had been in the military for twenty-one years and said that there he had learned to accept that some friends are certain to die. "But it's hard to accept this when it's something like your boy. I guess I looked at it like, this is terrible but it's like falling down in the gutter. You can stay down in there or you can get up on your hands and knees for a while, and then you stand all the way up. You have to work at improving. If you don't, you're gonna be down forever. I guess it's like if you've been real sick for a while, throwing up or something. You just feel so damn bad you don't know what to do about it. Kind of like an alcoholic; you don't drink today, you just figure tomorrow will come and you're going to feel a little better."

Listening to my tapes of these interviews, I was struck by how aware the parents are that they seem crazy or weird or miserable. This part of the grief process must be conscious. The decision to remedy the misery is certainly conscious. Sally Lambert "made the choice" to "participate in life." Brandt Jones made a "conscious decision to get on with other things." Emily Miller "consciously determined I couldn't live the rest of my life with such pain." Ruth Banick could "choose to do what I can while I have to live here." Tom Ford knew "you could stay down in the gutter" or "you could stand all the way up." Delores Shoda "learned to do things to help you get through the bad times."

Maybe time does heal everything, but these people aren't waiting for it. Maybe having been stunned by pain and confused by unnaturalness, they now want a sense of controlling their own lives. Maybe being alive carries with it a certain drive, a force, that makes people unable to stay flattened for long. Clearly they're aware of having family they're neglecting. So they decide, they choose. For me, the choice took the form of that metaphor, that I was like a fish on dry land, no water in sight, and the only alternative was to grow lungs and legs. The world I was used to was gone; adjust to the new world—though I hadn't a clue how to adjust, or how long adjustment should take, or what I would be like once I adjusted. And when I had, then what?

Researchers' answers to these questions are called models of recovery, the first of which was probably created by Sigmund Freud. In 1917, Freud wrote an essay called "Mourning and Melancholia," directed at other therapists, telling them how to distinguish between melancholia—what we call depression—and mourning. In the essay, he outlined the job of the mourner: the pain, he wrote, and "the loss of interest in the outside world," and the "turning from every active effort that is not connected with thoughts of the dead" must finally give way to reality. By "reality" Freud meant the understanding that death is final.

This finality, this reality "requires forthwith that all the libido shall be withdrawn from its attachments to this object," Freud wrote, "and when the work of mourning is completed the ego becomes free and uninhibited again." Libido is, to modern ears, sexual desire; to Freud, libido was more general, an intense emotional energy that attached itself to certain objects. The mourner, therefore, has to detach emotional energy from the dead person, and when this happens, mourning ends and the mourner is free.

Freud's simple model had great power. For seventy or so years, researchers and therapists accepted it as defining the normal pattern of grief. And so in 1944, a distinguished psychiatrist, Erich Lindemann of Harvard University, studied 101 grieving people and defined the grief process, or "grief work," as "emancipation from bondage to the deceased, readjustment to the environment in which the deceased is missing, and the formation of new relationships." And in 1983, another respected psychiatrist, Beverley Raphael at the University of Newcastle in Australia, wrote "when the finality of the loss is accepted, then the work of undoing the bonds that built the relationship commences." Raphael adds: "Each one of the memories that bound the bereaved to the deceased is brought up, then painfully relinquished. It is, perhaps, the reverse of love." If bonds are undone and memories relinquished, then Raphael is right: it is indeed the reverse of love. I suspect that Freud's model still affects the usual social expectations for a bereaved parent: cry, then put away the pictures and get a cat or have another child; detach and reinvest.

Any parent who has lost a child knows that defining recovery as detach-and-reinvest is at best a matter of defining "detach" and "reinvest." Do parents ever undo those bonds? Do they reinvest that same emotional energy in anyone or anything else? Can they ever reverse love? I don't think so, and I'm not sure Freud did either. In "Mourning and Melancholia," he was apparently talking about a parent's death. Forty years later, when his own grown daughter died, he wrote to a friend that duty and habit would "see to it that things go on as before," but, he added, "Quite deep down I can trace the feelings of a deep narcissistic hurt that is not to be healed." To Freud, a narcissistic hurt was a wound to his innermost, most self-interested self, and that wound, he thought, was irremediable.

Whether or not the Freudian detach-and-reinvest model accurately describes parental grief, alternative models aren't thick on the ground. The main alternative, called attachment theory, explains the nature of human attachments; it describes grief but not parental grief. The only model for recovery of which the parents themselves seemed aware was some version of Elizabeth Kübler-Ross's. In the late 1960s, Kübler-Ross, a psychiatrist, described the process of facing your own death and has since extrapolated that description to the process of grieving someone else's. She said, as do the Freudians and the attachment theorists, that people go through specific stages. Kübler-Ross's stages are denial, anger, bargaining, depression, and, finally, acceptance. One parent told me, "I think I'm in the acceptance stage now."

Researchers do more or less agree that the symptoms of grief change with time; some use the words "stages" or "phases," some don't. According to researchers, the general change moves from numbness and shock to intense pain and longing to despair (which includes depression, anger, restlessness, irritability, guilt, and sadness) to some sort of resolution or adaptation.

Most researchers also warn against taking these changes as law. Some researchers worry that the idea of phases gives parents erroneous expectations, and that a parent who after ten years still has flashes of anger will feel stuck in an early, undeveloped stage, like a child who still crawls when everyone else its age is walking. And even researchers like Raphael, who wrote "the bereavement reaction may be described as comprising a series of phases," deny that those phases are fixed or sequential or necessary or even clearly identifiable. Maybe those phases occur, maybe they don't and others do. In 1984, the Institute of Medicine convened a committee of national experts in bereavement and concluded, "The grieving process does not proceed in a linear fashion."

Researchers now seem less inclined to prescribe recovery and more inclined to describe the effects of grieving. Accordingly, they study whether the bereaved are more likely to get sick or die, or to depend on alcohol or drugs. They test what emotions people feel. They try to decide if men and women grieve differently. They study whether the symptoms of grief depend on how the child died, or on how old the child was. They compare losing a child to losing any other member of the family. They study the effects of grief on marriages and on surviving children. They keep trying to define "pathological grief" and failing, though they know that some bereaved parents are far too unhappy far too long. The results of all these studies will come as commentary in the chapters ahead.

And researchers do try to find some end point of grief, and call it "resolution" or "adaptation" or "adjustment" or "completion." They pretty well agree that the word "recovery," if it means returning unscathed to normal life, is meaningless. The Institute of Medicine wrote that "recovery" implies wrongly that grief is an illness from which people emerge unchanged; the Institute's report sanctioned the word only if it meant recovery of hopefulness, pleasure, and investment in life. The sociologist Robert Weiss agreed and expanded the list to also include recovering the ability to feel energy for life, to be generally free from pain, to function adequately.

In spite of researchers' descriptions of resolution or acceptance, however, they are in fact unsure whether grief has any end point at all. The duration of grief, they say, seems limited only by the length of a study; the more time a study encompasses, the longer the duration it finds. Maybe grief is limitless. Lindemann had set a limit; he found that "with eight to ten interviews in which the psychiatrist shares the grief work, and with a period of from four to six weeks, it was ordinarily possible to settle an uncomplicated and undistorted grief reaction." (What "settle an uncomplicated and undistorted grief reaction" means, Lindemann doesn't say.) The majority of studies covers only the first two years, but the few studies that extend to four or seven or nine or thirteen or more years still find people talking about pain and loss. One study of parents whose children had died from cancer seven years earlier found the parents functioning well but feeling what the researchers call an "empty space." "Thus, a precise end point in time," the Institute of Medicine report says, "cannot be specified."

Maybe the difficulty in specifying an end point to grief is at bottom only a confusion about definitions. Maybe what researchers call resolution or adaptation, the parents call the break point, the turning point. Maybe what the researchers call the ability to invest in and take pleasure from life is the decision parents say they make to live as well as they can in the new world. But neither researchers nor parents believe that grief ends.

"The grief that follows the death of a child seems peculiarly resistant to recovery," wrote Weiss. "When it is a child that has died, the parents' protective feelings, which make for a near-permanent need to save the child from hurt, produce a protracted phase of protest and search." Later in the same article, Weiss summed up: "Loss is inescapable. Deaths, estrangements, and separations are part of life. Recoveries tend to be either more or less adequate; only rarely can they be said to be either complete or entirely absent."

Dennis Klass, a psychologist who is both clinician and researcher, spent ten years working with a local chapter of The Compassionate Friends. "The bereaved parent, after a time, will cease showing the medical symptoms of grief, but the parent does not 'get over' the death of the child," he wrote in 1988. "Parenting is a permanent change in the individual. A person never gets over being a parent. Parental bereavement is also a permanent condition."

One of the nicest illustrations of this permanence came from a parent I did not interview. One day while stepping off a curb I fell, cut my knee badly, and went to my family doctor. He began stitching up the cut, and because he's a gregarious fellow and he knows I'm a writer, he asked me what I was working on. I told him about this book. "That's a subject no one wants to talk about," he said. "People suppress that."

I thought he meant people who had not lost children don't want to talk about children's deaths, agreed with him, and let the subject drop. He made a stitch.

"I lost a child, you know," he said.

"I didn't know that," I said. "I'm so sorry."

"Well, it was a long time ago. It was just a few months old, bad congenital heart problems," he said in the off-handed, seen-it-all way that old doctors have. "I never think about it."

"How long ago?" I asked.

"Thirty years," he said. "It doesn't affect me. The reason I think it doesn't is, you don't have a chance to get close in just a few months."

"What about your wife?" I asked.

"I don't know," he said, "we never talked about it. We mention it once in a while, casually. I don't really know how she feels about it. It doesn't bother *me* though."

I don't remember him referring to this baby as "he" or "she," only as "it," an age, and a fatal condition. I thought, "OK, maybe he didn't get close and thirty years is a long time," and I dropped the subject again.

"Are you going to put me in your book?" he asked.

"I'd love to," I said. "I've had trouble finding fathers who will talk about it. The interview would take several hours."

"I'd have to be anonymous," he said, then made a tricky knot and reconsidered.

"No, I don't want you to interview me," he said. "I don't want to talk about it. I don't want to dredge it all up. It would hurt too much."

I thought I'd let that pass but couldn't. "If it didn't bother you too much," I said, "maybe it wouldn't hurt to talk about it."

He gave me a look and started laughing. "You really know how to hurt a guy, don't you," he said. "Now I'm going to have to go see my psychiatrist."

So before I left, I made a bargain with him. I would ask him again in a month, and if he still said no, then no. Then I went out to my car and wrote down everything he had said because I was so impressed with it.

A month later, he still said no. "It was so long ago," he said. "Time is the great healer and I don't want to open up those old wounds."

"Thank you for considering it," I said, and thought, thirty years and a baby he didn't get close to, and the wounds can still be opened.

He even used the same metaphor as Freud, a wound. Time isn't such a great healer after all.

He's not unique. According to the parents, the effects are not only permanent, but also far-reaching. The social worker in pediatric oncology who sees so many grieving parents and whose name is Julia Marcus, lost two daughters herself, one who was twenty days old thirty-three years ago, and the other twenty-five years old, six years ago. "I'll sum it all up," she said. "I think there's no part of you or aspect of your life that isn't changed. I've worked with grieving and I know all kinds of things about what you are supposed to do." She meant the detach-and-reinvest models. "But that's all wrong. It affects *everything*."

Delores Shoda, whose son died of melanoma seven years ago: "I don't think you're *ever* going to get over it. You make yourself go on with your life and do what you have to do, and you *are* happy. But you're not ever going to get over it. You'll never be *as* happy. You talk about getting better and the pain going away. I don't think the pain will go away until you die. When you take your last breath—then, it's gone."

Betty Jones, whose son died fourteen years ago: "There's always a void, a pain and a void that will never be filled again in your life. Even when life right now is going well, it's never fully total, complete happiness like there once was."

Sally Lambert, whose daughter died six and a half years ago: "Very much in the beginning I felt completely dead inside. Now I don't feel completely dead, but I feel that there's a part of me that is *gone*. That's a cross you bear. A weight in your heart, a heaviness. An underlying sadness that's *there*. And you can feel the weight of it where you didn't have that weight before. But if she died and I didn't carry the weight, it would mean she didn't mean very much to me. And that's not so. But yes, I get tired of carrying the weight. I'm sure any parent who's lost a child has that."

Ruth Banick, whose daughter died six years ago: "You're scarred forever. I don't like it, I hate it. I feel like every morning I get up with this extra fifty pounds tied to my heart and I have to carry it. And there's no relief. You build the muscles after a certain length of time, carrying this weight. But I feel like it's always *there.*"

Chris Reed, whose daughter died ten years ago: "I just think that Mary's death changed me. It's something that will be with me forever. I'm still the same person basically but—it's difficult to put into words—but I'm changed from what I was before she died."

Chris is right: this is all difficult to put into words. What do these people mean by "it affects everything," or "you can feel the weight of it," or "you're scarred forever," or "I'm changed"?

The explanation of what they mean is an explanation of the effects of losing a child. These parents' marriages have changed. Their relationships with their other children and with other people in general have changed. They now feel guilty because as parents they are responsible for their childrens' lives, and the deaths must mean they've done something wrong. Some of the guilt is part of a larger attempt to lay blame, to attribute the death to some cause, to make sense of it. This attempt eventually affects the parents' relationships with God and changes their perspective on life. The change in perspective entails a change in priorities.

Such fundamental, sweeping changes are a measure of the depth and breadth of the bond between parents and children. This particular bond is so strong it doesn't break, even after death, and the parents find some way to continue the bonds with their dead children. Nine years after Walter Farnandis wrote that letter to Compassionate Friends, he wrote another letter. This letter told newly bereaved parents their children would not want them grieving forever, and then added: "After my prayers each night, I talk to my son. Tell him little things I think may be interesting to him. This does give me a feeling of closeness and it helps."

Chapter 2

MARGE FORD'S MARRIAGE

∞

O ne of the first and most obvious effects of a child's death is on a marriage. Marge Ford's history is not at all typical of bereaved parents, but the stresses that drive her history are.

Marge and Tom Ford weren't getting along and had already been separated for several months when their son David was killed. Eight years later, I interviewed both of them, but separately. In the meantime, they decided to stay married. To be honest, they didn't seem made for each other: they could hardly have been more different. Marge was diffident, talked mostly in a small, hesitant, almost dreamy voice, and cried quietly throughout most of the interview. Tom had been a pilot in the air force and in the Air National Guard for twenty-one years, and talked with ease, with little emotion, and with military authority and abruptness. The differences between the two were on the surface, however, and fell away when they talked about David and about their grief. With a few exceptions that were more apparent than real, what they said separately was almost identical. Since the interviews, they have moved south, to a new house in the sunshine.

This profile is Marge's, but Tom is all the way through it.

24

"David was sixteen, almost seventeen," Marge said. "He died October 12, 1984, and he would have been seventeen that November. He was the youngest of three. Jeffrey was nineteen and Terry, his sister, was twenty-one."

Marge recounted the story of how David went out riding with a friend on a motorcycle. Tom and Marge, even though they had separated, agreed that the friend who had been driving the motorcycle was too wild for David to be hanging around with, and both had told David so, but David hadn't listened. The friend, said Marge, "was not big enough to be driving the machine, he shouldn't have been driving it. And David was not there with my permission or my husband's." The friend lost control of the motorcycle and hit a utility pole, and both he and David died. Tom and David's brother, Jeffrey, had gone to the hospital, Jeffrey had identified David, "and really," Marge said, "I don't remember a whole lot."

Tom's version of David's death was more detailed but otherwise identical. David was living with Tom. One night when Tom was out playing racquetball, David went motorcycle-riding with the wild friend. Tom came home and didn't check David's whereabouts, so that when the police came and asked if David were home, Tom thought he was upstairs. The police asked if Tom would check because David had not been carrying indentification, and Tom came back and said, "No, I thought he was in bed but he's not." Tom and Jeffrey went to the hospital, where Jeffrey identified David's body. "I never looked at my boy," said Tom. "My other boy looked at him. He says, 'You don't want to look at him, Dad.' At the funeral, I didn't see him either, closed casket."

I had asked Marge if afterward she had people she could talk to.

"No," she said. "No."

"Could you talk to your husband?"

"No," she said, "we never did. He just never felt the need to, apparently. I don't know how he did it. I just never saw him shed a tear."

Tom disagreed. "Some people are more private in what they think. When David died, I didn't cry in front of other people. But I cried on my own some. Marge says I'm kind of hard anyway; she thinks that I should feel more than I do right now."

Then Tom went on to agree with Marge, that she does feel more than he does: "I think it bothers Marge more than it bothers me. And I think it always will. Maybe I'm a fast recoverer or something." Later, however, talking again about the early days of David's death, he refined the who's-bothered-more issue: "I was reading a book and it had a list in it about the worst things that can happen to you and it gave you points depending on what happened to you—the death of a child, change of jobs, moving, accidents. I added up all the points, and I thought to myself, 'Holy smoke, you got a lot of bad things going here for you; you'll just have to watch yourself. Probably better off if you didn't read the damn thing because that makes you worry about it and that adds to all the other numbers that add up on you.'"

"Does that kind of thing make you feel more vulnerable?" I asked.

"That does," he said. "Once you start thinking about it. I think farther in the article they say how to alleviate the problems. Says relax. So you try to do that." Tom laughed. "It's hard to relax."

Though Marge and Tom both agreed that David's death was more difficult for Marge than for Tom, the death was difficult enough for Tom. But Tom said he wanted to focus, not on the difficulty, but on his ability to do what was necessary. "I felt pretty ratty for a while," he said, "but I think, really, after I accepted this thing, which I did a lot sooner than Marge did, I didn't dwell on it that much. It was like, protect yourself from things more. There's things that you really have to do. Because at the time of my son's death, I was broke—I had to borrow money to bury him. So you have to pay off the debts that you accumulate. And you have to make sure nothing like this will happen to your other two children."

Soon after David's death, Marge moved back in with Tom. "If David had not died," Marge said, "we would not be together today. Because we were barely on speaking terms. I do believe we would be divorced today if we hadn't been forced to communicate. We had to make funeral arrangements, we had to write thank-you cards, we had to talk about insurance money. Then Tom asked me if I would be willing to go to counseling again. We decided to try one more time and see if it would do any good. Tom did give a lot, and it was not easy for him. Except we never talked about David. And we still don't."

Tom's account of their history agreed with Marge's, except when talking about David. "It's absolute fact," he said. "Had David not died, we would have never gotten together again. And I like being married. It was talking about things that gave us the opportunity to get back together. And I guess when we were talking, mostly we were talking about David."

Did they talk about David or not? Probably they're both right: their styles of talking about painful things could be different enough that Tom would think he was talking and Marge wouldn't. Marge later refined the who-doesn't-talk issue. "The counselor we were seeing was a marriage counselor. She apparently had no training whatever in grief therapy because the first time I talked to her, David had only been dead three weeks, and I started to cry, and she said, 'Oh, you're still grieving?' So who was I going to talk to? I couldn't talk to Tom, the counselor didn't think I should talk, I guess most of my friends were embarrassed to talk about it."

Then she went on to say she couldn't talk about it anyway: "I'm still amazed—sometimes one of the talk shows on TV will have a parent whose child died recently—and the parents can talk about it. How can they *do* that? I couldn't even say his name for about two years."

I asked, "Do you mean you couldn't say his name without crying?"

Marge whispered, "Yes." She'd been crying off and on, and now she started crying again.

"There's still pain," she said. "It's just not as intense. And there are some days I still feel a sinking feeling in the pit of my stomach, or a weight on my chest. It's when I think I'll never see him again. But most of the time, you know, OK. And after four or five years, one day I said to Tom, 'If it hadn't been for David's death, I think I could be happy.'"

"Do you have certain times that are painful?" I asked.

"I guess just about every time I think about David," she said, and began crying again. "I try to think of the good things so it's not so painful. And then you just wonder *why* couldn't he have been given another chance? You hear of people who get seriously injured but *recover*. And this is not a nice thing to say, but when they were growing up, Jeffrey was always the one to take chances. I always thought if something happened to one of my children, it would be him. Not that I wish Jeffrey would have died instead. One time when Jeffrey was in trouble and giving us a hard time, he said, 'I guess you wish it had been me that died instead of David. The wrong son died.' I said, 'Oh, Jeffrey, how could you say such a thing?'"

"Do your kids talk about David's death?" I asked.

"No," Marge said. "In fact, I think that's the only thing Jeffrey's ever said about David. I think that they're afraid to make me cry."

Marge was still crying. Her crying didn't interfere with talking. She seemed in no way unwilling to talk but gave short answers, every answer preceded by one long silence, followed by another.

I went on to my next question: "Do you think your relationship with your other kids has changed since David's death?"

"Oh yes, very definitely," Marge said. "At first my daughter, Terry, would not even speak to me. At the funeral, she refused to even sit next to me in the church, and she made that very obvious, very pointed, switching places with somebody so she didn't have to sit next to me. She blamed me, I guess. For not being there, I guess, when David died."

"*Why?*" I asked. I thought Terry was extremely unfair.

Marge didn't blame her, though. "If I had been living in that house," Marge said, "David would not have gone out that night. I would have been there to say, 'This is a school night. You don't go out on school nights.'"

I asked, "Have you and Terry settled this?"

"It took a long time. It wasn't until after I moved back home. Even then we didn't talk or visit—I guess it was a couple of years. It was a gradual thing. It just evolved. And Jeffrey is not one to talk about things very much either. But when I was separated from Tom, Jeffrey would come over to my apartment for dinner once in a while. So my relationship with Jeffrey didn't change much after David died, until I moved back home, and then I was after him to keep his room neat. Nobody did that when I wasn't there. The house was, aaagh," and she rolled her eyes and laughed. "I don't know how I moved back in."

She was quiet for a minute, apparently thinking about her relations with Terry and Jeffrey, because she began talking about problems she'd had with David before he died. "My relationship with David was strained right before he died—very, very strained. We had a couple of incidents. This was bad."

She took a breath and continued. "He was one of the main reasons I left home. On one occasion, he knocked on our bedroom door at five in the morning and he proceeded to tell us that—." Marge interrupted herself to backtrack.

"He had worked part-time for a restaurant washing dishes, and sometimes he would get home after we went to bed. We found out later that he would come in, take the keys to my car, and go out joyriding. He didn't even have a driver's license."

Then she jumped back to the morning he knocked on their bedroom door. "That night he took my car for a joy-ride, ran it off the road trying to avoid hitting an animal, and got stuck in a ravine and couldn't get out. He spent all night trying to push this car out. Well, I had AAA, they got the car out, fortunately it wasn't damaged. I was taking David to a counselor at the time because he got kicked out of his private high school because he wrote on the walls, things like that. He was a very angry young man. When I told the counselor about the car, she said, 'You have to report that to the police. That's a crime. It's just not fair letting a kid get away with these things.' So against my better judgment, I did tell this one policemen who knew there was friction in our family. And David was furious about that. Next time we went down to see the counselor, he kicked a hole in the wall in the office. And the counselor said, 'That should be reported too.' And I said, 'Then you do it, I'm not doing it any more. I don't want him to hate me.' Then a couple days later he was suspended from school for a couple days, I don't remember what for. And then he asked my husband and I to lend him money to buy a new stereo that was on sale. I said,

'No, I'm not going to reward him for getting suspended from school by buying this thing.' I said, 'Tom, that's totally wrong. There'll be another sale.' So I left for work and when I got back an hour and a half later, David had the stereo. I told Tom, 'You're not going to supersede my authority over what I thought was a mutual decision and reward David for bad behavior.' I said, 'This is the last straw.'"

Marge's quietness had vanished; she was still angry about this. "I left right after that," she said.

And now her voice got quiet again. "So as I said, my relationship with David was very strained. That was in June, and he died that October. I had seen him a couple of times. I went back to the house one time to pick up something—Jeffrey had made me a pair of bookends which I hadn't taken with me when I moved out—so I put them in the bag and was going to take them with me. And David came charging at me. He said, 'You're not taking anything from this house.' I said, 'These are mine, I've already talked to Jeffrey about it.' And he was—"

She stopped and thought about how to describe David—"out of it. I was not going to take those things, and he tried forcibly to stop me. And I went to the phone and I said, 'Don't you do this to me'— he even kicked at me—I said, 'I'm going to call the police. You let me leave this house with this.' And I picked up the phone and I dialed the police station, and he ran out of the house. And the police said, 'Come in and tell us what happened.' So I went down there and they said they were going to talk to the police officer who knew David. And then they called my husband and me and David into juvenile detention to talk to a counselor there, and she said, 'We're not going to do anything about these incidents at this time, but let this serve as a warning if you do anything, David, you're going to probably wind up in juvenile hall.' So we left there. The last thing David said to me was, 'I hate you. And I hope you're going to be so poor that you live on the street like a bag lady.' That's the last thing he said to me."

And Marge, understandably, started crying again. After a while I said stupidly that the incident must still cause her pain.

She didn't hesitate: "Sure."

"Even though you know he didn't mean it," I said.

"I know it wasn't true—but those were his feelings toward me, the last thing he said to me."

Marge cried a little more, then stopped, and I went on to my next question, about whether she felt guilt or self-blame: "I don't mean you have reason to," I added, "but you did have people blaming you."

"I know what you mean. I'm sure I have a lot of guilt. Even though I *know* in my heart that I didn't do anything intentionally to bring about this set of circumstances. But the facts are there."

I didn't understand her answer. She felt guilty even though she knew she didn't intend this set of circumstances? Which set of circumstances? David's anger with her? David's death? I couldn't tell, though the next thing she said implied she meant his death: "I think as parents we always think we could have done something differently so he wouldn't have been in that place at that time." So if the set of circumstances was David's death, then what did she mean by "the facts are there"? Because she moved out and because David blamed her, she's responsible for his death? She didn't explain further, I didn't want to ask, and we sat without talking.

After a long while, I continued my questions. "Some people say they now feel more distant from their child, some say their child is present and they'll never let go. Do you feel one or the other or neither?"

Marge answered by telling a story about a friend whose son, Jimmy, had been killed in a school bus accident. "I remember the first time I talked to her, she told me, 'I miss Jimmy but I know he's with me. I'm not very religious, but I feel his presence all the time.' And I said, 'Really!' because I do consider myself religious and I never feel like I'm communicating with David, or that he knows what's going on. I wish I did."

Marge sat quietly again, then went on. "I think part of the grief is not *knowing* where they are. If we knew for certain that the afterlife is a reality, that it's a place of refreshment-light-and-peace, it would be easier to accept. Being Catholic, some of my friends say it should be easier for me because I do believe in an afterlife. But I think it's harder, in that we believe in hell and purgatory. And according to the teaching of the faith, David was not in a state of grace at the time of his death. And that makes me feel bad—"

She waited a minute, then went on. "—because maybe he's still in purgatory. Or maybe he didn't even make it that far."

She waited again. "And that's a terrible thing."

I thought this was terrible too, and said that I couldn't think God would judge a sixteen-year-old so harshly.

"It doesn't sound like a very loving God, does it," she said.

"Has your feeling about God changed?" I asked.

"I go back and forth," she said. "Sometimes I feel that it must be a loving and forgiving father, and other times, I'm afraid that He's more of a taskmaster and is going to hold us accountable."

She thought for a while. "And some people say God didn't take David, He received him. That's a good thought."

Marge definitely had more she could have said about David and an afterlife, but she equally definitely was not going to say it, and neither silences nor direct questions on my part would move her. Tom did say it, however, and though I suspect the two of them didn't talk much about this together, he almost seemed to be talking for her.

I had asked Tom whether he felt any guilt or self-blame, and he said no, but then added: "There was one bad thing about it. He was gone before I got home, and you always think, maybe if I was there I could have stopped him from going out. But I probably couldn't have."

I interrupted because I hated to hear parents blaming themselves. "I think parents feel to blame regardless," I said.

"Well," Tom said, "you think, if I had been harder on him maybe, that maybe you don't know if he had done everything he wanted to do. You don't know."

Tom usually talked with military directness, but now he was confusing and hard to follow. I think he meant that if he had been harder on David, then David wouldn't have tried to go out and do everything he wanted to do. Next Tom made one of those abrupt transitions that people make when they're following their own thoughts and not worrying about being understood.

"The Catholic Church, which I go to, says you know what you're doing when you're six years old," he said. "So sure as hell a boy who's *sixteen* knows what he's doing. He's going to do it unless you have a lotta, lotta influence against him."

I was getting lost, so I repeated, "David was sixteen and you no longer had that much influence over him?"

Tom didn't really answer. "Well, we had enough to keep him angry at us a lot of the time."

In spite of not liking to hear parents blaming themselves, I wanted to know whether Tom really believed the church was right and David knew what he was doing, or whether Tom blamed himself for not having more influence over David. But Tom didn't want to talk about it, and the interview went on to other matters. Tom digressed easily, and at one point, he was talking about taking a night school course for which he had to read aloud a poem he chose.

"One of the kids that David went to school with brought this poem after the funeral," he said. "He read it then, that kid. It's a neat poem. It makes you cry. I have it somewhere, but it was neat, it was really good. It was about God calling away your child. And it wasn't real short, it was about a page. Hard to read. Hard to read out loud. I read it to that class and I couldn't talk when I was about three-quarters through it. Guy wanted to read it for me. I said, 'No.'"

I wanted to know more about what the poem said. First Tom said he couldn't remember, then he said, "Oh, it had to do with God calling away a child. The child was only here on loan and He decided He wanted the child back. Something to that effect. It was really neat. It's my favorite poem. But it wouldn't make me cry now."

"You don't think so?" I asked. "You don't think it might just hit you?"

"No," he said, "I don't think it would. Because it's really a nice poem. It makes you feel better. Kind of makes you feel like he went to heaven. Like he didn't go to hell. Which is supposedly the big deal if you listen to them in church. That's supposed to be what it's all about. According to them, it's how you end up."

"I don't think there's a chance that a sixteen-year-old boy's going to go to hell," I said.

"I don't know," Tom said. "I don't know. You're not supposed to run around, do things your parents don't want you to. And who knows? Maybe he was having intercourse with some girls he wasn't supposed to be having. That's considered nasty in the Catholic Church. I don't know. There shouldn't be too much chance of his going to hell. But it doesn't really bother me. I think it bothers my wife. She'll say a couple times, 'Where do you think he is?' And I say, 'What do you mean, where do you think he is.'"

"Does she mean, do you think he's in heaven?" I asked.

"Yeah," Tom said. "And I say, 'He's all right. Look at all the Mass cards you got for him. I wish they were for me.'"

Tom was circling a specific chain of logic: If the church is right, then David knew what he was doing and Tom wasn't responsible for him or his death. But in that case, the church would also be right about the boy going to hell. And though Tom dismisses Marge's worry about David in hell with a flippancy—he wishes the Masses were being said for him—he's still talking about it.

What Marge and Tom are agreeing on is the complicated issues of guilt and religion, which I think are at bottom the single issue of attribution—why did the child die?—and are the subjects of later chapters.

I asked Marge, "Do you think you're more selfish?"

She talked briefly about spending more on food and clothes for herself than she used to, and added, "I guess mostly I'm more selfish about my money and my time. I never did much volunteer work before now."

Not everyone would equate being more selfish with doing more volunteer work. So I asked her questions about how she used her time and about her job. Marge sells real estate, so successfully that she is a lifetime member of the Million Dollar Association. Since David died, she says, she still does a good job, but "I don't knock myself out to sell the million dollars every year. After I got my lifetime Million Dollar Associates, I decided there were more important things to do.

So I volunteer at a place called Joseph House, which is an outreach to the poor in Baltimore City."

"How did you start at Joseph House?" I asked.

"Long time ago at Christmas time, I was talking to a friend and said, 'We would like to give a donation to some charitable institution where the money is going to go to help the poor and not into the administrator's pocket.' And she told me about this Joseph House. And I started contributing on a fairly regular basis. And then, about four years ago, they said in the newsletter that they needed volunteers. And that's when I called and started doing that. We work out of St. Michael's Church in east Baltimore. It's a rough neighborhood; we always go in pairs when we go any place."

It is indeed one of Baltimore's roughest neighborhoods, full of the same drugs, crime, neglected children, and chaotic families of the rough neighborhoods of any large city.

"I can't say it's emotionally rewarding," Marge said, "because a lot of times it's very frustrating. The people don't seem to want to change much. But you do the best you can and try to improve their situation. We know that some of the people that we give food to will go out and sell the food and buy whisky. But it does more good than harm. So . . ."

She seemed to have run out of things to say, but I wanted to know more about a four-year personal investment in such an unrewarding place. So she elaborated.

"We have a policy of making home visits to people. We try to stabilize family life, or help to. So the first thing we do is schedule a home visit. And usually that's what I do when I'm there, is go out and make a home visit. We try to find out a lot of different things. We get information about what they pay in rent, gas and electric, food, what their needs are. And then we usually invite them to come into the Joseph House. There we have bags of groceries, not a hot meal, but things they can take home to prepare meals with the family."

Marge went into detail about the people she helps, and the troubles they have, and how she and her colleagues at Joseph House teach

35

parents to budget and to interact with their children, to nurture and, at the same time, to build up the parent's self-esteem. She sounded happy and competent and in charge.

"So you're trying to stabilize families?" I asked.

"Yes," she said, "get them back on track. And it's not something that happens right away. But we see the same people sometimes for three years, once a week. We try to befriend them. We're not just there to hand out a bag of groceries and say, 'See you next week.' We really like to help them change their lives. I'll tell you the truth, I get a lot more than I give. For one thing, I see how damn better off I am than they are."

I asked if she saw a connection between David's death, keeping families together, and Joseph House.

She whispered, "Oh *yes*. Sure. Sure." She started crying, as unobtrusively as always. "We try to keep the families stabilized. And maybe that is a connection. My own family was in such a—" and now she switched from crying to laughing, stuck her tongue out, and made a raspberry sound. "So I put other families back together."

Chapter 3

FATHERS AND MOTHERS,
HUSBANDS AND WIVES

Changes in the Marriage

M arge talked about many things other than her marriage: her emotional isolation, her sense of guilt, her worries about God. All these things came up in interviews with the other parents as well, and are the subjects of later chapters. Marge's marriage, however, and its effect on her other children and on David were clearly on her mind. In fact, her preoccupation with them was great enough that she spent years helping to keep other families together.

A few of the things that pushed Tom and Marge apart were evident in other parents' marriages: the mother takes the death harder, the father doesn't cry and doesn't talk, and the couple argues about the whole thing. Common wisdom says that the deaths of children are harder on mothers than on fathers. It also says that those deaths are hard enough on both parents that marriages often break up. Common wisdom usually contains some truth, if only because people believe it and act accordingly.

To give common wisdom its due, it has supporters among both bereaved parents and researchers. Tom thought that Marge felt more about David's death and that she recovered less quickly than he did. One mother said, "I think a mother who carried the child has much more feeling than a father. I mean, they've *got* to." Another father agreed because, he said, the child had been at one time a physical part of the mother.

Some researchers agree with these parents. A number of studies from the 1970s and early 1980s found that women feel the symptoms of grief more intensely and for a longer time. One large 1982 study of parents whose children had died of sudden infant death syndrome found no difference in how long mothers and fathers took to recover, but found also that fathers showed more anger than mothers, feared loss of control more, and desired more to be private, whereas mothers showed more sorrow and depression. Another study, however, found that mothers showed more anger, and still another found mothers and fathers equally depressed.

In a Scandinavian study done in 1987, mothers reported feeling more anxious, self-reproachful, and sad than did fathers; mothers also had more trouble sleeping. Mothers and fathers reported being equally angry, restless, and involved with work. Both mothers and fathers agreed with the earlier studies, that the mothers' grief was more intense and lasted longer. The Scandinavian researchers suspected, but couldn't prove, that the differences were the result of the fathers simply not reporting their emotions.

A later study, done in 1990, didn't settle for parents' reports of their emotions but instead gave the parents psychological tests for these emotions. On tests of all grief reactions (which researchers call "grief indicators")—including despair, anger, guilt, anxiety, loss of control, loss of vigor—mothers scored higher. The only test on which fathers scored higher was denial, that is, fathers were more likely to handle an emotion by denying its existence. "This finding," the researchers wrote, "may account for husbands' mean scores being lower than wives' scores on most other grief indicators."

Still another study, published in 1991, of Israeli parents whose sons had died in the Arab-Israeli wars, found men reporting fewer effects of bereavement and suggested the result had "much to do with styles of monitoring and acknowledging difficulties." The same study found women's level of discomfort improving over time more dramatically than men's.

My prejudice before beginning these interviews was that the effect of losing a child must be equally great for fathers and mothers. My prejudice—as prejudices often do—survived the interviews intact. The fathers to whom I talked are, like the mothers, at the limits of their capacity to take pain. Tom said David's death bothered Marge more than him, but he also said he'd never "had any problems that big before." He used those vivid metaphors of being down in the gutter, and of being sick and throwing up. And when I asked if perhaps some part of him had died, he said that on the contrary, David's death made him "drive harder to do what you're supposed to do." Could the effect on Marge be deeper or longer-lasting than that? Fathers still think about their children, still love their children, and most of them said the deaths have changed them profoundly.

Mary Norris's son, Theodore Junior, died at age twenty-seven, after his body rejected a transplanted kidney. Three years later, Mary's husband died of a heart attack. I asked her if during those three years, her marriage changed. "My husband used to grieve a lot," she said. "He and the son, they were so close, you know. My husband used to love to get off to himself. Instead of him and I sitting together, he used to go by a stream of water, just sit and think, you know. He used to grieve to his own self."

"Where would he go?" I asked.

"I really don't know," she said. "He was a motorcycle rider and he used to take that motorcycle and go all over the woods. Just sit by the stream and think. And come home. But he would never come out and tell me what's on his mind. He just kept it inward."

"Did you ask him?" I said.

"Yeah, I asked him. He says, 'No problem. I'll get over it.' That's what he always would tell me, 'I'll get over it.'"

"Did he mind if you talked about it?" I said.

"No," she said, "he didn't mind."

What Mary said is what I heard most frequently: mothers and

fathers differ in what they do about their grief, how they show it. This is what the later research studies found, and it is what Tom meant when he said, "I think after I accepted this thing, I didn't dwell on it that much. It was like, protect yourself more."

The differences between fathers and mothers in their styles of grieving are, of course, the differences in the social roles that decree how men and women handle emotion. According to researchers, bereaved fathers put their grief into a compartment separate from the rest of their lives. They feel they need to console and protect their families and so need to submerge their own grief. And they dislike being overcome by intense emotion and feel that talking about the emotion only makes it worse. They deal with grief by thinking about something else, by doing something else, and when they do cry, they cry alone in the garage, in the car, at the cemetery.

The parents I interviewed agreed that the fathers do these things. Agreement is hardly surprising, since social roles wouldn't have the impact they do unless they were widely accepted. My problem is that half the fathers I interviewed weren't following the male social roles, and many of the mothers were. This problem could easily be the result of a statistically small sample of people: the number of exceptions can equal the number of the people that follow the rule.

Everyone agrees, for instance, that men don't want to talk about it. Of the six fathers I talked to, five volunteered under pressure from their wives or from me; the sixth, Walter Farnandis, had raised his son alone. Tom and Marge both said Tom didn't like to talk about either David's death or his grief. Three of the fathers—Mitch Dudnikov, Brandt Jones, and Chris Reed—had stayed in either Compassionate Friends or Seasons long enough to have a combined total of forty-four years experience with grieving parents, and all three said that men don't like to talk at meetings, and don't even like to come to the meetings in the first place. When men do come, they say, they're coming to make their wives happy.

"Walter, my husband, went with me to Compassionate Friends the first time," said Elaine Levin, "because he said, 'I don't want you driving out there by yourself at night—you're upset, et cetera, et cetera.'

So that was his reason for coming with me. And he came every time after that."

According to those three fathers, Walter is an exception in one way: generally when men do come to the meetings, they don't come back. "We went down to one of those Compassionate Friends things one time," Tom said. "Maybe it's good for some people but it wasn't any good for me. When I go out with a bunch of people, I don't want to talk about bad things."

But when Mitch, Brandt, and Chris described themselves, they all three said they wanted to talk. Of the three, only Mitch said he talked less than his wife did: "Renee is very emotional, everything comes right out in her. She would talk and talk and talk about Marc, and I would just listen and I would think to myself about Marc." On the other hand, Mitch was president of the local chapter of Compassionate Friends for years.

"Men are different from women in grieving, in that men tend to suppress their grief," Chris began, then explained how he was different. "But I felt I needed to get it out. I didn't want to keep it suppressed."

"Do you think men feel grief as deeply as women?" I asked.

"Oh, I'm sure," Chris said. "Speaking for myself, yes. I felt it very profoundly. And I believe other men feel it just as deeply. It's just that men, particularly in our society—because of the image of men's being strong and somewhat macho—grow up with the idea of big boys don't cry. But that's awful difficult to deal with when you're faced with the suicide of a *child,* not to cry. Many times I've had people say to me, 'How's Helen doing, Chris?' Not 'how are *you* doing,' like I'm the big strong guy, I can carry on. But my wife being a female is weak and she needs support and comfort. That's very difficult to deal with, at least it was for me."

Chris went on to say that he began going to Seasons because he particularly wanted to talk to other men, and at Seasons, he found men who would talk: "They were able to forget the feeling of big-boys-don't-cry, and be willing to talk about their grief." In fact, even Tom, the "fast recoverer" who is "more private in what I think," said that at the time of David's death, "there wasn't a whole lot of people I could talk to, except I had a few friends, one or two guys from work, that I could talk to. I had one guy that I always talked to."

Another point on which researchers and parents agreed is that men submerge their own grief to take care of their families. "The big problem is this thing drilled in," said Brandt, "that you're the father, you're the one that's got the answers. So you sit back and say, 'What are the words that are going to make all this better?' There are none. But you have this driving force that says, 'I've got to make this better because I don't want to see them suffer. What do I do to *fix* that?' I was concentrating so much on what to tell Betty and what to do for Betty that it was tearing me up inside subconsciously, that I wasn't thinking about what it was doing to me."

Brandt was the only father who was explicit about this, both about submerging his own grief and about taking care of his family's. Tom implied something similar: "There's things that you really have to do," he said, which included paying off debts and protecting his other children. The only other parent who was as explicit as Brandt, however, was a mother, Elaine Levin. Talking about the year that her son was losing the fight with osteosarcoma, she explained, "I had to be strong because everybody else around me was falling apart. I knew if I let myself go, that would be it, we'd all go under. My approach was, 'OK, so this is what he has. How are we going to get him better?'"

The third point, that fathers deal with grief by distracting themselves with jobs, hobbies, duties, pleasures, is certainly true. Chris said he was back at work in a week because he didn't want to sit around in the depths of his grief. Mitch said that even eighteen years later, "I plunge myself into my hobbies now. There, before, I used to plunge myself into work. I didn't even care what I was doing. It does help you because you've got to keep going."

But this was equally true for mothers. "It's the old, 'Let's keep busy,' said Brandt's wife, Betty, after fourteen years. "To this day, I go to bed with a book so I can read while I fall asleep. And I always have a book with me when I'm in the car and someone else is driving. Or else my thoughts will immediately turn to the fact that my son is dead." Emily Miller repeated Betty nearly verbatim: "To this day, I need to be busy. Free time is not good for me. I get depressed. I'm at loose ends—" and she shook her hands to show how her hands nervously need to be occupied.

If these arguments do not illustrate the dangers of drawing conclusions from small numbers of people, then maybe they suggest that differences in the way individuals grieve are greater than the differences in the way the sexes grieve. Do Marge and Tom show grief differently because they are Marge and Tom, or because they are female and male? Certainly every person grieves differently. Certainly men and women have different styles. I haven't a clue which difference is greater, and no researcher has done this study.

Partly because the parents contradicted their social roles, partly because researchers haven't separated out differences in social roles from individual differences, and partly because researchers contradicted each other's findings, I'm wary of drawing conclusions about differences in mothers' and fathers' grieving styles.

For what it's worth, I was surprised to hear fathers saying two things I did not also hear mothers saying. One was that they had become more sensitive to other people's feelings, more aware of pain in other people. Mothers said this too, but didn't emphasize it and didn't seem to see it as a big change. Increased sensitivity to other people was not a question I asked; the fathers volunteered this response to general questions about how they had changed.

"It made me more aware in general of what's happening to other people," said Tom. "How, when something happens to them, it's a shame they're going to have to feel that bad."

"I think I've become a more caring person," said Chris. "I have less focus on myself and more focus on other people."

"It's made me much more perceptive, certainly, about other people," said Leight Johnson.

"If Marc were alive," said Mitch, "I think I would have been more of an introvert."

"I became more people-oriented than I was before," said Brandt, who was an officer in the navy. "I became more concerned about the feelings of the individual I gave an order to. Because I had been up to that point, 'Dammit, this is what I want done. And I don't want any arguments out of you, and you're not leaving here until you get it done.' I found myself backing off from that mindset. Later, I'd go in and say, 'Look, here's the job, we've got to have it done by this date, this is what I need you to do. You got any questions?' and work it that way."

The other thing fathers said that mothers didn't was that they missed a sense of lineage, of their children carrying their names on into the future. At least part of the reason is obvious: children take their fathers' names, not their mothers'.

Probably the only reason for caring about men's and women's differences in handling grief is what those differences do to a marriage.

I have an odd ignorance on this subject. My husband is not T.C.'s father. T.C.'s father and I had divorced six years before T.C. died, and the distant working relationship we had before T.C.'s death faded quickly afterward to nothing at all. So my husband is T.C.'s stepfather. He loved T.C. and invested as much in him as any stepparent ever has, and more than most I know. He grieves T.C. and misses him. By his own report, the effect on his life of T.C.'s death is unparalleled. I can say nothing to him about my own grief that he doesn't understand. But all the same, I have been happy that he isn't T.C.'s father. I feel less selfish asking for his support than I would otherwise. I don't know what it's like to look across the dinner table and see someone else hurt to the limits of his capacity to be hurt, and I'm glad I don't; it must be a depressing sight. What I'm saying is, even though my husband and I grieved differently, I could ascribe some of those differences to the offset in investment that a stepparent has with a stepchild. In short, I doubt that I understand exactly what kind of problem those differences cause.

The size of that problem, in any case, is anything but clear. A grief therapist I went to for my own marriage problems after T.C.'s death told me that 85 percent of marriages split up after a child died. The word at the local chapter of Compassionate Friends was that 75 percent split up. One study said that most marriages were worse off; another said that with time, people felt better about their marriages. A 1989 study said that bereaved parents were more likely than nonbereaved parents to divorce; and that 30 percent said their marriages were worse, 40 percent said better, 20 percent said the same, and 10 percent didn't respond. The same study said that marriages appear either to get better or to get worse, one or the other. A 1988 review of all studies said different studies showed ranges from 24 to 70 percent, and that the divorce rate among bereaved parents is more talked about than understood.

Part of the reason for the confusion is that the studies report two different things: one is a negative change in the marriage, the other is the rate of marriages that don't make it. Another reason for the confusion is that those studies that talk about a change in the marriage measure that change in different ways, either by psychological testing or by asking people whether they felt better or worse about the marriage. Why no one agrees on the simple number, the rate of divorce among bereaved parents, is a mystery.

Most of the thirty parents I interviewed have remained married. Three marriages had broken up before the child died; one of those parents has since remarried. The Fords, who had already separated, got back together. Four marriages broke up after the child's death. Each of the four that broke up was, not surprisingly, unique.

Diana Moores's daughter, Mindy, died when Diana's husband was changing the radio station while driving and ran into the back of a parked truck. Diana reacted by not having any emotions at all, and on the advice of her psychologist, checked herself into a psychiatric hospital. When she left the hospital, two years later, she didn't return home, but moved into an apartment.

"I knew I couldn't go home," Diana said. "We had had some problems before the accident happened. And afterward—we'd been married for twenty-three years and I still loved him *very* very much—but I knew with all these mixed feelings and the trouble we had before, there was just no way I could live with him. I think my love for him and compassion for him, having been in the position that he was, is so

45

huge that I get past the anger 99.9 percent of the time. I keep it very well controlled, I never have shown any rage toward him, I love him to death. We're *best* best friends and we're both so careful and so gentle. But how can I forgive him? I mean, how can I forgive that negligently he took my child away? Sometimes I think about getting back together with him and ask him about it. But when I sit and am real honest with myself, I know that if we were together we would drag each other down to the point where neither one could function. Because what we have most in common now is Mindy's death. That's what we have a need to talk about with each other because no one else understands. I think if we were together all the time, it would just be overwhelming." Recently, Diana and her husband divorced.

A woman whom I'll call Nancy and her husband are just divorcing, fifteen years after their three-year-old son, Jimmy, died. Jimmy had wandered off, Nancy went looking for him and found him drowned in their swimming pool. "I felt partly to blame," Nancy said, "and I also was blamed. He would say, 'Oh no, you shouldn't feel guilty.' And yet all of his actions then said that I should. Like a couple of weeks later, a puppy of ours was missing. I looked for that puppy, but boy was it hard. When you've looked for a child and then you have to go look for something else, it's awful. He said to me that night, 'You didn't bother to look for the puppy just like you didn't bother to look for Jimmy.' And our whole relationship was built on guilt and blame. Because I killed his namesake. Being told I'll never understand what it is to lose your namesake—don't ask me to know, because I *can't* know. And there are things that *he* can't possibly know. I think you have to work it through individually, but then again I also think you have to work it through together as a couple, to be able to survive."

Nickie Copinger and her husband separated for a couple months after their son, Adam, died of an inherited immune deficiency. "My husband and I grieve Adam completely separate," she said. "The barrier it put between us in communication was horrible. We stayed together, but we were really putting a distance between ourselves."

After Adam died, Nickie's husband sold a business: "His work record hasn't been steady since," Nickie said. Four years after Adam died, Nickie and her husband had another son, Alex.

"We got to the point where we felt the only thing we had in common was our child," Nickie said. "And my husband felt if we didn't have another child, we probably wouldn't stay together." But another child didn't pull them closer, partly, Nickie said, because she immersed herself in Alex: "I had an easy out. I had a baby to care for."

Later, they found out that Alex inherited the same immune deficiency that had killed Adam. And somewhere in this chronology, Nickie's husband had an affair, which Nickie learned about last year. "Last year I was willing to give the marriage up, didn't bother me a bit," Nickie said. "I didn't want to be married, I just didn't want to be there." But Nickie and her husband are still married and trying to work things out.

Anne Perkins' marriage was already in trouble when her son, Robert, was killed in a car accident: "I think that Robert's death hastened the breakup of something that should have broken up a long time ago." Anne and her husband differed over visiting Robert's grave; Anne didn't want to, her husband did. They differed over how to remember Robert; Anne thought her husband was glorifying Robert, making him into someone he wasn't. "And there was just a feeling I had," Anne said, "that whatever it was, he thought I was not doing it right, or enough of it. Both of us needed to be taken care of but you don't have the strength to take care of the other person. Everything was difficult."

Dennis Klass, the grief researcher, says that people who divorce after the child's death say that the death wasn't a central factor. "Marriages don't die with the death of a child," he wrote, "but often they receive an overdue burial." The reason divorces happen after the death, Klass says, is that people who had already been having problems find that those problems are no longer worth trying to solve. "After accepting the reality of the loss of the child," Klass wrote, "accepting the reality of the prior death of the marriage is a small step."

What I noticed in the interviews was that the couples who divorced grieved separately, each handling the grief in his or her own way.

Nancy is right; no one *can* know exactly what the other feels. But in truth, all couples grieve separately. Depending on each person's particular psychological rules, he or she might need to talk about the grief or sidestep it, need to be alone or be angry or be depressed or pull away from people or get closer to people or all these things and more at different times. And it's hard not to assume your particular way of grieving is everyone else's way. Even couples who usually work out disagreements have trouble not making judgments: one grieves too selfishly and indulgently, the other doesn't really love the child. The child's death pushes parents to their limits, and people need to handle themselves with whatever resources they have. "When a child dies, both parents must grieve in their own ways," wrote Klass, "for the death of a child is a matter of the self in its solitude."

Moreover, people are hurt so personally and deeply that they need to tend only to themselves. For a while they stop loving anyone; they neglect each other. But because couples also expect nurturing and attention from each other, they feel neglected themselves.

Betty said she and Brandt, early on, "had some difficulties. I couldn't help him and he couldn't help me, which is a horrible situation. And I didn't care about his feelings. I hurt so bad that if he put his dirty clothes on the floor, I fussed at him, whereas before I would have picked them up and put them in the hamper. But after, I just didn't care how he felt."

Brandt agreed they had had difficulties. For his part, Brandt said, "what bothered me most was that she didn't handle some things the way I thought she should. I was on pins and needles for a while because her tact and diplomacy went right out the window. It was just as if she cut people right off at the ankles. So that bothered me. She still does it to a certain extent but now I understand it."

Julia Marcus, the social worker who lost both a twenty-day-old baby and a twenty-five-year-old daughter, said she honestly didn't know whether the deaths changed her marriage. "I'm sure it has," she said. "Everything that happens to you changes it. I'm sure there were times that we were both very depressed and expecting a lot of sympathy and didn't get it because the other person was too depressed. But we've been around a long time and we've each developed some other people that we count on too. So the fact that we weren't as dependent on each other probably helps. Plus every now and then I would rally forth some good social work principle, like, 'You can't expect your husband to be supportive to you, he's too busy grieving himself.' We're just very different kinds of people, too. I don't know exactly how he feels. He doesn't have the problems some men have about crying, or saying how awful he feels. I think how it affects your marriage probably depends on what stage of your marriage you're in. I think a certain number of years earlier, it probably would have played havoc. But now, in some respects, I think it's made us closer. I don't think we take *anything* for granted any more."

What Julia is saying is what most of the parents said. Every couple, regardless of whether they split up or not, had a period of not being able to get or give the necessary attention. The couples that stayed together went on to say what Julia did, that they asked other people for support, that they tolerated each other's differences, that something they now have in common has made them closer.

Ginny Mitchell's son Joel died of a cancer of the kidney called Wilm's tumor, at age twelve. "My husband, Fred, that winter after Joel died, refinished our basement," Ginny said. "He got very angry, initially, after Joel had died. He pounded his way through the first winter. I've seen families that go apart. Sometimes, especially when Joel was ill, we were both just so mentally drained, physically drained, I guess we didn't have too much time for each other. When Joel first died, you're that way too. That puts a strain on the marriage. We kept going and doing things. So that was our salvation, that we each were able to be involved in our various activities. I think it's drawn us together more."

Leight Johnson, about a month after his son was killed in a car accident, thought that his wife was giving him "a real cold shoulder. So I said, 'Look, what is it?' And she said, 'I just can't understand why you're not grieving any more. Whereas to me, it's just so horrible.' I said, 'You just aren't with me when I cry. You're not with me when I

49

have to leave the office or when I have to stop the car because I can't see.' I remember thinking at the time, the marriage could have gone the other way if I hadn't asked her what was wrong. We could have just kind of drifted away—probably stayed together but never quite had the relationship."

Chris and his wife did a lot of talking, he said, "mostly about Mary and about suicide and about grief. I think we both felt the loss very, very deeply. Much of my grief was taken up with my guilt. On the other hand, much of my wife's grief was taken up with anger. She was and still is angry at God. She thinks He should have protected her daughter. And I never felt that way. So we were on somewhat different wavelengths. But I don't have any problem with that. It would be nice if she'd go to church with me, but I respect her feelings. I mean, it's just a given; she has been angry at God for ten years and probably is never going to change. But we were never so totally out of synch we couldn't understand each other. We were always willing to talk about it. If I didn't feel like talking about it, I'd at least let her have her say. And she'd do the same with me."

"We had a really bad time the first year," said Sally Lambert. "Oh, it was bad. I mean, we *argued*. His way was to stay very physically active. And I'm sure when he came home and took a look at me, he didn't want to see that. I thought he wasn't grieving. He *was* grieving, in his way. For a short while, I went for therapy, and the therapist said to me, 'Sally, you're just going to have to accept that the person you want most in this world to be able to grieve with, you just cannot do that.' I feel like we have a *real* strong marriage after going through that. I guess neither one of us talks about it much now. Sometimes he'll bring it up himself. The subject is not forbidden. But maybe I've gotten the same way. I don't talk about it either. It's not that we don't talk about Lisa, but just not about the death and about how we're feeling now. He did tell me, years later, he said, 'You know that feeling of sadness we were talking about, that you feel it coming over you. It'll just *hit* me.'"

Walter and Elaine Levin, like Anne Perkins and her former husband, disagree about going to the cemetery. Walter has gone every

Sunday for sixteen years. Elaine said, "I always tell my husband, 'I don't have to go to the cemetery, Merrill's in my heart.' Going there, it's just a stone. On Merrill's birthday I go. One day Walter said, 'I know you were out at the cemetery, I saw flowers out there.' I said, 'Yes, I was. But when the time comes in the hereafter, Merrill's going to greet you and say, 'Hi, Dad, I see you every week, but who's the fat broad?'"

If the problem is separate ways of grieving, the solution is obvious: talk about it, grieve the way you must, and allow the other person the same privilege. Compassionate Friends repeats this over and over. "You don't have to grieve the same way," said Mitch. "If you have some tolerance, you can handle it easily." Between the obviousness of the solution, and the repetition of it, I doubt that grieving would break up people who wanted to stay together.

I'm not saying these marriages are living happily ever after; people and their relationships are more complicated than that. But even couples like the Fords, whose grief has pushed them a little inside themselves, who do not present a united front, still have a certain extra commonality. That is, they seem to have an unspoken agreement to handle grief, separately when necessary, but fundamentally the same way, together.

I wouldn't argue that this added commonality has kept the Fords or the majority of these parents together. But I suspect about them what is true for me. My own marriage to T.C.'s stepfather seems deeper because we've gone through this together, and I value him more because he too still loves T.C. What remains of the child is memories, and the only other person who stores those memories is often your husband or wife. And you've changed now, and the only other person who understands the reason for your new attitudes and preoccupations is your husband or wife.

Delores Shoda's son died of melanoma at age twenty-eight. In the seven years since, she and her husband, she said, "are maybe not as close as we used to be. You find you don't have as much to say, maybe you're quieter. That could be true, because there's things maybe I would like to talk about and I won't say it because it's going to make

51

him feel pain and I don't want to do that. We don't talk as much. Though we don't like to be separated from each other."

"I think my husband's not the same person he was," said Elaine Levin. "I think my husband would have been a more carefree person than he is. And it's sad for him. As much as he does, and he does a great deal, he's not 100 percent there. Walter was *never* 100 percent after that."

Walter agreed: "I would say, to some extent, I keep more to myself. The part of my life that I shared with Merrill, no one would ever replace. And the fact is, sometimes I just go into my own shell and think my own thoughts. To that extent, if it had been a more emotionally open relationship before Merrill died, it was a bit less so thereafter. I'm just satisfied to stay in that relationship and do what I can. I care for Elaine a great deal, and my daughters. But I still have that—aloofness is the wrong word—that small portion of my own private world, where I think my own thoughts and mourn my own loss. Probably as a result of the loss of my son. I hear myself saying 'my son' and I shouldn't say that"—meaning he should more appropriately say "our son."

He continued: "If that's an answer, and probably it's not, but at least it's my answer."

"When you said your marriage used to be more emotionally open," I asked, "did you mean that you feel more distant from each other now?"

"I would think so," he said.

"Your way and Elaine's way of grieving are very different?" I asked.

"No question about that," he said. "I felt I couldn't really talk to her about what the loss meant to me, and that, at that time, set me distant and I never really came back from that. It may have been different had she said, 'OK, break down and cry in front of everybody.' But she said to me I should get over it, so I just sort of put up a wall, not an insurmountable wall, but a barrier. I understand and appreciate that she's doing things differently than I. I don't think she misses him any less than I."

"Do you understand why Elaine grieves the way she does?" I asked.

"I really *don't* understand," he said. "But I don't even try to understand. I know she feels it strongly because on his birthday, she can't do too much. But, you know, I feel each to his own."

I asked, "Do you and Elaine talk about Merrill?"

"Not frequently," he said. He sat for a minute thinking over his answer.

"Now that I think about it," he said, "she does it more freely than I. She, in passing, will say, 'Merrill, he fell out of the crib—he crawled—,' as though he were alive. Which is probably good."

He thought for another minute, and added, "Between us, we talk."

He thought again: "I'll tell you the truth, in my dotage I'm forgetting a lot of our talking. See, I've also forgotten some of the things Merrill did. And she has a good memory. So I'll say to her, 'Just tell me again, about when he was confirmed.' Or I'll say, 'Tell me about the vacation to Florida, to Disney World.' Then she tells me, she tells me."

I thought about Walter's longing for Merrill, and could hear him asking Elaine to tell him a story and bring Merrill back for him, and Elaine who had been married to Walter for so long, knowing what he wanted and knowing the same story would bring Merrill back for her too. Worse things could keep them together.

Chapter 4

BRANDT JONES' FAMILY

∞

As Marge Ford had said, David's death affected not only her marriage but also her relationship with her other children, David's brother and sister. Brandt Jones talked about similar things, but at greater length.

Brandt was a career military man and a "geographic bachelor," he said. He and his wife, Betty, decided their children, Bruce and Donna, should grow up in one place, "some place where they would have roots," he said, "and I would come home when I could. Luckily, for a good portion of Bruce's life, I was stationed close by, where for five years anyway, I could come home every night. Bruce and I did a lot of things together, but if I had things to do over again— Monday morning quarterback—I would have spent more time with him than I did. It was unavoidable, it was a career decision that Betty and I made together. But that's rough on a kid when he's two years old and his father's gone for almost a year. And various points throughout his life when I would have liked to have been there, I wasn't there, I was in Vietnam or Southeast Asia. But all in all we had a pretty good relationship."

Sixteen years ago, when Bruce was seventeen, he and his grandmother drove out west, partly to visit relatives, partly for Bruce to visit some colleges he might attend. On their way back home, they were hit by a truck. Bruce's spleen was ruptured and a broken rib punctured his left lung. "They took him to a clinic in Deming, New Mexico, then medevaced him to El Paso," said Brandt. "When he got to Paso, he was in irreversible shock and there wasn't a thing they could do. He bled to death."

"Betty's mother came through the accident?" I asked.

"She came through the accident," Brandt said. "She had some broken ribs and a broken shoulder and collar bone. And of course she was on a guilt thing. 'Why not me instead of him? I've lived for all these years and he's just seventeen years old.'"

Brandt went back to his story about Bruce's accident and its aftermath.

"Military people understand how to operate with people that have lost children," he said. "So when Betty and I went down to El Paso—they had sent Bruce's body to the morgue at the civilian hospital there—I didn't know what else to do, so I went over to the army hospital at the base there. I saw the duty officer and told her what happened, and you'd have thought they blew the roof off that place. She said—" and Brandt imitated her snapping out an order—"'You sit right there.' Out she went. Next thing I know, there's two other guys taking down addresses and calling over to the morgue, making arrangements to ship his body back to Baltimore."

"These people taking charge had no connection with you?" I asked.

"None at all," he said. "Just all of a sudden that network of the military fell in place. The commanding officer at the army hospital said to me, 'Why the hell didn't they send him here to the army hospital?' I said, 'The only thing I can think of is, I found his ID card as a military dependent in the bottom of the car, so it must have come out of his wallet and they didn't know to send him here.' He said, 'Damn! If they'd sent him here, maybe we could have done something.' I said, 'Don't tell me that.' He said, 'No, I've looked at the autopsy report, there's nothing we could have done by the time he got here. But we

55

could have handled things a lot better than they did.' They also got hold of the navy chaplain. He came over and saw me; next thing he did, he went over to the hospital and he talked with Betty. He also had a church that he was the pastor of, and the ladies from the church visited my mother-in-law the whole time she was in the hospital, and then made sure she got to the airport to get home. The military jumped right in. The military was great.

"I call it an advantage—all of the men I worked with were Vietnam veterans. They all showed up at the funeral home. The military is a brotherhood—you support the other guy because he's in the same boat you're in. The colonel I worked for was a prince. Anything I needed was no problem. He eased me right back into work. Nobody stopped talking about kids while I was there. And if I got up and walked out of a meeting, they understood. A lot of places you work, you don't have that advantage. The things that we learned later on in Compassionate Friends that were helpful, these guys were already doing. They talked about Bruce, they asked what he liked to do. So that helped me a lot to work my way through some of it."

Much of the interview with Brandt was like this: stories of how people, men in particular, stand by each other. Brandt was in his early fifties, had thick brown hair, and sat slouched in the chair. He had a happy, easy voice.

"I guess it was a good six months before I could focus on what I was going to do to fill that void in my life," he said. "He died in August and it must have been right around his birthday, somewhere in March, that it must have dawned on me, 'Hey, there's a void here. You're avoiding the void.' That's a pun in there. Anyway, I got involved in going through the line as an officer in the Scottish Rite, involved with the Shrine and the Masonic Lodge, worked a little bit with the DeMolay. It was selfish on my part because it was a lot of male companionship.

"And I also tried to fill the void with the Scouts, because the thing that came to mind was, 'Now, he's gone. What of him can I pass on?' And I think with the Boy Scouts, I could teach them things that *he* did. Like canoeing was one. There's a thing called frogging, that's what the kids call it, or gunnel pumping. You stand barefoot on the gunnel on the back of the canoe and bounce up and down, and move the canoe across the water or in circles. That's one of the things that Bruce always did. So I showed the little ones how to do frogging. It was just to pass on knowledge that he had. That was where I channeled the love for him, I guess, that's where the love comes in."

But though Brandt's enjoyment of the Scouts and his gratitude toward and appreciation of the men in the military were notable, he eventually got out of the Scouts and became impatient with the military.

"The biggest thing that changed in my career," he said, "was that things that had been important became rather mundane. The position I was in was chief of communications on a nuclear aircraft carrier. I had seventy-eight enlisted personnel and five officers. And the majority of my time was talking with these enlisted people. 'Why did you buy this car when you can't afford the payments? How come you're not sending money to your wife?' I had everything from guys robbing 7-Elevens to the one who wouldn't take a shower. I might as well have been a psychologist. I was like my Aunt Ruth—I was the matriarch. I had to solve all disputes, and I always had people that would come in with, 'Chief, these pens don't work.' I'd tell them, 'The supply room's over there. Start thinking for yourself a little bit. I'm not here to be your father confessor, I'm not Mom.' I didn't have the patience at that time to deal with being Dad for a twenty-year-old."

Brandt went on to explain how this impatience, six years later, led him to retire from the navy—"suddenly it just wasn't important any more, it was no more fun, I was tired of counseling, and it was time to retire."

I don't know whether Brandt's impatience came from the mundanity of the situations or from the necessity of acting like a father when his son had died. He talked with equal intensity about both. In any case, he was feeling the same combination of appreciation and impatience about his family.

"I grew up in a close-knit family that *dealt* with each other," he said. "My cousin that lives on the Eastern Shore has the annual party and seventy-five or eighty people show up. And it's five generations of the family, and they all know each other. My mother is the matriarch of the clan now because she's the oldest one of the sisters that were the mothers of all the rest of us down here, down in later generations. Before my mother, the matriarch was her other sister, Aunt Ruth. Aunt Ruth ruled the roost from the time I was this big, and if Ruth said, 'You guys stop the fighting,' everybody stopped the fighting."

Brandt said he was "Aunt Ruth" not only with the enlisted men, but also with his brothers. "My father drilled it into me since I was this big, that I was the oldest and anything ever happened to him, I was responsible. And my brothers will listen to me. Because he drilled it into them that I was in charge. But deep down, I have the feeling that life's short and why should I make myself feel bad inside to put on a good front to keep peace and harmony here? So when they get into one of their battles, I call them both up and say, 'Settle it. Get it over with. You're both wrong. Get it out of your system. Get back to doing things that keep the family together. Settle it.'"

"So they should work it out themselves," I asked, "like the enlisted men with the pencils? And you're back out of the father role again, right?"

"Basically, yes," he said.

"Does that mean that the family means less to you?" I asked.

"No," he said, "it means more to me. The family is feeding down to the fifth generation and now the sixth generation is coming along. And their knowledge all migrates down. The thing is, my mother's generation had miscarriages and stillborns and my mother's youngest brother was killed when he was eight years old. There were a lot of child deaths within the family through the twenties, thirties, forties. I had a cousin who drowned when he was twelve. And the family talks about all of the dead ones. The stories come up. 'Do you remember when Bruce did this? Do you remember when Jack did that?' So all this goes on down through, and the little ones hear this. So when that type of atmosphere is in the family, it makes a big difference.

"See, I think from the beginning, people have expected their children to live beyond them," he explained. "It's an inborn hope. But when you look two generations back, the loss of a child was damn near an everyday occurrence. My grandmother's time, people would lose two or three children—miscarriages, stillbirths, flu, cholera. But now we've had it ingrained in us, children don't die. So we come up into a generation that doesn't have that corporate knowledge that says, 'These things happen.'"

"What does that knowledge tell you?" I asked. "Because of Bruce's death, what do you know that you didn't before?"

I didn't know how Brandt would answer this, but his answer was surprising nevertheless. "I think I've had to look at the finality of my future that I had already preplanned," he said, "and now have to replan."

I heard the phrase "finality of my future," and asked, "Do you mean that you've had to face your own death?"

No, he didn't mean that. "Not my death," he said, "my projected future. It's a major re-compute of my projected future. I had all these brilliant plans, where Bruce was going to get through four years of college, he was going to marry this girl down the street, they were going to have these kids. And all of a sudden, no more."

Brandt was facing not his own death but the death of his "projected future," which was Bruce's future. I wanted him to explain a little more, so I asked what he missed most about Bruce's future.

"I miss the things he could have been," he said. "I would dearly have loved to watch him be the master counselor of his DeMolay chapter and to be raised as a master Mason with my father and my brothers there."

I asked, "So you miss that line to the future that your son would have been?"

"Oh sure," he said. "I'm the last Brandt Jones. My father had two other sons, so the name will go on. But this is one branch of the family tree that when I go is gone. Because my daughter, Donna, married into an Eber family, so that's an Eber family tree. And my little branch of the family tree is going to stop here. You know, I think every man in his core wants to feel that he's perpetuating the line. I had fully expected Bruce to go on and have grandkids for me. I knew that wasn't mandated. But I had fully expected him to be what I was to my father—to be able to say to my son, 'If something happens to me, you're the man of the house.' And he's not there to do that."

Although Bruce's trajectory had stopped, Brandt's had not, but Brandt's future had subsequently changed. Now what? Brandt continued, quoting himself talking to himself.

"'Now. OK, Brandt. This part is stopped. This part over here, yourself, is going to keep going, but you're probably going to put more emphasis over here on the one that's left, your daughter.' Now, do I tell my daughter, Donna, that she can't do an activity, or she can't go on a trip? Knowing that suddenly, life is short, that possibly it could happen to her, God forbid, but it could?"

Every parent, unasked, brought up their worries about their other children. Was Brandt saying that his daughter, who seemed not to have been the line to the future his son had been, was nevertheless just that and that, moreover, he now knew that such lines are fragile? I couldn't think fast enough to ask the question, and just let him talk. Eventually, in bits and pieces, he answered. Of course Donna was a line to the future; so was her husband, so was her son, Nick. And because Brandt was his own father's line to the future, Brandt's line to the future included his father.

"Donna was kind of pushed aside for essentially three years, with this grief process going on," he said. "And she received help from her friends, but she sought out friends that we didn't particularly care for. I mean, her friends were into *everything*. And Betty would get vocal about it. There were a lot of arguments. But her last year in high school, she started to come around. She had a year of Social 101 at Frostburg State College and that got the rest of it out of the way. So then she came back home and went to Howard Community College. Her biggest problem was that she couldn't form a close relationship with any of the boys. She was always afraid that if she got close to them, they were going to die."

Betty told the same story but in greater detail. "Our daughter was fourteen, just starting in high school when her brother was killed," she said. "We noticed that when she began dating, she'd never date a boy for more than about three weeks. These were nice boys she dated. So after seven or eight years of this going on—throughout high school and into college, all this short-term, never falling in love—she finally realized that she was afraid of making a close relationship with anybody. She'd decided she was never going to be hurt again. The boy she finally married pursued her for almost five years. She went to Hawaii for six months and he moved into her basement apartment in our house while she was gone. She went on beach patrol in Ocean City, Maryland, for four years, and he managed to get on beach patrol so he could be there. He hung in there. She finally fell in love with him; she was twenty-four. The impact of Bruce's death lasted that long. Now they've been married for a couple of years."

So Donna married into the Eber family, and had a child named Nick. I asked Brandt if Bruce's death had changed his relationship with her. "It's changed in that we're pretty close," he said. "Donna does day care, so I go over and watch the kids in her day care for an hour while she works out, and the kids and I all have a good time."

Brandt was underplaying his own generosity: Donna cared for five children, ranging in age from one to five. "I found out how to operate the Barney tapes in the VCR," Brandt said, "so we don't have any problem. We put Barney and Winnie the Pooh on, and we're home free. We have a good time. And Donna and my son-in-law have no qualms when I call up and say, 'I'm going someplace, how about I pick Nick up and take him with me?' So I go put the car seat in the truck and the two of us go off. The Shriners have a Christmas party for the kids. So my son-in-law, he and I packed Nick up and took him to the Christmas party, had a hamburger and hot dog and got balloons. It was a couple hours we spent. We had a good time."

Apparently reminded by his son-in-law, Nick, and the Shriners, Brandt began to talk about his father.

"Also after Bruce died, I got closer to my father than I'd ever been in my life," he said. "My father loved me dearly, but he was a strict disciplinarian, old German from the word go. I had been all my life a lot closer to my mother than to my father. I felt I needed to be closer with my father because he worked shift work at the steel company and he missed a lot of things when I was growing up. So now I shifted some emphasis over and spent some time with him. I found things that I could do with my father that alleviated that disciplinarian type of feeling. The last two months of my father's life were a bout with lung cancer. And here again, I had a close relationship and it was ending. And for, hell, a good three months after Dad died—the Scottish Rite up here at Thirty-ninth Street would do degree work and I'm the prompter, and my father used to sit in a particular seat—well, for three months, I'd look at that seat and the tears would come because he wasn't there."

"You're describing the situation with your father in almost the same words that you described the situation with Bruce," I said, "that you and your father both missed a lot of things with your sons. Do you make that connection?"

Brandt took my question to mean, did he make a connection between his relationship with his son and his relationship with his father?

"I didn't," he said, "not consciously. But I guess I do. Because suddenly I had somebody I could do things with that I would have been doing with my son. I needed a relationship some place."

"That's wonderful," I said, meaning that these kinds of unconscious connections are wonderful.

"It was wonderful to me at the time," he said, meaning he loved carrying on his son through his father.

Then he returned to the subject of his family. "Consequently, that void is starting to be filled," he said. "Because now my brother is getting closer. And of course I've got my grandson and son-in-law—my son-in-law and I get along real fine—so they're coming into the fold. That's all working in that family-clan thing."

"So I guess what it boils down to is," he said later, "you throw yourself back into others."

Chapter 5

BROTHERS AND SISTERS,
SONS AND DAUGHTERS

Changes in the Relationship with Other Children

∞

Brandt seemed to be maintaining a balance that no one else I interviewed did. On one hand, he was increasingly impatient at being put into the role of a father, or "Aunt Ruth." On the other, his own father, as well as his daughter, son-in-law, and grandson became more important. He seemed to be saying that Bruce's death not only removed him from the role of father but threatened to break the line from the past to the future. Brandt didn't particularly mind not being other people's father, but he wouldn't let that line break.

I have no other children. I wanted only one, though I knew that I ran a risk: common wisdom says you should have more than one child in case something happens. The parents I interviewed sometimes felt sorry for me and sometimes said so.

"You lost an only child," said Leight Johnson, "and I think that's harder than losing one of five, even though the others don't make up. But still, I've got four other kids to love."

"With having another child, that makes it easier," Delores Shoda explained. "It doesn't make me not miss him any more. But maybe in

63

my mind, my daughter's a reason to make me go on. She makes things brighter for me."

Maybe my life is harder without more of my own children to love or to live for; I can't know and don't care. But researchers do find parents who lose an only child scoring higher on measures of grieving. So when one child dies, why not have another? Common wisdom also says that if you are still of child-bearing age, you should have another one. "Talk about clichés," said Julia Marcus. "People say, 'You can always have another child'—of all the *wrong* things to say, as if you can make a substitution."

Common wisdom seems to be coming in for a hard time in these pages. Researchers say that parents' relationships with what they call "replacement children" are often troubled. Studies find that parents compare the new child unfavorably with the child who died, they overprotect the new child, resent the child's being alive, or use the child to deny that the first one died. The problem with these studies is that they are done on "replacement children" who sought psychiatric care; the studies thus overlook those "replacements" who grow up well and happy. All researchers know, then, is that replacement children can have problems, not that they inevitably will. In any case, some researchers recommend that bereaved parents wait to have another child until they've recovered from the loss. The Institute of Medicine's 1984 report on the effects of bereavement pointed out the obvious flaw in that reasoning: "Being treated as a replacement is certainly apt to be burdensome to a child, but waiting until there is recovery may not be the solution either, especially since it is often observed that grieving for a lost child never entirely ends."

I didn't talk to the parents I interviewed about replacement children. Most of the parents' children died as teenagers or young adults, so these parents were, like me, past the usual child-rearing age. The parents who were younger when their children died didn't talk about replacement children and I didn't think to ask. The only thing that some parents, like Julia, said about the whole issue was that no child is replaceable anyway.

"I still marvel at our four sons," said Ginny Mitchell, "how *different* they all are with the same genetic makeup. Each one is so individual-ized. That's why another child—another three or thirteen—could never take the place of that one you lost."

I did go through a period of wanting another child. I decided against it, partly because I felt my parenting days were over, but mostly because I finally understood I was confusing wanting another child with wanting T.C., and T.C. was gone for good.

The upshot of all this is that I began the interviews in ignorance, with unrealistic expectations of how parents get along with their sur-viving children. I thought parents and children would have the same initial problems with distance that husbands and wives did: at first, everyone is hurt badly enough that they have to take care only of themselves. This was certainly the case with Brandt, Betty, and Donna. But later, I thought, the relations would regularize and everyone could take up where they left off.

I should have known it wouldn't be that simple. In the first place, I have several middle-aged friends whose brothers or sisters died as children. One said she felt then and since that her parents could never love anyone any more, not even her. Another said she thought the loss was all her parents' and she hadn't understood until recently, twenty years after her brother's death, that the loss was also hers; she began crying when she told me this. And the third said her mother recovered, kept a neat house, saw her friends, drank too much, and died at the earliest opportunity. This particular friend not only didn't cry when she told me this, she also didn't bother to visit her dying mother's bedside. These reactions and relationships are anything but simple.

In the second place, after a child dies, everyone in the family changes, parents and children alike, and no one takes up anything where they left off. Brandt, Betty, and Donna seem to have had as sta-ble and supportive a family as possible, but even in these best condi-tions, Donna took ten years to reconcile herself to running the risk of loving someone.

What follows is a look at a subject from one side only: what hap-pens to the children and to the relations between parents and children, through the parents' eyes. I didn't interview the parents' other children. Nor did I ask the parents what they thought the effects on their other children were, though the parents talked about it anyway. "Sets you back," said Tom Ford. "Also sets the kids back. They don't always act like it but it does."

I'm aware of the limits of seeing the children through their parents. By rights, the effects on the other children should be seen through their own eyes; the subject deserves its own book.

To begin, I'd been right about some parents having a period of pushing the children aside. Brandt, for instance, had talked about pushing Donna aside for "essentially three years." Betty agreed. "The parents are hurting so badly it's hard for them to help the siblings," she said, talking first about her experience with Compassionate Friends, then about herself. "I was no help to my daughter. The biggest wrong thing I did was to leave her home when we went out to get his body."

Diana Moores, whose six-year-old daughter died in a car accident, has a second daughter, named Kristin, who was twenty at the time of the accident. Since then, Diana's relationship with Kristin, she said, "has taken quite a journey. I considered her an adult. Kristin had a lot of needs, but I refused to take care of anyone but me. I refused to mother; I resented it very much. She'd have these emergency situations and I'd pull her out of them, but as soon as she was out, I pushed her back on her feet. I didn't want to be taking care of anybody any more. I think she was kind of put out, feeling like I wasn't paying any attention to her for the first few years, which I really wasn't. Then when she became pregnant, then I became closer and closer, and now there's so much more we have in common that we're very, very close now."

Sally Lambert, whose daughter committed suicide, had another daughter, who at the same time got divorced and moved back in with Sally. "It was a sad thing for her," Sally said. "Her marriage was falling apart, but I was so caught up in my own grief I never realized how hard it was for her. Here she had lost her own sister, her marriage had collapsed, and she was back home with her parents. She was a very independent soul, but she was crushed. But in my own misery, I didn't really get upset for her like I would now. You can only feel so much."

With time, of course, when the parents can pay attention again, this initial distance resolves itself one way or another. What happens next depends partly on what's happened to the children in the meantime.

Most research on children's grief is on children whose parents die. Researchers know less about children whose brothers or sisters die, and much of what they do know comes from the parents. One study found that 70 percent of the siblings returned to normal in a short time. Other studies find problems, but don't say how long they last. The most frequent problem seems to be that these children feel guilty. The reason, researchers say, is that children are naturally ambivalent about their brothers and sisters. The children wonder whether their ambivalence somehow caused the death or if they could somehow have prevented it.

According to researchers, these children are prone to a long list of unhappinesses. Like Marge and Tom Ford's son, Jeffrey, the children can think "the wrong son died." They think that if they had died, their parents might not be so unhappy. And they worry that, if children can die, *they* can die too, and they often fear death. They feel unloved and ignored. Or they feel overprotected and smothered. They get depressed, sad, and lonely. Their grades in school fall and they get into trouble. They're prone to accidents. They feel different from other children, sometimes more mature. In one study, 73 percent of the parents thought their remaining children suffered negative effects, and half thought those effects were extremely negative. Their children dropped out of school, took drugs, got depressed, withdrew emotionally, even tried suicide. The same study compared the effects of the death of a sibling and of a parent, and found death of a sibling as hard as, or harder than, the death of a parent.

But much of this is the children's reactions as seen through the eyes of the parents; only one study asked the children themselves. The study asked children whose brothers or sisters had died in accidents or homicides about the symptoms of post-traumatic stress syndrome. Anywhere from 50 to 95 percent of the children had the syndrome's intrusive thoughts, flashbacks, distress at symbolic events, estrangement from others, and avoidance of feelings. Their parents, when asked, were unaware of the children's symptoms.

Notice the contradiction between the fairly grim reports by the parents of some children and the apparent ignorance of the parents of children with post-traumatic stress syndrome. What the parents know, of course, depends on what they notice and what their children tell them. Dropping out of school, drugs, suicide attempts, and emotional withdrawal are all noticeable. Maybe the more subtle symptoms of post-traumatic stress are harder to notice and harder for the children to talk about.

I think the harshest story I heard describes most vividly what the researchers say about siblings' reactions. A reminder: this is a parent's view of her children. Octavia Johnson Pompey, a school teacher, had three sons. As I wrote earlier, the youngest, Erin, was a star basketball player just graduated from high school. Three days later, during a summer league game, he outscored another player who became angry, left the game, got a gun, and returned and murdered Erin.

"At the time, Erin was nineteen," said Octavia, "my middle son, Bryan, was four years older, and the oldest, Chris, was two years older than Bryan. Bryan and Chris were the sons of my former husband, but they and Erin never considered themselves as half brothers; they were just brothers—because I raised them all together as a single parent. When Erin was killed, the two of them had so much bitterness to build up in them, and they knew by going out in the neighborhood, kids there would get them weapons. The night Erin was killed, when he was still at the hospital, Bryan was at work and someone told him about Erin, and he came down to the hospital and he said, 'Where is he?' meaning where is the boy who killed Erin, and I said, 'Bryan, I don't know, I don't know about this boy.' Now I didn't know this until months later, but Chris and Bryan had gotten a gun and they left the hospital with some friends and they roamed the streets all that night. They didn't know this boy, so they wanted to find some of the kids on the team who knew this boy's name and where he lived. And they said the police aren't looking for this boy because to them it's just another black boy being killed. But I kept telling them, 'Don't look at it that way, they're doing their job. It's not a thing where it was drug-related and Erin was out here doing something wrong.' And after that they kind of cooled down."

While all this was going on, Octavia continued, Chris and Bryan were also going to visit Erin's grave. "For a while they were going every week, which wasn't good because it would take them so long to get back to normal after they'd gone," she said. "And especially Chris, because I'd come home and he'd be just sitting there. He'd be holding a picture of Erin and tears would just be flowing. It was always just after coming back from the cemetery. And I would tell them, 'Don't go, don't go yet, wait a while.' And they would go and they wouldn't tell me."

Not long after, Erin's killer—"this boy," Octavia called him—was caught and tried.

"Erin was killed in June; the first day of the trial was the following April," she said, "so it was almost a year. Chris was sitting in court and I didn't want him to go because I didn't want him facing this boy. So when the coroner got on the stand and gave the autopsy report, Chris just got up and ran out of the courtroom. He couldn't stand to hear any more. I didn't see him all that night. What I didn't know was that he had come in sometime during the night, gotten keys for the car, and wrecked it. He had called home and Bryan answered the phone. Bryan woke me up, said, 'Mom, it's Chris on the phone. He's a couple of blocks away from here—he had an accident. We got to go find him.' So Bryan brought him home. The car was wrecked something terrible. I said, 'What did he run into?' He said, 'A pole.' I said, 'Chris needs some help.'

"So I called Compassionate Friends and they referred me to a psychologist, and the psychologist called me back that same night and I explained to him what was going on with the family. He said, 'I want you and the two sons to come in the office tomorrow and talk to me.'

Bryan wouldn't go. He said he was all right. And at the time he was doing pretty good, he was kind of holding things together. Chris and I went, we went every week for about a month. The psychologist would have sessions with both of us and then he would talk to us separately. He said, 'Chris is going through a lot of guilt that's not founded, but to him it is. He feels that he was the oldest, he should have been there to protect his little brother. If he had been there, the boy wouldn't have done it. I can't get him to understand that the only thing that probably would have happened is that he would have gotten shot too.' So he said, 'Chris needs to be put on some antidepressant medication along with the therapy.' This psychologist had a psychiatrist he worked with, so he set up an appointment to go see him, which we did, and the psychiatrist put Chris on the antidepressant medication. In the meantime . . ."

Octavia sighed and was quiet for a minute, then went on. "I went back to teaching in August. I'm at school trying to do my job, trying to keep it together. I didn't know whether I was coming or going. And then Chris's psychologist called me and said that Chris had just called him and was really in a bad way. He said, 'I'm fearful that he's suicidal.' He said, 'I'm going to call and have him admitted. Which hospital would be more convenient, University of Maryland Hospital or Sinai?' Well, Erin died at University of Maryland and I didn't want to see University of Maryland any time soon, so I said, 'Sinai would be closer to home.' And Chris stayed six weeks there and it seemed to help.

"As soon as Chris seemed to get better, Bryan took an overdose of some medicine for neck pain. He was working four to twelve midnight, he came home and usually he would go to bed. And this particular night, I could hear him moving around. But I kind of dozed off and then around two I woke up—something was not right. And I went in the bathroom and I saw this medicine bottle laying in the trashcan, and I remembered what these pills were and I remembered that just the other day this bottle was full. So I went in his room and he was just sprawled out on his bed with his clothes on and I tried to shake him and he was just out of it. So I called 911. So the ambulance came and the police came; so they had to rush him to the hospital to pump his stomach. He had taken fifty-some pills. The doctor told me the medicine would not have killed him but it would have done just what it did, knocked him out. And they kept him at the hospital for about five days and they wanted him to see a psychiatrist. I talked with the doctors and told them what was all going on."

The problem for both brothers, Octavia explained, was guilt. "They would say things like sometimes, 'Ma, it should have been one of us and not Erin because he was doing all the things he should have been doing. He never caused you any problems.' Well, the two of them got into all kinds of things when they were teenagers, but Erin *was* doing all the right things and he made me proud. He also made Chris and Bryan proud too."

Erin's killer was convicted and jailed. And within the next few years, some of Chris's and Bryan's old friends had gone to jail themselves. "I got a call from the Maryland Penitentiary," said Octavia, "from a boy who grew up with Erin and Chris and Bryan and who was doing two life sentences for murder. 'Miss Johnson,' he said, 'if that boy that kill Erin come this way, what's the worst thing you want to happen to him?' I got a similar call from Hagerstown. I got calls from Jessup. But that call from the Maryland Pen, he said, 'I'm doing two life sentences; there's nothing more they can give me. Because I will waste him in a minute.' I couldn't believe it. I mean, I have letters from boys that knew Erin: 'Miss Johnson, I have a friend who's in Jessup, I have a friend who's in Hagerstown, they'll take care of him.' Stuff that you'd hear about on TV. I couldn't believe this, I really couldn't believe this.

"And then Chris and Bryan are also getting these letters: 'You have to revenge your brother's death.' I said, 'They didn't need this. They got enough of that already built inside. They didn't need any encouragement.' I got mad and I said to them, 'If something happened to this boy, the first one they're going to come to look for is one of you. Think about that. If you went out and did this to him, what makes you any better than him? You're a murderer too. Think about that. It'll just mean that Erin's gone, you'll be in jail for murder. It just means I don't have any sons any more. Think about that.'"

Octavia sighed again, then started to laugh. "As it turned out, this boy got life plus twenty-five years. Hopefully he'll do at least twenty of those years. By that time, I figure Chris and Bryan will be too old to want revenge."

By now, five years later, Bryan is back at work, working double shifts and, Octavia said, "making a life for himself. He's doing pretty good." But Chris, she said, "hasn't been right since. Right now, I haven't heard from him in about two weeks. He's just not coping well at all. He's hanging with the wrong crowd and I don't really know what they're into. And when the phone rings late at night, I expect a call from him or about him. I can't even reach him. I don't exactly know where he is. Bryan probably knows more than I do, and what Chris is into Bryan knows, but he's not going to tell me unless he has to. Bryan was up here yesterday and I asked him had he seen his brother. He said, 'I saw him the other day.' And the only thing he will say is, 'He's OK.' The pastor said, 'You just have to put him in the hands of God and hope for the best.' And that's what I do with him. Chris is thirty years old and I can't hold his hand forever."

Octavia sighed another one of her deep, long sighs. "When they say victims of crime, it's not just the person killed. That bullet just did a whole lot of damage."

Octavia's sons live in an unusually violent world, and their reactions are unusually dramatic. Their attempts at suicide, however, are not unique. One other mother, after asking me to turn off the tape recorder, told me that after the death of her son, her daughter tried unsuccessfully to commit suicide.

Octavia's sons' guilt at still being alive isn't unique either. When Marge told how Jeffrey had said that the wrong son died, Marge said she protested, but thinks that's the only time she and Jeffrey talked about David.

Julia said her son also felt guilt after his sister, Simone, died. "Every now and then," said Julia, "he feels guilty about having things when Simone can't. The guilt is *just* awful. He really just needs to talk about it. It's good therapy for him, it's good for me; we usually have a little cry together. What we both decide is, the person that would be most pleased by his having what she couldn't is Simone. And he believes that, as he should. I think that he started about a year ago, really having survivor's guilt. So he went to this psychiatrist, which has been really helpful to him."

Besides the guilt, the parents see their young adult children having trouble committing themselves to every step of the whole life cycle: getting jobs, having romantic relationships, marrying, wanting children of their own, worrying that their own children will die. The parents attributed this to several causes. Maybe the children thought that they, too, wouldn't live long enough to carry out commitments. Maybe they thought that the people they loved would inevitably die. Maybe they saw their parents' grief and didn't want to go through that themselves. Betty and Brandt both said their son's death made his sister, Donna, unwilling to get romantically involved, and Betty added, "She wants three children. She remembers what it was like to become an only child. She does not want her children to ever become only children."

Joan Gresser had two sons die, Steven first and then Teddy, and still has one daughter, Jody. "When Steven died," said Joan, "we never included Jody in anything, we farmed her out. She has very little memory of her brother's funeral. But in Teddy's death, she did everything. Because when Teddy died, I knew that moment that I had done everything wrong when Steven died. I knew later that all of us were going to pay because of that. And we did. My daughter, she was very fearful of having children because (a) she lost her brothers and (b) her mother and father lost both of their sons. And we just forced her to look at her reasons as to why she didn't want to do it. And it all came out: fear. The fear was for good reason, yes, but we can't live with fear. Now Jody has two wonderful children, little girl, little boy. So I feel very good, and my husband also. We feel very proud that we were able to get her to take the chance."

Loretta Marsh's nineteen-year-old son, Mike, was killed by a drunk driver six years ago. Mike's younger brother, Eddie, was then in ninth grade. "Eddie deliberately failed the ninth grade," Loretta said. "I got him to a psychologist, he picked up his grades, and he went through by the skin of his teeth. He left school when he turned sixteen and joined the fire company. And the psychologist used to tell me what him and Eddie talked about even though they're not supposed to, but he knew the situation. He said, 'He keeps talking about wanting to help people that are hurt. So I suggested the fire company.' Eddie loves it; he's there day and night. He talks about every call, how he helps them. I don't know if this helps him with his hurt, but he's got to realize he's got to make a life of his own. He doesn't make any money at the fire company. It's volunteer. He needs to go to college and pick up subjects. My husband, he thinks it's terrible to be twenty years old, dropped out of school, don't have a job. Sometimes I say to my husband, 'Well God, look at Mike. He was preparing and he got nowhere. Who says we're going to be here tomorrow? So let it be.' But I'm scared for Eddie. He's not trying, he's given up. No, maybe he's not given up. Maybe he has to go through this procedure. Then I think the hell with it. Let him be. He'll do it."

Several parents said their children had Eddie's problem, but they ascribed it instead to difficulty maturing. Marge said she guessed her son, Jeffrey, "might someday get married and have children, but it's not in the immediate future. I describe him as twenty-six going on sixteen, and he is. He still lives from day to day like teenagers do, makes no plans for the future, doesn't save any money—just day to day."

Ginny's son, Joel, died of kidney cancer after three years of treatment. His older brother, who was still in school during Joel's treatment, "almost totaled the car two times shortly after Joel died," Ginny said, "once about a year after Joel died and then again a year later. I don't know if it was related to Joel's death. It could be, because he was—looking back, his whole behavior—he has matured. Then he joined the air force, and when he got into the third year, he decided that was not the role he wanted to be in, so he got an early out

74

to go back to school and then he did real well. I know Joel's death had a long-range effect on him; it took him a long time to mature."

Several parents thought their children did almost the opposite: they grew up too fast. Ruth Banick said that after her daughter, Leslie, died in an accident, her other daughter, Laura, "who was the oldest in the family and a leader, she wanted to take care of me. So she didn't allow herself a lot of emotional breakdown because she had to be strong for me. She threw herself into law school and blocked out for four years. It wasn't until she graduated from law school that I think her grief really caught up with her. And now I notice that she'll cry easier, and she'll allow herself emotions. Now Laura is an attorney for abused and neglected children. I think she changed her direction after Leslie."

Leight Johnson thought his son took over where Johnny had stopped. Johnny had been on an emergency diving team to pull drowning victims out of the water, and Johnny's brother "kind of took his place," Leight said, and joined the same team. "It was against his own instincts," Leight said. "He didn't like it, but he did it anyway, went down and searched for bodies."

Occasionally the parent thinks—as Diana thought about Kristin—that the effect on the brother or sister is a general neediness. Mary Norris, whose son Theodore died after a kidney transplant, said she had to talk this out with her daughter. "His death put a hurting on my daughter," she said. "See, from the time he was twelve years old, he had this kidney. And my daughter—she was two years younger—she always thought we cared more for the boy than we did for her—you know how children are—because more attention went to him. She kept that in her mind for a long time, you know, until I really had to sit down and explain things to her. And after my son died, my husband took her out to dinner in order to sit and talk to her, explain to her just really what was happening. She was married then, just got married. I thought she had outgrown all that. Then I was sick, not long ago, and was in the hospital and had a operation, and she did say, 'I wish my brother or my father was living,' she say, "so I can have somebody to be here with me.'"

Three parents said their daughters felt overshadowed by their brothers' deaths. In all cases, the brothers were older and had been, in the parents' eyes, unusually intelligent and successful. "Merrill was probably my favorite," said Elaine Levin, "even though one shouldn't have. Merrill from the very beginning—I was too dumb to know that he was that special a child. He was extremely bright—walked at about seven months, spoke, read—extremely. I didn't know until Alison was born, how fast he was and how ordinary she was."

Elaine was talking softly because Alison, now an adult, was in the next room. Alison, Elaine said, "didn't have to be bright, because she was a sweet little girl and everybody loved her. And the problem arose after. Alison had to be everything because Merrill was gone, and she thought she had to take on the world. And she had a terrible problem. See, Merrill was wise enough to know when and when not to. I knew that if he went out on a Friday night and he took my car, I would rather he drive because I knew that he was responsible. I couldn't say the same thing for her. She would let peers influence her. Different children from the very beginning, totally different. Alison was Alison, Merrill was Merrill."

"And when Merrill died?" I said.

"Alison had to achieve," said Elaine. "She had to achieve. She had to be everything."

In another case, Mitch Dudnikov's daughter, "I think lived in the shadow of Marc," he said. "She's three years younger. I think she always resented her brother. Because he was so outgoing, had a lot of friends, he was a National Merit scholar, and early acceptance into any college he wanted. For her everything was a struggle. See, they had that sibling rivalry, and he made peace with her but I don't think she ever made peace with him. I mean, when he was seven years old, he was written up in the Cleveland paper. He had a memory that was unbelievable; he knew every president of the United States—seven years old. Now I think she resents even more his death. I think she thinks we're always doting on his memory. We keep telling her, 'We have you, we don't have him, so give us a little slack.'"

One can't help suspect, with these children who are feeling overshadowed, that their parents might in fact be, as Mitch said, doting on the memory of the dead child. In fact, throughout the interviews, I had to stop myself from asking the parents what part they thought they played in their children's reactions. To what extent were they unconsciously keeping themselves at a distance from their children, leaving the children to feel frightened or unlovable or unworthy or incapable? I didn't ask these questions because if the parents were unconscious of what they were doing, they couldn't answer; and besides, the questions are unpleasant and the parents felt bad enough. I also didn't ask the questions because, to repeat, the book is not about family dynamics but about parents' reactions. Nevertheless, Louise Lewis is a striking example of what might be going on with these parents.

Louise and her two daughters have an off-again, on-again relationship. This doesn't seem to be because, like Diana, Louise wants to stop being a parent. Louise says she feels close to her niece and nephew, to her neighbor's children, and to a number of other young people; she describes how they get together, eat dinner, do things. Rather, Louise and her daughters seem to have missed connection somewhere.

Louise's son, Michael, had just joined his father in the construction business and was inspecting a site when he was robbed and murdered. One daughter now is married and lives in Birmingham, Alabama, and the other is unmarried and lives in Atlanta. Louise's description of the situation with her daughters is a litany of mutual disappointment and misunderstanding.

"I think the first thing that I realized," she said, "was that I had to take care of me. I just couldn't function until I was OK. So when all of this happened, I told the girls, my girls, to get help, that I'd pay for it. You know, whatever they needed to do. The younger daughter, the one that's not married, she was in college at the time. And she took some courses on death and dying. So she's just dealt with it, I guess, in her way. She was a psychology major and now she's a therapist—that's what she does down in Atlanta—and lives a very remote, to me, lifestyle. Our married daughter, Heidi, doesn't deal with feelings at all. She was anorexic when Michael died. She became anorexic when she went off to college. So then I thought, well, maybe when she gets married, she'll change, but she's still anorexic. Once when we went down to visit her, we saw she got herself down—she's five foot seven—to about eighty-seven pounds. And my husband and I stayed up all night talking about it, and what happened next was, I got in touch with a doctor that she had been seeing, and I got very involved. I got help, my husband got help, and after we laid it all down and Heidi found out that I'd been in touch with the doctor, got simply *furious,* and that was the end of communication between she and me for two years. She doesn't know from what she was doing, destroying herself. She's forty years old, she weighs about in the nineties, and she looks like she just walked out of a concentration camp; she's just awful-looking."

Then Louise began talking like Elaine and Mitch. "Michael was the first child and only son," she said. "He stood up in his crib at four and a half months, he said 'Hi, Bye-bye' at nine months, he did all these things that I thought were absolutely not ahead of schedule—nobody told me they were. And then when his sister came along, we were thrilled it was a girl, but Michael was a *good* child and I think I did appreciate him as the boy in the family. I think Michael was the calmest, the most loveable. He had faults too, but he cared a lot for the family. And now my two girls are off doing their thing and they're going to be that way. And if that's how they have to deal with it, that's their problem. I think if the girls cared after this tragedy—I run stories through my head—that maybe they would have moved back to town to make us feel a little better. They would have taken care of us a little bit. And because they didn't, then my husband and I became independent of them. And I just don't think in terms of what happened, that it's the best situation."

The situation relaxed after Louise's married daughter, Heidi, adopted a baby. "So anyway, we were getting ready to go to Philly at two one Friday afternoon," Louise said, "and the phone rang and it's Heidi, and she says to me, 'Mom, I have Matthew David in my arms.'

I said, 'What?' She said, 'He's three days old and we adopted him. Can you come Tuesday for the *bris?*' I said, 'You just make the arrangements.' We went to Philadelphia and I did nothing the whole weekend but tell everyone we were grandparents. And the baby was named after Michael—Michael David, Matthew David. So would you believe, we go down there Tuesday and everything was like nothing happened. So the relationships have changed and now that she has a child that she's bringing up, it's better, it's better. He's adorable. Oh I love him dearly, and it helped the situation, my relationship with him."

Louise isn't worried just because the girls don't care enough or don't take care of her; she's worried that she's not taking care of them either. "I mean, there's nothing like family and my kids knew it," she said, "but they don't give a hoot now. Heidi's having a tough time raising her son; she and her husband both were out of work for a year. It hasn't been good. There's *no* family of her husband's down there, there's *no* aunts or uncles, no babysitters built in, nobody to help her. I talk to them on the phone, I see them once a year. But they chose that. I guess that's the hardest thing to accept, what your kids are doing. I don't know how different it would have been if Michael had been alive. I don't know that."

Louise is surely right to say she doesn't know what would be different if Michael had lived. She said only one thing that made me wonder if, for her part, Michael's death made a certain distance with her daughters more desirable. She'd been talking about her daughter "destroying herself" with anorexia, "looking like she walked out of a concentration camp," and not communicating for two years, and she interrupted herself to add, "I functioned better not having this communication because I was scared to death I was going to lose another child."

For every parent who has other children, the possibility of losing another child is real. For four of the parents I interviewed, the possibility was a reality. Lydia Frasca had two miscarriages, and her infant daughter and infant son died. Joan Gresser, Walter Farnandis, and Julia Marcus each lost two children in unrelated circumstances years apart.

79

The possibility of losing a child was just as real before the child died, and most parents rightly avoid thinking about it. But now these parents know it happens. As Brandt had said, "knowing that suddenly, life is short, the possibility that it could happen to her, God forbid, but it could?" During the interviews, I never asked if people were aware their other children could die. It is too harsh a question, and to be honest, because I had an only child, the question hadn't occurred to me. But though I never asked, the parents almost universally answered: yes, they were aware.

They brought it up on their own, in answer to different questions. The question to which it was most often an answer was, "Do you feel more anxious or more vulnerable in life?" When I asked the question, I had in mind a feeling of greater personal fragility, and thought the answers would be, "Yes, I worry more when I get on an airplane," or "No, I am less concerned about my personal health."

Instead, they answered like Estelle Lemaitre when I asked if she felt more vulnerable to bad things in life.

"To life and to the children," she said. "I'm paranoid when it comes to their well-being now. I've turned loose as far as giving them the freedom they need, so I don't know that they know how I really feel. When we're in Florida, the phone calls are back and forth to the children here; the cost doesn't mean a thing to me. All I need to hear is their voices, to know they're OK."

I asked Loretta if she felt more vulnerable. "Fearful," she said. "I was really fearful for a long time for Eddie. Couldn't handle him going out. I wouldn't *let* him go out. I made myself get over that."

I asked Elaine if she felt more anxious.

"Not today," she said. "I think at the very beginning—Alison was fifteen at the time he passed away—and of course she was just emerging as a young lady and beginning to date. And I would say to her, 'Look, I'm an overanxious mother. But we've been through a lot so humor me. You're going to have to call me, you're going to have to get up from wherever you are and call me. And if that's the biggest price you're going to pay for having a crazy mother, that's the way it is.' It doesn't seem to have hurt her."

I asked Delores what she enjoyed doing, and she gave me a list of what she didn't like doing: bringing work home, shopping, cooking. "We go out to eat a lot more," she said. "And I don't feel like spending a lot of money on the house or the yard."

Then she abruptly changed the subject: "You didn't think anything like this would even happen to you, and now it has, you're just so afraid that something else bad is going to happen. I'm always afraid something's going to happen to Laura. Or if my husband doesn't get home in time and doesn't call. You're always waiting for this other shoe to drop."

I asked Betty if she had the same interest in making plans that she used to.

"I do think about family death more," she said, "that somebody could be dead suddenly, and what I should do if that should happen. Also, all through my daughter's pregnancy, I had many more fears of something going wrong, which I never would have said to her. When I was pregnant, it never occurred to me that anything would go wrong. Normal, happy pregnancy, you have a normal, happy baby. But that whole nine months my daughter was pregnant, plus a couple weeks after the baby was born, it was like I was holding my breath thinking, I know so many things that can go wrong."

"More so than before Bruce died?" I asked.

"Oh absolutely, absolutely," she said.

As Loretta and Estelle said, this anxiety about their other children often has a period of high intensity, after which the parents give themselves a talking-to and control their anxiety.

"I'm active in Compassionate Friends," said Ruth, "and I *know* several people who have lost more than one child, and I thought, 'Oh my heavens, it *can* happen again.' As you can ask my oldest daughter, that was rough on her. Because now all of a sudden, she is an only child. We went through some rough times when she was going to the University of Baltimore. She was twenty-two when Leslie died and basically an adult, and I would just have these horrendous panic attacks that she wasn't going to be coming home in one piece. I remember one night in particular when she wasn't home when she was

81

supposed to be. That day she had driven to White Marsh Mall and ridden the bus into the city. So I went to the mall to look for her car, to see if she'd gotten back as far as the mall. They had an accident right there at the mall and a little red car was involved. She has a little red Nissan, and when I came up on it and saw this glimpse, this little red car almost turned over, I know my heart was beating 200 times a minute. When I got up on the accident and realized it wasn't her car and her car was still at the mall, I turned around and went home. I think it was ten minutes later that she came home. I immediately—which was wrong on my part, of course—jumped on her and said, 'Where have you been?' She said, 'I can't take you. You're just smothering me.' And I, of course, called her a little ingrate. I said, 'You just don't appreciate how devoted I am to you.' So then we had to come to this compromise that she would make an extra effort to call me and I would make an extra effort not to get hysterical."

After Lydia miscarried and after two infants died, she had a child named Tommy, who was born with a heart problem; then two and a half years later, she had a third miscarriage. "I stayed in the hospital for a good two weeks, went home without a baby to Tommy. And I didn't want to have anything to do with him. Because I *knew* that this child was going to die. So I had day people come in to take care of him. But I live differently now. Before, he stayed in my room with me for almost five years. I am more cautious with Tommy—sore throat, I go to the doctor—because of his heart. I lavish him more. But I can't live now as if he's going to die. He needed to live his life as normal as possible. Holding on to him wasn't going to bring my babies back. I never knew my babies true, but this guy was an individual and it wasn't fair to him."

Two things these parents say are striking. One is that they are aware of not imposing their anxiety on their children, that just because they themselves know that children die does not mean that their children should live in that shadow.

The other is that the shadow, even when it lightens, remains. Estelle, after talking about the phone calls back and forth to Florida, said, "And my granddaughter just got a job for the first time. She's only sixteen, and she only works like six blocks from our home. And I drive her whenever I know she doesn't have a ride, so that she doesn't get hit by a car."

"What are the big changes in your life?" I asked, thinking I was changing the subject.

"Well," she said, "I don't think I would be as paranoid now as I am. Probably more relaxed. Probably enjoying the retirement years without always thinking what may happen to the other children."

Maybe, even if they had not had children who died, Louise might still be having troubles with her daughters, Elaine might still want her daughter to call her, Lydia might still have been overprotective. But I suspect that anxiety, which almost every parent talked about whether or not I asked them, does affect the continuing relationship.

The effect of the anxiety is either increased distance between the parents and their other children, or the opposite, increased closeness. And being human, some parents feel both. One research study, done in 1989, asked parents how their relationships with their remaining children had changed. A third of the parents said they felt closer, a tenth said they were more distant, and a fifth said they felt no change.

"My children mean more to me," said Emily Miller. "But I don't always know how the children feel. I don't think we mean to them what they mean to us. I suppose that's probably normal. Our family, we're close but we've never been exchanging love emotionally, but when Sue died, we did. We were all a great support to each other. But as the years have gone by, it's slipped back into the old way. Nobody talks about Sue any more. I know why it is; it's too painful. And when I was talking to my older son, I asked him, 'Do you talk about Sue?' And he said, 'Well, I talk about her to Norman,' which is his brother, and he says, 'I talk about her to Gail,' which is his wife. He says, 'I don't talk to you and Daddy about her because it's just too painful.'"

Like Emily, one way some parents notice distance is that their children don't want to talk about the brother or sister who died. Janet Wright seemed to have a list of all the things she and her son, David,

83

said to each other about David's brother, Bill, who was killed in a car accident. The list was short and more notable for what they didn't say to each other than for what they did. "Unfortunately, the accident was David's fault," said Janet. "I sometimes wonder about him, because we've never really, you know, had any deep talks on that. David had come over to the house, and he and Bill left about ten-thirty that night and we got a call about one-thirty saying there had been an accident. An eighteen-year-old boy that hit him had a lot of traffic violations— the kid had been on the Hardee's parking lot spinning wheels, and had gone down the road and come back up. David was making a left turn. It was partly his fault. When we drove up, they had Bill lying there on the Hardee's lot. David was in the ambulance and the first thing he said was "How's Bill?" They took David to St. Joe's Hospital, and David didn't get to go to the funeral. When you're doped up like that, you don't know. Something came up not long ago. I said, 'David, I was going through a lot over losing Bill, and I *still* haven't gotten over it.' He said, 'I know,' but there was never any big discussion. Once I had put out photos of Bill and David together when they were young. On a lot of them, they had their arms around each other. And when David's wife was looking at the photos, she said, 'You know, Dave really loved his brother.' Which I thought was nice."

I asked Walter Levin, whose younger daughter was born retarded, whether he felt closer to her and her sister. "Obviously, I'm trying to get a little closer to my girls," he said. "My older daughter, I see a little bit of myself in her which I didn't notice before, a sense of humor. And my younger, handicapped daughter, tried to fill the void in her own way by either feigning or actually adopting an interest in sports. And so I go to the basketball games with her, where I went with Merrill, and she's really interested in it. We talk about the Orioles and the Terps."

Delores's son, Larry, died of melanoma. One of Delores's reactions has been an odd restlessness that makes it difficult for her to stay in one place for long. "I just think, I want to be going," she said. "But I don't know where I'm going or what I'm going to do when I get there." Her daughter, Laura, was an adult when Larry died. "We're closer to her now than we were before Larry died," said Delores, "because she is a person, just like my husband and I, that you know, you solve your own problems within yourself. But now she talks more about what's going on in her life. She met a fellow, a nice man who has a sort of a personality like Larry did. And they got married, and they moved to Florida. We could handle Florida because once she said they were going to California and I just about fell apart. Because she had no one in California and my husband has four brothers in Florida. We're still very close. When I go to my daughter's house and stay, I can sit on the sofa and read a book, I can lay out by the pool, I can walk around her neighborhood—I don't have that restlessness. I sleep at night."

Chapter 6

LEIGHT JOHNSON AND HIS FELLOW MAN

❧

Leight Johnson's first name is a family name and pronounced "light." Leight and his wife, Shirley, have one daughter and four sons, one of whom died. Leight retired nine years ago as an account executive, which, he says, "is a high-flown name for salesman, sort of an unsupervised salesman; I worked pretty much alone. I don't know that my son's death had anything to do with my wanting to retire. It might have just been that I was getting closer to sixty and wanted to do something else before I got too feeble."

Since Leight retired, he has had two missions: to take photographs and to spend time with hospice patients. Photography was something he and his son had begun together, he said, and after he retired, he continued it. He now teaches photography and has made slide shows of The Compassionate Friends and the hospice. "If you buy a camera, you have to have something to do with it. After a while, you took enough pictures and you've brought them upstairs and your wife has said, 'That's nice,' and you've put them in a drawer. You have to have more of a purpose than that. If I can get good pictures that really capture people, that's a means of expressing how I feel about things."

Leight has an easy voice, talks and looks straight at you. He's serious about wanting to capture people: when the interview was about two-thirds over, he began asking me questions about my own experiences, and by the time the interview was completely over, he knew as much about me as I did about him. Like many parents, Leight hardly needed to be asked questions; he knew what he had come to tell me. I did ask him questions, but the story he told was so coherent and seamless, I will interrupt him only rarely.

"He was Leight Junior. He was our first son. We called him Johnny just to make it easier in the household; we didn't want to call him Junior. Johnny and I did a lot of things together. We were both on ski patrol together. That's partly probably because he was the oldest boy. We had a good, easy relationship.

"He had left the house by the time he died. That was fifteen years ago, 1979, in May. He had been out for a while and moved back in— some problem with his apartment mate—with all of his gear, back into the basement. When he came back in, it was a little bit of a disruption. Came and went at his own hours, just dumped his laundry—little friction there, no question. Anyway, we encouraged him to move back out again, which eventually he did. But not much more than six months before he died. He had been to college, sort of in and out, probably the equivalent of three years of college. We begged him, for heaven's sakes, finish it. 'Even if you want to be a carpenter,' we said, 'at least finish it up and then you've got some more options.' He didn't seem much interested. He was interested in emergency medicine, rode ambulances professionally—that was his job—for the army. He was getting very accomplished at it. He was happy, he was content with the work he was doing. And like I said, we had a nice, easy relationship.

"And then on Sunday night when we had just gone to bed, we got the phone call. He was sharing an apartment with a woman who was just his apartment mate, not his girlfriend. And she worked at the same place he did. They were on opposite shifts and she was on her way home from work and passed a big accident on Route 40, which turned out to be his. He'd been driving on his way to work, and the woman who hit him was coming down the wrong side of the highway, taking a shortcut to a bar—she was a chronic alcoholic, very sad.

Anyway, she was in a big car, he was in a little one, they hit head-on, he was killed outright, she was out of the hospital in a day or two. Lesson here is, drive a big car.

"Well anyway, Roxie, the woman he shared the apartment with, was the one who called us. As I said, we had just gone to bed. My next son, Peter, who lived at home then, took the phone call. I didn't even hear it. About eleven at night, Peter answered the phone, and called my wife, Shirley, who got up, and I heard her talking, and she handed the phone to me and said, 'Johnny's been killed in an automobile accident.'

"You just don't absorb that. It's like you're reading something out of the paper. Well, I listened to Roxie. She didn't really tell us much. She said they were taking him up to Harford Memorial Hospital, wherever that is. In any case, I thanked her. And my first thought— this is ridiculous—but my first thought was, 'How should I dress to go identify my son?' Crazy thing. We all got dressed, the three of us, Peter, Shirley, and I, and drove off not saying very much. We still couldn't quite—it just *hadn't* sunk in yet. Fortunately.

"And we got up there about twelve-thirty at night. A whole group of his co-workers from the ambulance company got the word through their beepers, and they were all there waiting for us at the hospital outside, just to support us. I hadn't even met any of these young people before. One young couple—the man worked with Johnny on the ambulance crew—and the woman's mother had been killed on Route 40 only about a year before. Her name was Susie and she just put her arms around me. Both young people were so helpful, especially considering we were strangers.

"We were asked if we wanted to see him. They said, 'You don't have to, you don't need to identify him and he has been in a head-on collision.' So we thought about that. I said I'd prefer not to. And Shirley agreed, though later she said she wished she had. But I've never regretted that, that image would be in my mind and hard to get rid of. I didn't have that feeling like I had to see him to believe he really had died. I know people do say that, but it wasn't the case with me.

"We went on back home and told my other two sons, who had

been out for the evening. I had been scheduled to go to Chicago on a business trip the next morning, and it even occurred to me then, we won't have the funeral until Wednesday, so why not go? I did go into the office that morning. None of the people knew what had happened, and I went in to make arrangements for someone to cover for me, and then went back home. The rest of that week is kind of a blur.

"That Wednesday night we had the memorial service. All his friends from the volunteer ambulance company came, plus the ones from the army ambulance company where he worked, plus people from ski patrol. There was something like six hundred people in that church. And we had a eulogy written by a close friend of his—a young man I hadn't met before, Dennis Jones—who was sure he couldn't deliver it without falling apart. So we had another young man deliver it; he read the eulogy. And we had some nice music, and then we had a receiving line so people could say hello. If you had told me ahead of time that I would stand there for an hour and a half, I would have said I couldn't do it possibly. But I did it—we did it. All these people, not only the ones that you would expect, but business competitors of mine, *competitors*. And all of these people who said, 'You don't know me, but I worked with him,' or 'I went to school with him.'

"I want to tell you one thing more about Dennis Jones. We hadn't met Dennis before all this happened. But Dennis and his wife came over and spent Christmas eve with us that first year, even though they both have families here in town, just because they knew we would be lonely. That young people would think of a thing like that. And there was another young man who was just a kid at the time, Willy Gilbert, and every year for about four or five years he'd send Shirley a potted plant on the anniversary of Johnny's death. For a young teenaged boy, to think of things like this.

"Anyway, all that took up that first week very nicely, when I was kind of numb. It's when that ended, and the people stopped calling, that's when it settled in. It was a very warm week in May, that week, and I can remember lying on the grass out in front of our house looking at the tree overhead and just thinking, 'What do we do now? Where do we go from here?'

"I didn't go back to work that week, but I went over one evening to clear some things up. I went into the office and on my desk was a card, a prayer card from the Marianists, from the family that *cleaned* the building at night. I only knew them slightly and casually. I mean, people with no particular reason to do so, will do things like that. Like on the anniversary of the day that Johnny died, which was May 6, we go to where he was killed and generally put some flowers there, right along Route 40. And one year, maybe two or three years ago, there's a flea-bitten motel right there, an old kind of rag-tag motel. And this old black man came out, and after we walked back away from where we put the flowers, he said, 'Can you folks tell me? Every year I see these flowers here. I wonder where they came from.' And we explained to him. And he said, 'Well, I will make sure this little area is maintained now.' And the next year we went back, he'd cut the grass around where we'd put the flowers. I tell you, Ann, things like that make you feel maybe mankind's not so bad after all.

"I would say Johnny's death was certainly a watershed in my life. I went along fat, dumb, and happy for all these years. Because I was never really touched by tragedy of any sort. My father had died, but he was eighty-seven years old, so that's not really a *tragedy.* Johnny's death didn't change my life in any external way. I had been working, I continued to work. Maybe I overstate the case when I say watershed. But it just changed my attitude. I don't know, people say sometimes that a tragedy like this doesn't really change you, it just makes you more like you were before. I don't know. It may push you maybe in one direction or another. I used to avoid going to funerals before all this. I'd say, 'Well, some guy at work died, but I never met his family so what's the point of going?' Now I go to *all* the funerals. Anyway, it was that experience, the people who just show up at the door, just come and say, 'I don't know what to say but here I am.' I guess that's really how I got into hospice.

"Basically, I'm retired and I have a lot of time. I was on the medical ethics committee over at Liberty Medical Center Hospice, having to do with, should you pull the plug on a patient, that kind of stuff. I was on that committee for three or four years, and one of the men on that committee was on the board of the Visiting Nurses Hospice, and he said to me one day, 'Would you be interested in being on the board of the hospice?' I said, 'No, I don't want more meetings to go to. But I might be interested in becoming a volunteer.' I had known a lot of people who had cancer or whatever, and I would go to see them. I did that even before Johnny died. I found it not hard for me to do. The guy's dying, he knows he's dying, I know he's dying, I can still talk to him about the weather or anything he wants to talk about. I found that rewarding because I thought I was being helpful. After losing a son, and all those people being so helpful to me, I guess that combination of things—a natural inclination and my heightened compassion as a result of my own experience—I thought, 'I can do this, so why not try it?' So I did, but if Johnny hadn't died, I don't think I probably would have done that.

"This is a home-hospice operation. The hospice agency will say, 'This family could use a volunteer.' The volunteers simply do what-ever might be involved. Mainly it's visiting. Sometimes it involves sit-ting with the patient so the caregiver can get out for a while. Sometimes I get to know the caregiver because the patients are so nearly dead they can't talk much. If the patient is well enough that they can talk, then you visit with them.

"I've had some wonderful experiences. I had one patient down in the Dundalk area who lived in a rowhouse with his wife, and her sis-ter next door and her other sister right across the alley—they were a close family. I went in and the husband was there dying and I'd sit in the kitchen with her and talk. After her husband died, I kept after her for a while. One day nearly a month later, she said, 'My sister says I've got to stop crying, I'll make myself sick.' Which is such a dumb thing. I said, 'Don't listen to her, listen to me. You've *got* to cry. She means well; give her credit for that.'

"I had one patient whom I met, went down to sit with him so his wife could go out and play bridge. The first time I went to see him, we chatted away, two or three hours passed quickly. The wife came back and she said, 'I had a great time. Can you come again next week Friday?' I said, 'Sure I'll be back.' Three days later I got a call and *she* had died suddenly. So he then was left alone. They sent him down to an in-house hospice. But he was still well enough to get out and around. So a couple of times I took him out. We went downtown to his old neighborhood where he had grown up and went to Sunday school. He wanted to go eat at a certain restaurant. We stopped in to see a couple of his old neighbors. That was *fun,* that was *fun.*"

And Leight went on to tell me story after story about people he had met through the hospice. One man asked Leight to hold his hand for a while, and said nothing much was wrong with him except for the cancer. One woman, a black woman, died just before he got to her house. He passed her body being wheeled out on a gurney. So he went on into the house and asked the woman's niece if she would like to be hugged. The niece said she would, Leight hugged her, the niece cried a little, and Leight left. The point of this story was how surprised the niece had been to see a white man walk into her house and hug her, and how surprised he was that he'd done it.

One man hadn't been out of his apartment in years. Leight visited him on and off for about a year, then one day took him to the doctor, and afterward the man said, "Now I think I'm ready to go out."

"So yesterday we went," Leight said, "and this was his first outing in three years. He wanted to go to the International House of Pancakes. He said afterward, 'That was just great to be able to go out in the sunshine.'" Leight drove him out to a lake and took his picture with the lake in the background, and the man told Leight the story of his career. "That kind of thing is fun to do," said Leight. "Anyway, that's what I do."

"So this hospice work is not only a way of helping people, it's also a way of getting to know them?" I asked.

"Oh yeah," Leight said.

"Hospice work is such an unlikely thing for a man to do," I said, "and you seem to enjoy it so much. Is it connected in some way with Johnny?"

"Oh I'm sure it is," he said. "I'm sure it is. I think the one thing that contributed most to my ability to do this was the support that I got from his friends, like those people that waited for us at the hospital, or Dennis and his wife who invited us on Christmas eve, that kind of thing."

"That's a connection with Johnny's friends," I said. "Is there a connection with Johnny himself?"

"Like I said," Leight said, "we were really close. We even used to speak French together. I don't know, I guess the things that we shared, like the photography and the skiing and the sailing. I guess the closeness that we had. I was so grateful for that. He had talked to me on the phone just a couple days before, I have forgotten what about, but it was the usual conversation that we had. We were good friends, that's what I want to say, we were friends. We had gone beyond the father-son to the point where we were friends."

I didn't see the connection until I tried to think out my next question: how is doing things and having talks with dying people connected to being friends and having talks with Johnny?

Leight didn't wait for me to finish thinking. "One thing I found that triggers my grief a lot," he went on, "is certain songs, often just something in the lyrics. There's a Neil Diamond song, 'Hello my friend, hello, just called to say hello.' For some reason, that just throws me."

I asked, "Do you feel like you're carrying Johnny with you in some way?"

"Oh yes," he said. He sighed and stared out my window. "No. I don't know. There's a bird on your window sill. It's just a feeling sometimes that Johnny's with me. A lot of things, during the first year or two, you'd see something and you'd say, 'Oh, I want to show Johnny' or 'I got to tell him about this.' After a while you don't do quite that. You say, 'I *wish* that he could be here to see that.' I have that feeling still. When I dream about him now—and I do from time to time—most often he's about twelve years old. One time we had sailed our boat down to Gibson Island for a weekend, went on a late Friday afternoon, sailed down through the evening, and Johnny was with me, and I can still picture him at the helm, chattering away. And every once in a while now, I have a dream where he comes back, he's here, and I say, 'Where have you been?' He'll say, 'I've been away.' I say, '*Please* don't go away again.'"

Chapter 7

JANET WRIGHT'S BAD FRIENDS

∞

Janet Wright's twenty-three-year-old son, Bill, was killed in a car accident seven years ago. A teenaged boy with several traffic violations was showing off in another car, spinning wheels, and when Bill's car made a left turn, the boy's car hit it.

For most of the interview, regardless of what questions I asked, Janet told horror stories of how heartless her former neighbors, friends, and relatives had been in the years after Bill's death. The reason for the heartlessness, she said, was because she had "gotten involved with another man," and six weeks after Bill died, she left her husband of thirty years to marry this other man. The neighborhood was shocked by the divorce and sympathized with her ex-husband, who, in their eyes, had just lost a son when his wife walked out on him.

"It was one of these neighborhoods that you never find again," she said. "Thirty years ago it was a new neighborhood, everyone moved in at the same time, we all had babies together, we raised all the kids together. Nobody could believe that this divorce was happening. So nobody called and said, 'Janet, it's terrible that Bill died, this is a terrible loss.' My card group just about kicked me out, or made me mad enough that I told them how I felt and I got out. No one would have

94

anything to do with me. I lost every friend. I lost really that whole thirty years. I had no one to talk to. It's really true, nobody wants to see you crying. One neighbor was my closest friend—we were like sisters, our kids grew up together, we went on vacations together. When Bill was killed, I don't know what I would have done without her. She was a nurse and she came over, fed us, organized. But after the divorce, when I needed her she was not there. She said to give her a call sometime, and I never did.

"About two years after Bill was killed, I was talking to one of my neighbors. I was crying silently, the tears dripped down just for a second, and she acted like she didn't see this. She was telling me about her kid, and I said something about Bill, and she said to me just as cruel, 'I would think you'd be over that by now.' That was her answer."

The stories sound bitter and angry and reading them, one might suspect Janet of equal bitterness. But if Janet was bitter, she was cheerful about it. She laughed all the way through these stories and all the way through the interview. She was middle-aged, good-looking, and outgoing, and had none of the tight self-absorption that goes with such anger. Her whole manner was at odds not only with these stories but also with her description of herself.

"Probably it turned out for the best with the neighborhood," she continued, "because if they had stuck by me they would have ended up hating me. Because I had turned into such a nasty person. I don't know if I could handle watching these kids whom I had seen grow up with my son, go on to get married. I don't think I could. I used to have bitter thoughts. I thought, 'I want you to have the same,'" meaning she wanted their children to have died too. "I was probably mad that they still had their children and some of their children weren't as good as my child. It's terrible to be that way, to see I'm not a very good person. You're not supposed to have these thoughts, I don't suppose.

"I still feel the bitterness about kids I see speeding or squealing their wheels, thinking they were cute. Talk about killing someone, if I had had a gun, I think I could have done it to those kids. I maybe would have been sorry afterward as I was going off to jail. But I would get so angry with them.

"When my other son, David, got married, at his wedding my closest friend came over and—I guess with the emotion of the whole day—I looked at her and said, 'I really miss you as my friend.' And then I started crying. And then she walked away and left, and that's the last I've seen of her. Like I say, I'll have to cry a long while—she couldn't have told me that any better. It didn't exactly tear her up. Well, that did it. I can laugh about it now. What she did released it.

"Anyway, David was saying to me that I was supposed to be forgiving. Well, I never did forgive. I was bitter. I had lost a child. If I wanted to hate, I should hate. If I wanted to think bad thoughts, I should do that. You read about all these grieving parents who are not bitter any more and they've gone on and done some good in the world. I don't know, maybe I don't want to let go of my bitterness."

I finally protested: "But you don't seem like a bitter person to me."

"I don't?" she laughed. "You can't be bitter *all* the time. I just do the bitterness inside. I'm not trying to change. Don't most people stay bitter? I would think they'd have to."

Feeling bitter and angry over the death of your child and your friends' coldness seems natural. But being so straightforward and cheerful about bitterness and anger does not. I didn't understand Janet at all until after I gave up and changed the subject. I asked her if she felt any guilt about Bill's death.

No, she said. "I still feel that Bill was almost the perfect child and he did everything right." She laughed again, this time at her pride in Bill.

"One of the things I asked him—and don't ask me why I ever did this, I shudder when I think of it. When he was in college, he worked hard. This kid would stay home, I mean, maybe there are other kids like that, but I just thought it was strange, he would stay home and work and work and study. Kids would call for him to go out, and he'd say no, he had a big exam, or a paper to do. And I'd say, 'For God's sakes, Bill, why don't you go?' And he would get mad, 'Look it's my life and my career.' And I said, 'Suppose you drop dead after you go through this, what would you think?'"

She acted out his answer, deepening her voice and shouting: "He said, 'I'D BE *MAD*.'"

Then she returned to her own voice, still laughing: "He said it in such *a way*. I often wonder, whatever made a mother say that to her child? Then I think, he's mad as hell now wherever he is. And he has a right to be. When people say there's a reason why he died? They'll never ever give me a reason why this happened. No way would I ever accept something like that. He would have done well. He would have made somebody happy. And I *never* will let go. I never will stop being angry. I never forget that your life can be taken from you very fast. And as far as being a kinder, more understanding person, truthfully, I can't say that I have, though I read all these things, like the newsletter from Compassionate Friends, where you should be. I plan on being bitter. He's up there *mad*.

Chapter 8

CHANGES TOWARD OTHER PEOPLE

∞

Where Janet saw coldness and cruelty in other people and reacted with anger, Leight saw generosity and intimacy, and reacted with warmth. Their reactions were equally intense and exactly
opposite. I doubt that the reason for this difference is that Janet was a
hostile person and Leight friendly: both were similarly extroverted,
open, and easy. I suspect the difference was in their ongoing relationships with their children: Janet was living out Bill's anger at his unfin-
ished studies, and Leight and Johnny were chatting in the boat.

But more than that difference is going on in these stories. These
stories are also about the effect that a child's death has on the relationships with other people. Janet and Leight both spent most of the
interview talking about other people—not themselves, not their children, but other people. Janet and Leight were both a little unusual in
this, but not very. People almost outdo gerbils as social animals, and
our friendships are central to our lives.

People make friends with each other because they have things in
common: interests, experiences, attitudes, principles, desires, aims,
anything. One of the most pervasive commonalities between people
is children. Parents are bound to each other by their children. Rela-

tives have genes in common with the children. Close friends tell proud or worried stories about their children. Acquaintances and colleagues ask each other, "How are your children?" and strangers say, "Do you have children?"

What happens to these friendships, then, when a child dies? Is some part of the common ground for the friendship gone? Or do friendships intensify in sympathy and common feeling? As usual with human reactions, the answer is contradictory. But for the parents I interviewed, certainly, the common ground changes.

Throughout the interviews, one recurring phrase was "nobody knows." By this, people meant two slightly different things. The first was, nobody else knows how losing a child feels. In fact, the parents themselves wouldn't have known, and now that they do know, they can't communicate it well. The second was, they wouldn't have known by extrapolating from other deaths. No other death is adequate preparation, they said, not the death of a parent or a spouse or a lover or a sibling.

Researchers have recently been trying to distinguish parental bereavement from other kinds. One researcher compared people who had, within the year, lost either a spouse or a parent, or a child. "The death of a child produced the highest intensities of bereavement," she wrote, "as well as the widest range of reactions." But scientific research on complicated, contradictory subjects being what it is, another study found no differences between people who lost spouses and those who lost children. Yet another found bereaved mothers much more depressed than bereaved wives or daughters. And still another found the death of a child more stressful than the loss of any other close relationship.

Some unlucky souls I interviewed were in a position to make the comparison, having lost a child *and* a husband or wife or brother or sister or parent. Most of them said that losing a child is worse or that the grief is more intense, whatever "worse" and "more intense" mean. One sixty-year-old woman's son died, and a year later, her husband died as well: "It's just wrong, isn't it," she said, "a child dying. Losing a husband is not an easy thing, but at my age, you've come to expect it. But losing a child is just outrageous."

Such comparisons are unpleasant, however, and the people I interviewed would in no way say that anyone mourning a parent or spouse doesn't know what grief is: "If someone has lost a mother, and they've never lost a child," said Betty Jones, "then losing their mother is to them a great loss."

One after another, without being asked, the parents repeated "nobody knows," in its different meanings. "Nobody knows," Janet said. "Until you go through it and you can feel it, nobody can say how it's going to be."

Diana Moores: "I think people who haven't lost children think that you may have a harder struggle and more pain and it may take a longer time, but that you'll get to the place where you got after Grandma died. But it's a different place. It's not even in this world."

Betty: "My father died two years ago, and although I loved my father dearly, the impact was like, one hundred being my son's death and two being my father's death. There was just no comparison, none at all. I would never have believed there was that much difference until I'd been through it."

Anne Perkins: "Even though I didn't like it when my father died of cancer, it was still natural. I was close to my father and loved him. But it's really different. *Big* different."

Ginny Mitchell: "Since Joel died, I have lost my father, and lost Fred's father, who lived right next door, and his mother and stepmother. We have a large family, so we've had our share of deaths. But it just doesn't have the same effect."

Joan Gresser: "I don't think I will ever, *ever* experience that kind of pain, ever again. Except if anything happened to my daughter. Like when my father died, I was very close with my dad, I didn't have this intense grief. I didn't have this intense grief when my mother died or my sister. Maybe it's a protection, I don't know. But it's not like *that*. Definitely not like that."

Delores Shoda: "When we lost our son, I spoke to a friend who had lost a child before, and I said, 'I'm so sorry that I wasn't with you more and I wasn't more understanding.' She said, 'How could you know unless you'd been there yourself?' And I always think about that. That's what's such a help about Compassionate Friends; you know these people have been there. Counselors, unless they've been through it, are never very good."

Loretta Marsh's doctor gave her advice about managing her grief: "And I told the doctor, I said, 'I don't care what you say. You have two beautiful pictures on your desk of your two sons. You don't know.' 'But,' he says, 'I'm trained.' I said, 'God bless you, we need you. But, *no, you don't know.*'"

Walter Levin: "The words I remember, the words most memorable to me by someone who came to visit me while I was mourning, this is an old guy, he just touched me and said, 'There are no words.' And that's exactly right. There are no words. 'There are no words,' he said, and he left."

I remember a similar thing: after T.C. died, a colleague of my husband's was at a loss for words, as everyone is, and said only, "I don't know what to say to you." As Walter did, I liked this, that someone else knew that nobody knows. Someone else could recognize the blank incommensurateness between a child's death and anything else in life.

Dennis Klass, the grief researcher, says that at his first meeting of Compassionate Friends, he was unprepared for what he saw. "Clearly, here was a grief that had a different quality from what I had seen before," he wrote. Later he added, "I am still an outsider, and I am still not sure I can really understand what it must be like to have one's child die."

So, if the child's death is a nobody-knows experience for both the parents and for everyone else, is the common ground for friendships then gone? Not at all. This particular common ground is not as much the children themselves as a parent's involvement in them, and the involvement does not die with the child. The common ground between the parents and their friends isn't gone, just changed. Changed how? Must the parents' relationship with other people become inevitably different?

The answer to the first question is complicated and emerges gradually from the answer to the second, which is also complicated, but parents have a lot to say about it. What they have to say is all over the map, at least on the surface. Some parents get closer to certain other people. Some parents get more distant from certain other people. Some parents get closer to some people, more distant from others. Certain people to whom some parents feel closer are the same people from whom other parents feel more distant.

Below the surface, one motivation behind the greater distance or closeness is that the value parents place on other people changes. This change in the value of other people accompanies a change in the parents' priorities and is the subject of a later chapter. Otherwise, the motivation behind greater or less distance seems closely tied to the dead child.

Begin with the people to whom the parents felt closer.

Researchers haven't studied changes in the relationships between bereaved parents and other people. Some suggest anecdotally that parents get closer to other people. One researcher said that bereaved parents eventually valued personal relationships more and had an increased capacity for empathy and intimacy. Another said that after six years, bereaved parents were more tolerant, more sensitive, and more understanding of others' problems.

In some cases, parents I interviewed simply appreciate other people more. They empathize with other people who need help or are in pain. Like Leight Johnson, they are grateful to people who have helped them out or who have been kind. Their gratitude is intense, as is the pleasure they take in talking about these people.

"We lost our son around Passover-Easter time," said Walter. "And since that time, our closest friends, *dear* friends, have always had us to their home on the holiday, Passover, the first night, and the Jewish new year. They never missed. They didn't do it before, so I'm sure they instituted that knowing that it's tough at home. Same friends, year after year."

"That's nice, isn't it," I said.

"That *is* nice," he said, thinking it through. "*Very* nice."

"After Merrill died," said Walter's wife, Elaine, "people told me, 'You will lose friends, people will leave you.' We never found that. We found people were just marvelous. Even after Merrill's arm had to be amputated, the people he worked for, a family we never knew who had a little ice cream store, they let him work. He would scoop ice cream with one arm. It was marvelous of these people—after all, there were people coming into the store who might be turned off. And a very good friend of Merrill's, we heard that he had gotten married, and then last June, I got a phone call from him that his wife had just had a baby, and he wanted to know Merrill's Hebrew name because they had a little girl and he was naming her after Merrill. And he said, the day Merrill passed away he made a vow to himself that the first child he had would be named after Merrill, and now it's come to fruition. And then the nicest thing is, they brought the baby girl to see us, and his wife is a charming girl, and this marvelous, marvelous baby, and lovely, lovely—he was always a sweet wonderful boy. Charming boy."

Loretta knew a similar person. "This one girl, she and Mike just had started dating off and on," said Loretta. "She got married two years after Mike got killed, and not long ago she had a little baby. Every seventh of December, she writes us a note about how she's felt and different things this year. And I *love* it, I just—I love it that she's not forgotten him."

"Before Joel died," said Ginny, "the children at his elementary school were fantastic. It was a very small school, and they went through his illness for three years. When he lost his hair after treatment and wore his hat to school, every boy in the class wore his hat, you know, to keep him company. And then afterward, I think we're fortunate to have kept the relationship with my husband and I together, and with the children. Our family and real close friends have always been supportive and stayed that way. They're our precious few."

"I have a very good friend, she lost her daughter," said Delores. "We talk to each other an awful lot. I'm never afraid to talk about her daughter, and she's never afraid to mention Larry. And if she cries, that's all right. If I cry, that's fine. We don't see each other a lot, but I always feel like if I have a bad day, she's there to talk to me. My other friends, though they're good friends, I don't feel like that—I feel like there are things I want to say that I can't say because it makes them feel bad, and I don't want to make them feel bad."

Mary Norris had a friend like that too. "A lot of times, I was sitting at home and look like I started getting down," she said, "I used to call up a friend of mine. I said, 'I'll be over.' I go over, we sit down and drink coffee, you know, sit down, just talk, talk, talk. Right after he died, I used to call her up at night and talk with her about him. I used to wake her up, but she was very understanding. She's gone now, so I really miss her. She was there. Whenever I needed her, she was right there."

Notice that the intense appreciation, the extra closeness is directly related to the dead child. This was so for all the parents I interviewed. However, the question I asked—"Do you notice yourself more distant from other people or closer? Which other people?"—didn't specify any connection to the child. But because the context of the interview was the death of children, the parents may have inferred the connection. So maybe the parents might also feel closer to people who are in no way related to the child.

Many of the parents also felt more distant from other people, and in this case I have no doubt that the greater distance is related to the death of the child. Some parents acknowledge they originate the distance, others think other people do. If I'm certain of anything, I'm certain that both are right.

The basic reason for the greater distance lies in the full meaning of "nobody knows": nobody believes this can happen, nobody else knows what it feels like, no other death is preparation, the parents themselves wouldn't have known and now that they do, they can't describe it. On this one issue anyway, the parents live in one world, everyone else lives in another, and the worlds don't communicate.

This reason for distance is inevitable and originates with neither the parent nor the other people.

Emily Miller: "I'm definitely more distant from people. I can be in a crowd and I'm all alone. I still have good relationships with all my friends, but many times I'm there in body only. I act like I'm there but I'm not."

Anne Perkins: "I value the friendships and I'm fortunate that way a lot. But I'll find, much more than I did in the past, when I go to a party or go into a room with people I know, I just feel disconnected."

Another reason for the distance originates with both parties and is also inevitable: the parents are sensitized to emotional reminders that their children are dead. One unexpected reminder is their child's old friends moving through life's stages.

"All these people that we're friends with," said Delores Shoda, "all their children are about Larry's age and you see what's happening in their lives. That is a constant reminder of what your child would have been doing. And it's hard. Also I have a lot of trouble if I see the young men Larry went to law school with. We keep in contact with a lot of them, but it's very difficult to see these young men in their business suits walking around downtown. It's especially hard for my husband because he and Larry would meet for lunch, and he says, 'I see all young guys and I think, 'Where's Larry?'''

"When I see other people with their daughters, clearly their adult daughters," said Julia Marcus, whose adult daughter died, "I really just get *so* lonesome."

"My ex-husband gets a lot out of seeing Robert's friends," said Anne. "I see them this one weekend that they come to Baltimore to decide what projects the Robert Perkins Fund should give money to. I was close to them when they were all around; I like them and they like me. But it's not something I seek out. There is some pain attached to them. Robert has stopped in time; they've moved on through time."

Notice that these old friends of their children who have moved through time and are therefore painful to be around are precisely the

same old friends that Loretta Marsh and Elaine Levin found so comforting. Maybe the reason is that Mike's and Merrill's friends take pains
to remember them, and so include themselves in Loretta's and Elaine's
ties with their children. Whatever the reason, Elaine manages to feel
the opposite as well.

"Some friends of Merrill's kept friendly over the years," said Elaine.
"I think so highly of these kids. But when I would see them all like at
a wedding, this whole nucleus of kids, it really would upset me, it did,
it did. I had pleasure, but I also felt that longing, he should be there.
And there was one particular girl that liked my son, he liked her, and
when I heard she married, I had that same feeling, that sort of pang.
That describes it, it's a dumb word, but that's what I get, a pang."

These and other reminders of the children's deaths are everywhere
and in nearly every relationship with everyone. Everyone who has
children talks about their child's school, sports, bar or bat mitzvah,
confirmation, graduation, job, wedding, children—every stage of the
normal life cycle. Some people seem to have few other topics of conversation. For a parent whose child has died, all this is difficult.
"There comes a point where I'm just sick of hearing about other
people's kids," said Louise Lewis. The difficulty is painful for the first
few years, fades with time, and reappears sporadically forever (Louise's
son was killed seventeen years before).

"There was a good friend who was really close," said Anne. "Her
son was Robert's best friend all through life. And she was wonderfully
supportive, she was very helpful at knowing about how to be there
after Robert died. We're still good friends. But I just don't see her
that much any more. She and her son are different, they're not what
they were two weeks after when Robert's presence was clinging to
everybody, and that was wonderful for all of us. But now—there's
something that's harder."

"We had neighbors in our old house," said Elaine. "Our children
played with their children. They were very dear friends. When Merrill got sick, they would come all the way from Potomac, two, three
times a week, to Hopkins to see Merrill. They'd sit with us. I'm talking *good* friends. But after Merrill died, every time they would invite

us, Walter just, he would have another reason not to go. And it doesn't take a rocket scientist to understand. So I would see her occasionally, we would meet for lunch. But you know what happens, you know, 'the kids got married, the new grandchildren, blah blah blah,' and we no longer see each other. And that is a great, great regret of mine."

Elaine's husband, Walter, told the same story: "People say to me, 'My son went to here, my son has a this,' and when it's too much, I can just feel myself tuning out. I don't say, 'Go away from me. Stop talking.' I say, 'Oh, that's really great.' I feel that people are not sensitive. But I tell myself, 'For God's sake, Walter, you lost your boy sixteen years ago,' and when a fellow says, 'My son just got a great job and he has a lovely wife,' I'm sure they don't think about, 'Hey, Walter lost a boy.' But it's hard. We were very close to another couple with four boys, and the boys were very friendly with Merrill. After he died, we were friendly for a while, but we lost contact and we just didn't have the impetus to resume it. Primarily because the contact was our sons. We've cut off our relationship only because there isn't that common thread any more."

"Or maybe the common thread is painful now?" I asked.

"Yes, now the common thread is painful," he said. "Absolutely. The common thread is painful."

Meanwhile, what's going on with the people who are telling Walter about their sons who went to here or have a this?

Even though Louise said she was sick of hearing about other people's kids, and Anne said there was something that was harder, and Walter said he tuned out—that is, even though these parents are clearly pulling away from other people—my impression is that the greater distance between the parents and their friends is mutual.

On the parents' side is pain. When Walter said that the common thread between the Levins and their friends had become painful, he implied that the thread is still there. And that's true: the thread is the children and the parents' involvement in them. The Levins have not suddenly become a childless couple who have no common ground with a couple with children. Instead, the talk about the great job and lovely wife reminds the Levins not of Merrill's life but of his death. So the thread is now painful. This pain, which now pervades the common ground, changes it.

But surely everyone knows this about this pain, or at least senses it. Then why is Walter's friend telling Walter about his son's lovely wife and great job? Why are the friends also distancing themselves? Maybe the only distance here is time: maybe after sixteen years, Walter's friend has simply forgotten that Merrill, too, would have had a lovely wife and great job. I remember an acquaintance telling my husband at a party that she had just dropped her daughter at the station to take the train up to college, and that she was always relieved when her daughter took the train, which was so much safer. The acquaintance knew that T.C. died in a train wreck on the way to college, and when my husband said, "Yes, we used to feel that way too," the acquaintance was horrified by what she had said. Truly, she had forgotten, and why not? People have their own lives, their own stubborn troubles, and how could they possibly stay eternally aware of yours?

But other people also distance themselves from bereaved parents more actively, out of social awkwardness or confusion. People are afraid to talk about your child to you, afraid of reminding you, afraid of disturbing your equilibrium. They are uncomfortable and confused. "Our friends," said Estelle Lemaitre, "if they accidentally say Robby's name, they look like they want the ground to open up and swallow them."

When I asked Ruth Banick what she thought people meant when they said, "You'll have to get over this," she laughed and said, "I hate that expression. I think it means that people face life with 'here's a problem, here's a solution.' And this is a problem for which there is no solution, and it makes them uncomfortable. I think they want us back the way we were, and it's such a stupid thing because we'd *love* to be back the way we were, *much* more than they. I always think it's ironic that they're uncomfortable with it and they're only around me a little bit. I'm around me all the time."

Leight: "I had my son's picture up on my wall in the office, and the secretary said, 'Gee you're brave to have that picture there constantly reminding you of it.' I said, 'Nancy, I don't need a picture to remind me that I had a son.'"

A friend who is a secretary had a two-year-old daughter die, and while she was still on leave, her employer asked me if he shouldn't remove the daughter's pictures from her desk, so as not to remind my friend. I said what Leight did.

I don't think my friend's employer and Leight's secretary or Estelle's friends were as stupid as they sound. Maybe people don't know that parents feel a difference between being reminded of their child and being reminded of their child's death.

Then too, maybe people know that one way to deal with irrevocable pain is distraction. Maybe this hesitancy to remind you of the child is not the idiotic assumption that you've forgotten the child but is instead a more subtle recognition that you may not want to be distracted from your distractions. And maybe when Leight and I and most other bereaved parents say, "Don't worry about reminding us, it's always right here," we're also saying, "The distractions don't work very well anyway."

People also distance themselves actively because they must. A child's death is bad news of the worst kind, and no one wants to hear it. Even people in fearless professions have trouble with this: Dennis Klass did his research at Compassionate Friends' meetings along with his graduate students in social work: "Though I hear stories each meeting, I find that my students (most of whom have children) and I protect ourselves from full identification with the experience," he wrote. "I am not a member and must hope that I never become one."

People need to stay away from that sort of news. Joan Gresser said, "Don't you think when somebody says, 'You have to get on with it,' that what they're probably saying is, 'Oh God, please get better because watching you is killing me; I don't know what to say to you; it could have been my kid and thank God it wasn't; so look, if *you* get on with it, then *I'm* going to be OK.' That's what I think they mean."

That's what I think they mean too, and I don't think they can help themselves. In some primitive, hard-wired thought process, people suspect that bad news is contagious: you have something catching and they better avoid you. After Lydia Frasca's infant daughter and infant son died, she consoled herself by making two baby books. "It took me a long time to do it," she said, "because I didn't have very much to put in them. So a friend was looking at one of them and said, 'What is this?' And I said, 'It's a baby book.' And she said, 'For *whom?*' And I said, 'For my children.' And she closed it right up and said, 'This is for a dead baby. If I look at this, it might happen to me.' She actually did say that."

Therese Rando, a practicing psychologist and a researcher, calls this fear of contagion, "magical thinking," and an "attempt to ward off the anxieties generated within themselves." She writes that "bereaved parents represent the worst fears of other parents, and consequently they are subject to intense social ostracism." Some parents call this "shying away," and the metaphor is apt. People in these circumstances act like horses who come up against something frightening and abruptly change course. The result is a huge gap in many conversations, a huge subject that has to be ignored and circumvented. When the subject does arise, it usually stops conversations in their tracks.

So maybe other people are not simply forgetting, but are forgetting because they're rightly frightened. In fact, they might not be forgetting at all. Many bereaved parents suspect that their bereavement remains uppermost in other people's minds. "You know, once that happens to you," said Julia Marcus, "no matter what else people know about you, that always, I think, is in people's minds." Anne said she thinks people look at her the way she used to look at people whose children died: "It was always one of the first things I'd think about when I saw them, that they lost their child. That would always be very much that person's identity."

I suspect that Julia and Anne are right about most people most of the time. And the reason for people to put this out of their minds and forget it is justified. Even the thought, let alone evidence, that a child can die, is terrifying. This is the second way the common ground between bereaved parents and other people changes: the other people are terrified.

So even though "nobody knows" is true, I think anyone who has children has a pretty good idea. I have a friend, a man with two grown sons, one of whom is going blind. Five or six years after T.C. died, this friend asked me, with sympathy, when I would be done mourning. I told him I was happy in my life, but I couldn't see a day when I would stop mourning. He said this was because I was a woman, that men were bastards, he said, who could easily forget their children. I laughed, as he meant me to.

"Now, my older son," my friend went on, "if he died, I'd feel bad for a while, but I'd get over it."

Then he thought for a minute. "My younger son, though, the one who's going blind," he said, "if he died, I'd have to die too."

"My point exactly, you old idiot," I thought, but I like this man so I didn't start anything.

Another occasion: a year and a half after T.C. died, I went to my gynecologist, a young woman. She knew about T.C.'s death and asked how I was doing. "Fairly unhappy," I said, "but physically fine."

She said, "I think about you a lot."

"Do you really?" I said, feeling touched.

"Yes," she said, "now don't make me cry."

"All right," I said, and prepared to change the subject.

"It's just having one child like I do, only one," she said, and started crying. "I'm sorry."

"Please don't be," I said. She stopped crying and went on with the examination. I thought later that she hit all the bases at once: I was on her mind, she was frightened for her own child, she was sorry for reminding me.

During neither of these occasions was I unhappy with these people. In fact, because they were so open about their fears, I felt they understood a little of my own feelings and I felt comforted. But too often, to bereaved parents, other peoples' distancing—passive or active, forgetful or terrified—feels like simple insensitivity. And now this understandable stand-off—pain on one side, fear on the other—becomes more complicated. The parents too often feel not only isolated or hurt, but also betrayed. For many parents, the greatest betrayal has come—they think—from the very people who owe them the most loyalty: their relatives.

"My mother asked me many times why I don't get on with my life," said Diana. "And when I was in the psychiatric hospital, my mother called and demanded to know why they were keeping me there. Finally I said to her, 'They're trying to keep me alive.' She started crying and she said to me, 'If you *ever* did anything to kill yourself, then you might as well figure you're killing two people. Because if a daughter of mine was killed, I wouldn't want to be alive.' She could not conceive of why I felt like dying, but if I died, she'd want to kill herself. Phenomenal."

My own mother said something less dramatic but similar: "You really are going to have to get on with your life. You don't know how hard it is for me to watch my daughter suffering." At first I was angry at her. How dim could she be, to want me to stop mourning *my* child so she needn't watch *her* child suffer? After a while, I understood that watching a child suffer was no fun, regardless of why, and stopped being angry. Diana, two and a half years later, now says the same: "I understand now how much she was hurting. And she and I have gotten closer and closer."

Ginny was more understanding than I had been. "I think your parents have a double hurt, a double grief," she said. "Which I can understand now that I have a grandchild. She's just three months old but I can see how if anything would happen to her, I would have the feelings for my children and then the feelings for the child."

Brandt also thinks he understands what's going on. "My mother says you have to get on with your life," he said. "And knowing my mother, I know what she's saying. To other people, that would be a crass thing to say. People don't couch their words. And the older they get, the worse they get. But I think she means she wants me where she can help me."

112

Little research has been done on the effects of losing a grandchild, and the little that has, agreed with Brandt and Ginny. The researchers found that most felt closer to the child's parents—their own children—and most felt pain for their children. The researchers suspected that the grandparents were grieving as much for their children as for their grandchildren. My mother and Diana's mother were saying precisely that. The normal response to watching a child in pain is to try to make the pain go away.

But not everyone is so forgiving as Diana, Brandt, and Ginny. In fact, I'm not, myself. Along with a sense of having been betrayed comes anger. I asked the parents no questions about anger at their relatives; the closest was, "Are there people who were once in your life that are now out of it by your choice?" But anger at relatives came up in most of the interviews.

Betty, who has led a chapter of Compassionate Friends for years, said: "I do find from Compassionate Friends, right from the first couple of months, family members are the worst offenders. And with my family, after fourteen years, that hasn't changed a bit. The family members *still* don't talk about my child, and if I bring up something about my child, the subject is changed—they will not continue that conversation on that child. You have that child all those years and you want to talk about all that child did, and people don't want to hear it. I've grown to accept it. I know that's the way it's going to be. It's not going to change. They can't do it."

Loretta: "I don't know about your relatives but I've never had a normal conversation with mine since Mike died. Never. My own family, a close family, they're afraid to mention anything about Mike. I talk and they just look at me. And that makes me feel, 'Is it me?' But it's not me. It hurts. When my father died, my mother would call me and she'd be crying, and I loved my father a lot, and I'd want to say, 'God Almighty, Mom, how many times did you call me after I lost Mike? I couldn't even talk to you on the phone.' And it's my own father! I didn't used to be a selfish woman. All my sisters say, 'Loretta what's wrong with you?' I say, 'Do you want me to tell you what's wrong with me? Do you really want me to tell you?' I say,

'For crying out loud, I'm not like you any more.' I don't wish it on anybody, but I wish every person on this earth could live for one day like I feel, just one day, one day. I told my own mother that, I told my sisters that, I told my brother that, both brothers I told them. I get the impression that people think when somebody's dead you should grieve but you should pretend it never happened. I can't do that, and I'll never do that."

In retrospect, I am most impressed by the amount of anger with which parents talk about their relatives. They had what they thought was a contract with their relatives to share life experiences, blood being so thick. And here was one of life's worst experiences, and the relatives said, in essence, "the child wasn't *my* blood." Normally I rarely bother to nurse grudges, but I am still furious, eight years later, at small, thoughtless things my relatives said and did. I'm uneasy about this anger. Maybe they did betray me, but surely out of either innocence or personal necessity. The most obvious explanation of an eight-year grudge is that T.C.'s death left me with a generalized, free-floating, unattributable anger, and the smallest, most forgivable be-trayal is a convenient target.

This same anger gets directed at friends. The sense of betrayal is similar: again, the parents thought they and their friends had a con-tract to support each other in hours of need. And here was the par-ents' hour of need and the friend said, like the relatives, "better you than me." These stories of betrayal and anger were so common that in my notes I gave them the name "horror stories."

Loretta said she wanted to be interviewed for this book because she wanted to help tell other people what it's like. "They withdraw from you," she said. "They make you feel like you have a disease. I would find myself crying. I ask myself, 'What is it? Is it something I say?' When I talk to people, I don't keep on the subject of Mike. But people are different to you."

So I asked her, "Are other people more distant from you or are you more distant from them?" The answer, apparently, was both.

"I'm distant from everybody," she said. "Everybody. I don't ever want to get hurt like I've been hurt. I think I looked for help for at least the first three years, from anybody. And I don't think I got help from nobody. Not that they could have helped. But nobody, family or friends, said, 'Let's go out, have a sandwich, sit and talk, I want to see how you're doing.' I don't think I ever got that. If I did, I don't realize it. Maybe people tried to do it and I just burst away. Maybe I block it out. But no, I don't want to get close to anybody. No. I think they don't understand. And I don't want no hurts, none, so just leave me be."

"It took me years to go to a baby shower," said Lydia, whose infant son and daughter died and who miscarried twice. "When I go, people talk about their labor and their deliveries and how awful and oh it's so painful, and I want to shake them. I hate it, I hate it. No one at a baby shower has ever asked me about my experiences, never, and I'm forty years old and I have four deliveries here, I have some input—that makes me so mad."

"Someone I was furious at," said Emily, "this person had not come to see us, we never got a phone call, and this was someone who should have come, a friend whose daughter had also committed suicide. My husband had gone over to him for months, console him, listen to him. One day we met him at the mall. He said, 'Hi, how are you?' I said, 'Oh, you're just the person I wanted to see. I wanted to tell you, I think you're a piece of shit.' He said, 'What?' I said, 'When Sue died, we never got a call from you. When Alice died, we came over, we came over for months.' Believe me, he knew I was right. That was two years ago, and I still feel good about it."

"I had one lady even tell me," said Estelle, "and this was during, maybe the second year after we lost Robby. And she said to me, 'Just think how lucky you are, you will never see your son grow old. He will always be young in your eyes.' I will never, never forget that remark, never!"

"I'd say my friends and my family were *very* supportive," said Sally Lambert. "I can't say that anyone has ever turned me off. Except a social worker in grief therapy used to talk to me at work. One thing she said, she said she felt that some parents want to make—how did she put it?—a career out of being a grieving parent. And that support groups should be for a period of time only. That really *burnt* me up, *really* burnt me up, really burnt me up. I thought, '*Who* in the world is she?' Because I was still going to support groups after two years. I thought, 'Who is she to say that?' Oh, she made me so mad—'they make a *career.*' Who wants *that* as a career?"

"While we were sitting *shivah* after Teddy drowned," said Joan, "all the different little stories about how their children had *near* accidents, *and by the grace of God,* they were *saved.* Well, what was my kid? If I believed that God had anything to do with this, which I don't, this was a little—I mean, really. I was in no condition to do what I would do to them now if I ever saw them. Especially the ones in the *water.* 'This is like on a *raft,* and the raft fell over. And oh yes, we saved him.' They at first were Johnny-on-the-spot, bringing in the trays, answering the phone, what can we do, what can we do. And then all of a sudden, no phone calls any more, get on with your life, it's been a year. There was a lot of desertion on their parts. I had a group of friends, social friends, and I don't have one of them any more, not the first one. And they did it ugly. They just dropped us. They didn't have the balls to say, 'Look, we can't be around you because it's too painful.' All of a sudden they were lying about they weren't having these Christmas parties any more and I found out they *did* have them. Isn't that ugly? I think the *worst* statement was, 'I know how you feel.' That's what used to get me. The person who's saying it to us, we want to whomp them one. Or say to them, 'Do you want to really know how this feels? Give me your kid, I'll show you how it feels.' Does that mean I would want you to experience grief so you would know what I felt? I'm sure I did at some point."

I had a friend who argued with me, after T.C. died, that I should have another child. I didn't know whether I wanted one, I told her. "But you need to," she said. I was sure it would be years before I could love another child, I told her. "You're getting older and you better do it soon," she said. I was furious, and my response was a slightly more polite variant of Joan's "then give me your kid" and Janet Wright's "I wish they had the same." I asked her, "Can you put the name of your daughter and the word 'dead' in the same sentence?" My friend just looked at me. "You can't," I said, "and you shouldn't have to, but until you do, you shouldn't tell me what to do."

Like Joan and Janet, I regret my brutality but I probably would do it again.

Clearly, in some of these horror stories, the other people are killing the bearers of bad tidings, or at least avoiding them. And just as clearly, in others of the stories, the parents are reacting with fury to foolish words kindly meant. This fury, this anger, is much more general than any particular reaction to insensitivity or even betrayal. The subject comes up again in a later chapter.

Although friends and relatives are often the most convenient target, Chris and Emily both mentioned another kind of anger: anger at the child who died.

"Some people at Seasons are quite angry at the person dying," said Chris.

"At a *child?*" I asked.

"At the child," said Chris. "They say, 'He caused me all this pain and hurt. I wish I could get ahold of him and shake him.' Not unusual."

I don't mean to imply that anger at the child is common; I heard it only twice during the interviews, and then as reports of what other parents said. I only mean that parents occasionally feel so much unfocused anger that any target will do. I remember one mother at a Compassionate Friends meeting saying she was lucky in having a job where she could easily take out her aggressions on her co-workers.

Few of the parents, however, seemed to live in the anger. Though they don't forget, they do seem to forgive. They tell themselves that their friends and relatives might not always be kind or sensitive, but they are not malicious, they mean well. After all, the parents say, nobody knows, and what they do know is terrifying. And in any case, they're not necessarily going to be much help. Most parents sensibly return to the idea that they wouldn't have known either.

"Look," said Joan, "just recently a dear friend of mine lost her husband, fifty-one years old, arrhythmia; he was gone like that at a baseball game. Being Jewish, we all go over to the house for *shivah,* every single day, day in and day out. And do you think I knew what to say to her? Do you think I had magic words for her?" By this point, Joan was so angry at her own ineptitude, she was shouting. "All I said to her was, 'I'm sorry.' And then I said, 'If there's anything I can do, please call me.' *Bullshit.* We're just as guilty as these people."

And other parents take "nobody knows" one step further and try to explain to people what they do not know. "You can't expect other people to be sensitive for the rest of their lives," said Louise. "I've heard parents in Compassionate Friends say, 'Oh, they see me coming down the street and they cross over.' But it's mostly those parents' fault—I am so convinced of that. Because they could make those people feel comfortable. After Michael died, if it was a day to play cards, I would say to my friends, 'I'm going to get back in the card game, but I have to tell you that I'm feeling very sad.' Or I would say, 'Girls, I have to tell you I am so upset today, and I have to tell you why.'"

I protested, "But you said you have to make people feel comfortable? Wouldn't bringing this up make them uncomfortable?"

No, Louise said. "I think by my saying that, they feel more comfortable. Because I'm not just very quiet, and they're wondering what is wrong. And in the beginning, I told people, 'You know, I might cry, and I might leave the room, or I might have to talk about Michael, so please bear with me.'"

"And then in return, you ask them about their kids?" I asked.

"Yup," she said. "And they feel more comfortable. I do think they feel more comfortable."

I have a friend who grew up in a village in the mountains of Lebanon. He told me that when someone died, the whole village converged on the house of the bereaved in a Lebanese version of sitting *shivah.* And after everyone was there, a singer, usually a certain blind man, would arrive, accompanied by his adolescent child, boy or girl. The singer would ask the child, "Who's here?" The child would look around the room and name every person there, one by one. Then the singer began to sing: "This one is here and remembers when his mother died. This one is here and still thinks of his son.

This one is here whose husband died only this year." The singer reminded everyone there, one by one, of his or her own grief. Soon, my friend said, everyone in the room would be crying. Bereavement is universal, the singer was saying. You escape grief no more than you escape your own death.

What Louise and the Lebanese singer are both doing is finding a way to erase the distance created by what nobody knows and to maintain the common ground between people. They know the common ground has changed so that it's full of pain for the parents and fear for everyone else. The solution to this problem is sensible and simple. The parents are themselves tolerant and understanding, and they back off from their anger. In turn, they ask other people to recognize what no one wants to know, that children die.

Chapter 9

CHRIS REED

∞

Chris Reed is about to retire after thirty-two years as a tax accountant. He says he's been working since he was sixteen years old and now wants to be able to loaf: "I don't see anything wrong with that. If I get tired of loafing, I'll find something else to do. As long as I feel financially comfortable, I'm looking forward to it frankly."

Chris talks formally. Sometimes he almost seems to be reciting, describing his grief and the days surrounding his daughter's death with the same stock phrases you hear at Compassionate Friends and in books and pamphlets on grief. Though some people use such formality and stock phrases to cover what they feel, Chris seems to hide nothing. He just seems less interested in being original and more interested in being accurate. He has a voice that would sound good on the radio, and he talks with open and calm sincerity.

Chris is a practicing Catholic. He says, "I'm told my love of God is supposed to exceed all others, but that's not in the concrete world. God's not there physically. So aside from that, I guess the love of a father for his children and his wife is the most compelling emotion in his life."

"I had a daughter, nineteen-year-old daughter, Mary, who died ten years ago, April 2, 1984. She died in April and she'd been born in April. Her death was a suicide. She died from an overdose of antidepressant pills on top of some alcohol.

"About a month and a half after she died, my wife, Helen, and I found an organization called Seasons, a support group for people who have lost someone to suicide—some are parents, some are spouses, some are children, some are fiancés, all kinds of relationships. And I found tremendous outlet in Seasons. Because there I could go and talk with people who could understand what I was talking about. And more important, they were willing to let *me* talk. It's awful difficult to deal with, when you're faced with the suicide of a *child,* and not to cry. I had trouble concentrating at work, concentrating and just getting through my routine. And yet society as a whole seemed to be saying, 'We don't want to talk about this, put it out of your mind.' And I couldn't do it. No, no, it's just overwhelming."

I interrupted him and asked, "So in your personal world, who did you talk to about Mary?"

"My wife and the Seasons group," he said.

Seasons, I know, meets once a month, and Chris's wife was surely as overwhelmed with her own grief as he was with his. Then I asked if in addition to Seasons, had he also been to Compassionate Friends, and if so, did he find the two groups were different? He had gone a few times, he said, and yes, he did think the groups were different.

"I think a death by suicide has its own unique grieving period," he said. "I don't want to say that it's more profound because it probably isn't. But a child dies by an accident or an illness, it wasn't intended. Death of a child by suicide—I felt in some way I had some control over what happened to my daughter. That caused a lot of guilt in me. Now I've heard parents whose child has died by other than suicide express feelings of guilt also. But it seems to me that the guilt of a parent after the suicide of a child is probably—what do I want to say?— probably more justified.

"I felt that as a father, it was my role to protect my children. And when my daughter died, I felt that I had failed to protect her from

121

herself. And I had a lot of trouble dealing with that tremendous feeling of guilt. And in that respect at least, I think the grief of a parent surviving a suicide is different. Does that make sense? It took me a long time to get over that overwhelming feeling of guilt. I still feel it after ten years, that if I had done some things differently, maybe, *maybe,* Mary would still be living. I have no assurance of that either. But I told myself I wish I had been more aware of certain things going on in her life."

I hadn't asked Chris about guilt; he got into the subject by talking about differences between Compassionate Friends and Seasons, that is, between parents whose children die from all causes and those whose children kill themselves. Since he'd brought up the subject, I asked him if he would mind telling me what he felt guilty about.

He sat silent for a while. "I don't quite know how to put that into words," he said finally. "About two years before she died—she was a senior in high school—we got a call from her counselor at school. And the counselor said that Mary was in the counselor's office and talking about suicide. That was the first indication that we had that she was ever in trouble. Obviously, she had been in trouble for quite a while. But I think parents often miss those signs of trouble."

I interrupted, not wanting him to blame himself for missing what so many parents miss: "The kids *hide* it," I said.

"They hide it, they hide it," he agreed. "But I think sometimes parents don't want to recognize that there are problem signs. Anyway, the counselor suggested that we get her some professional help, so we did. She began seeing a psychologist weekly. And there were things going on in her life that we were not aware of. She wasn't telling us, and the psychologist, because of professional confidentiality, wasn't telling us either. And it was quite a while before I realized she had a drinking problem. And I talked to the psychologist about it, and he said, yeah, he was aware of it and they were working on it. And I guess I just put too much faith in what he was telling us, and I guess I had too much confidence in my daughter as a good person, to really recognize how deeply troubled she was and the extent of her drinking problem. Her problem was that she would go to singles bars with her friends—which is not unusual for an eighteen, nineteen-year-old—and being somewhat of a shy person, she seemed to feel that if she had a couple drinks, she could lose a little bit of that shyness, she'd become more outgoing.

"I never really saw her come home. I'm a person that goes to bed early and she often came after I'd been in bed. I'd hear her come in, and she'd go up to her room, and I'd assume everything's all right. But apparently everything wasn't all right. And I look back and I think, 'Well, I should have been more aware of what was going on.' When she came home so late I should have used the occasion to check on her condition. And if she really wasn't in good condition, I should have done something to get her some help. And I didn't. I just was too trusting or naive maybe even. And then about a month before she died, I talked to her and asked her to stay away from her drinking friends for a while and give herself a chance to get herself together. And she did.

"Then the day before she died, on a Sunday, she went down to Harborplace on a Sunday afternoon, came home for supper, and then went out with her friends and said she'd be back early. Well, I went to bed at my usual time and she wasn't home. She came home at two in the morning. And I said to myself a number of times after she died, 'Why didn't I recognize that something was going on here? I mean, she said she was coming home early, and she *wasn't* home early. Why didn't I call up that bar and say, 'Mary, are you OK? Can I come get you and bring you home? Do you need help?' And I chided myself for that. It just made my guilt feel overwhelming, that somehow I'd failed her."

I interrupted again: "But she was an adult—at that age you have to leave them alone."

Again he agreed, then explained: "I know you do. At that age you can't follow them around and you have to loosen the reins. But I told myself, 'Yeah, loosen the reins. But when she's in trouble and needs my help, I should have been with her.' So many should-haves. It just kind of compounds my grief. In spite of my best efforts to try and be a good parent, somehow I hadn't done enough."

Chris's voice began breaking up and he had to clear his throat a few times, though he kept his composure. "It was very difficult to deal with that," he said.

I asked if he still had periods of guilt, even though he'd already told me he had.

He contradicted what he had said earlier: "No, not really. I've gotten beyond that. I still believe I should have done things differently. But I reconcile myself to the idea that I made mistakes; we all make mistakes. There's a God, and He forgives me. So I believe I can be forgiven. I can forgive myself. I still believe I should have done more. I'm sorry that I made the mistakes. But now I live the rest of my life. I no longer scold myself for making those mistakes. So I'm not still overwhelmed with the guilt. I've forgiven myself."

I wasn't sure I believed him. He *had* said earlier that after ten years he still felt guilty; and the language he was using was full of clichés, phrases that require no thought to roll off your tongue. But what would I have believed: that this calm, careful man was wracked by agonies of guilt and lying about it, to me or himself? I didn't believe that at all.

I went on to the next question: "Do you feel more vulnerable or anxious in life?"

"No," he said. "No, I can't think of any way I'm more vulnerable or anxious. Maybe aware."

I was surprised at this: awareness didn't seem related to vulnerability or anxiety, and this was the fifth time so far he'd used that word. "Aware" was what Mary's counselor had been and what he felt he hadn't been. For once I didn't interrupt, just paid close attention and let him talk his way through it.

"Mary was the third of four children, and my youngest is now twenty-two, still living at home. She was twelve when Mary died. And so I tried to become more *aware* of what adolescence is like. Because I wanted at all costs to avoid the youngest one going through the same problems that Mary went through if I could at all possibly help. I guess awareness is a better word. Not really vulnerable. Anxious, yes, I guess there's always anxiety with children growing up, particularily the teenage years are difficult. But I was anxious more in the sense that I wanted to be aware of what was going on in her life and try to have a better relationship with her. I wanted to be closer to her, not more—I don't want to say distant, but not more trusting maybe. Well, I wanted to trust her, but I wanted to be more aware of what was going on so I had more basis for my trust."

So Chris set about finding out how to become more aware of his teenager.

"I'd been brought up in a home where the parents set the rules and that was it, no back talk," he said. "And that was the kind of parent I had been pretty much, not that I was mean, but I just didn't tolerate any infraction of the rules. So I thought, well, maybe there's a different way. And I became aware of this communication business and I did a lot of reading on it. Then I took a course on parent effectiveness training, which basically is to teach you how to communicate with your adolescent children.

"I found that a tremendous help. In the past, where I had been more inclined maybe to raise my voice and as they were growing up I didn't hesitate to smack them on the behind, I got away from that attitude and was more willing to listen, really listen. Maybe there was some reason why she didn't do something that I expected her to do. Let's listen to her reason, instead of being so fast to punish. It made for a good relationship and she's often commented, 'Gee, Dad, you never holler at me. Other parents holler at their kids.' And it was true, and I'm glad I did it. I think it's turned out quite well."

I asked, "Do you feel like you know what's going on in her life?"

"Sort of," he said. "I'm just more aware. Let me give you an example. Several years ago, she was fourteen, and she was supposed to be spending the night at a girlfriend's house, which was fine. I got a call about twelve at night from this girl's mother, 'The girls aren't here. Where are they?' Ohhhh!" and Chris reenacted how worried he'd been. This had resonances with the night before Mary's death: "*I don't know where they are.*"

But this time, Chris went and got his daughter. "So I get in the car, scour the neighborhood," he said. "About an hour later it turns out that several of the girls had been to one other girl's house and they fell asleep on the girl's living room floor. There they were, all asleep. Well, I went to pick up my daughter. And a neighbor father went to pick up his daughter and hollered at his daughter, threatened to throw away all her Madonna records. And I wasn't upset. 'Let's go home. It was an honest mistake. I wish you had called me and let me know where you were.' So we go home and I say, 'OK, look. I want you to recognize that you need to be more responsible. I want you to stay home this weekend.' She said, 'OK, that's reasonable.' And that was the end of it. Even now that she's twenty-two years old, because she lives with us, she usually lets us know, not always where she's going, but what time she'll be home. So I'm pretty pleased with my relationship with my youngest daughter. I think she got through the teenage years pretty well."

Like the other parents. Chris was anxious not for himself but for his other child. So he read books and took a course to make himself more aware and help his child through the difficult teenage years. I thought, "Maybe that's why God could forgive Chris his mistakes, because Chris took his mistakes to heart and found a remedy"

The next question I asked was whether he thought he'd become more selfish.

No, he didn't feel more selfish; in fact, he said, "More the opposite. I think I'm more aware of other people's feelings and concerns." By now, this word, "aware," had become outright noticeable.

The reason for his increased awareness, he said, is "because I went through a period where I found so many people didn't want to talk about Mary and my grief. I took that attitude that I don't want to be avoiding people in *their* times of difficulty. I wanted to try to be more aware of their hurting, maybe offer a few words of encouragement, maybe do what I can to help them in some small way. I guess in the past if somebody was telling me about a difficult time they were having in their life, maybe I took the attitude that we all have problems, no big deal. I'm not the kind to futz in other people's business, but I'm more willing to listen to people tell about their problems without cutting them short."

"Do you have some way of carrying Mary's memory on?" I asked. I thought I was changing the subject, but he wasn't finished thinking about people in difficult periods.

Yes, he said, he did have a way of carrying her memory on: "My activity with Seasons. I feel that I'm long past the stage where I need a support group. But I feel that with Seasons, maybe I can help some newly bereaved people get through the difficult periods. For the past two and a half years, my wife and I have been the moderators of the local Seasons chapter. And I do phone calls from people who had somebody who just recently died in their life. It's been an enlightening experience, it's been a rewarding experience, it's been a difficult experience."

"Doing phone calls" means publishing your name and number as someone to be called whenever people need to talk. These phone calls come any time of the day or night, and the callers don't leave messages and you may not tell them you'll get right back to them. Moreover, "difficult" is a modest word to describe talking to people whose relatives have just committed suicide. Shortly after I interviewed Chris, I had a phone call from a woman whose son had AIDS and had just killed himself with an overdose of pills. I found myself way over my head; she was so incoherent I couldn't tell whether what she said was the truth or craziness. I took her phone number, hung up, and called Chris. When I told him she seemed almost insane, he said that this was often the case, and he'd call her right away. I felt, as he meant me to, that I'd consigned her to good hands.

The next question on my list was, "Has your relationship with God changed?" Earlier, Chris had told me that his wife was angry at God; she felt, he said, that "God shouldn't allow these things to happen. Why didn't God stop this?"

"But you don't share your wife's anger?" I asked.

"No, not really," he said. "My feeling is that, I don't think I should blame God. I believe that we have free will to do what we want. So consequently, if I'm overwhelmed by the burdens of life and I try to escape from those burdens by putting a gun to my head or whatever, it's still my free will. God may not want me to do it, but it's not His role to step in and say, 'You can't do this, I'm going to stop you.' Because then He takes away our free will.

"So I just feel that what Mary did was, she didn't—*I* believe that Mary didn't want to die. She was hurting so deeply that she was looking for an escape. And to get away from her hurt, she swallowed the pills; this was going to make her go to sleep. Well she did more than sleep, she died. And I don't think it's God's part to step in and say, 'I'm going to stop it.' I don't know if this makes any sense."

I asked, "So it was Mary's choice?"

Yes, Chris said, "It was her choice. Ultimately, it was her choice. But I don't think she consciously said, 'I can't stand this any more. I want to die.' Although she left us a note, she knew what the result of this was going to be. I think basically she was trying to escape from her hurt. But I don't know what her hurt was. I don't think one person can possibly know what another's innermost thoughts are. After she died, I asked myself many, many times, 'Why, why?' And I began to realize there really is no answer. I don't know why. I don't know what was going on in her mind. I just have to accept the fact that I'll never know. I just believe that if it's possible to consider suicide is wrong—and I don't believe it is—but if it's possible to consider it's wrong, then God can forgive her."

Chris has two related questions: how can he live with his guilt over Mary's death, and why did she die? His answer to the first was God's forgiveness and his own remedies. His answer to the second was more complicated. To a Catholic, suicide is a mortal sin. But Mary hadn't meant any sin, she only wanted to stop hurting, and anyway, God allowed her that choice. If God gave Mary the choice to die, then even though Chris didn't understand why, he could allow Mary that choice too.

I asked one more question: "Some people feel more distant from their child, other people feel closer. Do you feel one or the other or maybe both?"

"Maybe I can explain it this way," he said. "I like to think that she's still with us in spirit. When we sit down to the Christmas dinner and

I can't see her there across the table, I like to think that in spirit she's there with us."

"Is that how you think of her now," I asked, "how you think of where she is?"

He said, "I like to think that there's such a—I don't want to say place—there's such a condition as heaven. And I like to think that she's there. I like to think that she's found her peace and her happiness that she was lacking in this life. That she's found that in heaven."

Chapter 10

ON GUILT

I asked these thirty parents, "Do you feel any guilt or self-blame?" Twenty-two said they felt guilty; eight said they felt no guilt. Of those eight, five later told me what they felt guilty about. That left three who said that they didn't feel guilty, but two of them added that they couldn't say the same about their husbands. Small number statistics or not, I think the generalization is correct: bereaved parents have a problem with guilt.

Chris felt guilty because he was unaware that Mary was in trouble and because he didn't pick up on the clues he did have: her frequent late homecomings and the Sunday night she didn't come home when she said she would. Like many bereaved parents, he feels not only responsible for his child's life, but also implicated in her death. His sense of guilt, he says, is "probably—what do I want to say?—probably more justified."

Chris's suspicion that parents whose children commit suicide have more trouble with guilt than other bereaved parents is backed by research. One study compared parents whose children died of accidents or chronic diseases with parents whose children had committed suicide and found the effects—that is, the health problems and emotional distress—on both sets of parents to be similar. Another study looked at the same groups of parents specifically for differences in the amount of guilt, and found it. In parents whose children had died of chronic diseases, 71 percent felt guilty; of accidents, 78 percent; of suicide, 92 percent.

Three of the parents I interviewed had children who killed them-selves—Sally Lambert, Emily Miller, and Chris—and all three talked about guilt.

On New Year's Eve, before Sally Lambert's daughter, Lisa, hanged herself, Sally and Lisa had had an argument.

"Lisa was in her junior year at college and had started to date one of her instructors," Sally said. "She didn't tell me, but she had gotten a little ring and I found out later she had showed it to all the neigh-bors. She said she was engaged to this instructor. The argument was about that, because we'd gone to my cousins' and they were telling me what she had told them, that the wedding was set up. She told us that he was coming down New Year's Day. I was absolutely furious, and that's what we argued about. So my last—."

Sally went silent, not finishing the sentence, which must have been a repetition of her last words to Lisa, then jumped ahead a few days. "So in the beginning, I almost felt like I had killed her. The guilt at-tacks were heavy. I mean it wasn't the first time we argued. But it *was* the last.

"She told Bob, her father, that this instructor was coming down the next day to talk to Bob about it. But it wasn't true that he was coming here the next day. I don't know. Was Lisa planning all this, to go around and show this ring and have this story so that she could have this good feeling because she was going to end it all in a week? I don't *know*. Or maybe, if she was telling everyone this and it wasn't true, did it get to a point where she just thought, 'I have to get out of all this?' I don't know. It's one of those things where you say, 'I've thought and thought,' and then you just say, 'I don't know.' And I'm not *going* to know."

This last is almost word for word what Chris said. And although she'll never know for sure, Sally, like Chris, has a next-best explanation of why Lisa needed to die: Sally had adopted Lisa as a child, but before the adoption, Lisa had been neglected, not held or talked to. The early neglect seemed to leave her with unfillable needs.

"When Lisa was in therapy in high school for a rebellious type of depression," Sally explained, "her therapist said to me, 'She's like a cup that has a hole in it. And you can't fill it up.'"

"How did you settle that guilt?" I asked.

"I don't know if it's settled," she said. "It still comes back every once in a while. I still feel guilty about it. When I think about it. I try not to think about it. And I say to myself about that argument, 'I had a right to be angry.' And then I think, 'Why didn't I keep my mouth shut?' My husband wanted me to wait until the next day, but I was so mad, my Irish was up, and I—."

Again, Sally stopped before repeating her words, and sighed instead. "To me, that made it even worse, that I felt so responsible. And then I felt, being a nurse I should have recognized some signs I was seeing and gotten help. She had attempted suicide before. And she had an eating disorder, which I suspected but didn't want to make any confrontation. Then we saw—" and once more, Sally paused, avoiding too concrete a memory—"we saw evidence of it. I had talked to her and we had an appointment at an eating disorders clinic for a week after she died. I didn't even want Lisa to go away to college because I just didn't know that she could handle it. Yet she said she loved it. But I think she was having a lot of problems, social problems. It's all such a jumbled-up mystery that I've kind of trained myself to put it out of my mind. And I have been able to do that pretty well. There's some things that it doesn't really help to know.

"See, when your child takes their life, you feel like there's something very wrong with *you,* very wrong, that that happened and you couldn't prevent it. Or they felt like they *had* to take their life and you were their mother. I don't think about that much any more. But in the beginning you have to ask, it's just normal, you go over and over. And then it comes to a point where you're not getting any further with the answers. And you just accept what is, you don't have to like it, but it *is*. And then you can kind of just go on from there."

Emily Miller never said how her daughter, Sue, killed herself, and I didn't ask. Sue was twenty-five years old, had a law degree, and "was not well," Emily said, "though that was no one's fault. She couldn't find happiness in life."

"My daughter had had emotional problems for a long time," she said. "She had made a couple of suicide attempts. But I never in my heart believed this would happen. I think the last time—"

Emily paused because what she was about to say was not about the last time she actually talked to Sue but about the last time she tried to reach Sue.

"The day Sue died," she continued, "I had called her up and left a message because her therapist had called me that afternoon and asked if I had spoken to her recently, and I said, 'She spoke to my husband yesterday,' and the therapist said Sue hadn't been to work yesterday or that day and she was concerned. My first thought was—my daughter had a substance abuse problem—and I thought she went back to drugs, but the therapist said she was worried about suicide. So I called Sue and left a message on her answering machine, 'Sue, I'm very worried; please call me back.' And why didn't I, when I called, say '*I love you.*' Why didn't I say that? But she was gone already. She didn't hear me. I mean, reason and emotion are two different things. But that's not—I mean, she was lost."

Emily jumped to the present, five and a half years later, and began talking about a movie she'd watched on TV, about a daughter who had a last talk with her mother before committing suicide.

"It was sort of I guess somewhat cathartic," she said. "Or perhaps wishful thinking, that maybe Sue could have had this dialogue with me so that maybe I could have—"

Emily stopped again, rethinking. "Though I know there was nothing I could have done about it. I know that. But yet I feel there are things I should have done. I regret that and feel guilty. But it's not going to bring her back. If it would, I'd feel guilty every day. I realized that I am entitled to be happy, that Sue made her choice, I didn't make it, and I'm entitled. I did the best I could for her. It may or may not have been enough, but it was the best I knew how."

Emily seemed to go back and forth between feeling guilty and letting herself off the hook. I believed she meant what she said, but some of her phrases had the sound of lessons learned in therapy: "I'm entitled," "it was the best I knew how."

Emily had indeed spent time in therapy and still checks in, she said, for problems with life. "After a year, I wasn't feeling better," she explained. "I didn't begin to feel better until four years. Five years. I started letting go. I have a wonderful therapist who's been a big help. Without him, I'd have been in the rubber room a long time ago."

She doesn't seem to have let go of the guilt, however, and she doesn't say she has. She thinks the guilt, like Sue's death, is a fact of life. "The guilt is because of the natural order of things," she said. "The child should still be here and if anybody should go, it should be the parent. You feel guilt about *anything*."

When I changed the subject and asked her about her feelings about God, Emily continued her internal dialogue about guilt. "I do believe He's a good God and doesn't do things to punish people. But even God can't be everywhere. And if He can't, how can you?"

I don't think Emily is tormented by the worry that she should indeed have been everywhere, should have intervened in Sue's death; but I do think she's occasionally distracted by it. Emily is the person quoted in an earlier chapter: "Peace is the best thing you can wish someone who's lost a child."

Parents whose children commit suicide do feel more guilt than parents whose children die in other ways. But regardless of how their children died, bereaved parents feel guilty. If researchers agree on nothing else, they agree on this. One of the earliest studies, done in 1944, found that all bereaved people, not just parents, feel guilty. Several studies since then have compared people whose spouses or parents have died with people whose children have died, and found parents with more feelings of guilt.

134

Parents of babies who died of sudden infant death syndrome still have, years later, what one researcher called a "gnawing sense of responsibility for the child's death." Parents of children who died suddenly feel more guilt than parents of children whose deaths were anticipated, and parents of children who committed suicide feel most guilty of all. Parents of older children feel more guilt than parents of younger children. Fathers and mothers feel equally guilty. Less religious parents feel more guilt than more religious parents. Even grandparents feel guilty.

In general, the researchers say what Emily said: parents can feel guilty about *anything*. Sally and Chris felt guilty for the usually harmless, completely human reactions of anger and inattentiveness. Emily felt guilty for not having said, "I love you," even though her daughter had already died. Perhaps their guilt over these specific instances stands in for guilt over general argumentativeness, inattention, and insufficient affection. But what parent is innocent of any of this?

So much of bereaved parents' guilt seems so unreasonable. Ruth Banick worked two jobs to support her daughters and argued with Leslie, who died at eighteen in a car accident, about going to college; Ruth felt guilty because she worked two jobs and argued with Leslie. Mitch Dudnikov's son, Marc, was a medical student working on an ambulance that got hit by a train; Mitch felt guilty because he hadn't pressured Marc to work in a steel mill instead.

Elaine Levin, whose son, Merrill, died of a bone cancer at age seventeen, said, "I don't feel any guilt. I think we gave him the best medical care that was available. But thinking about it, maybe we did too much. Maybe we should have given him a couple more months of enjoying his friends. We were doing all these things that made him sicker really, and to what end?"

Elaine's answer followed a typical pattern: "No, I don't feel any guilt, except for the things I feel guilty about."

Some parents feel guilty over heartbreakingly small instances. Mary Norris's twenty-seven-year-old son, Theodore, died after his body rejected a kidney transplant. "I don't have guilt," Mary began, "because I did just about everything I could do. I don't have no guilty conscience. One thing that I feel guilty about is, the time that he had his kidney transplant, I was in West Virginia. And when you have a kidney transplant, they just call the patient and he goes to the hospital. And I couldn't get back here in time. That's the only guilty thing I have. But I did make it back later. They had a kidney transplant that day, and I was back the next day."

Brandt Jones had wanted his son and mother-in-law to drive a bigger car, "the brand-new van that I had sitting in the driveway, and they took my mother-in-law's little Fiesta. Of course, when he was killed, I went on a guilt trip that was out of this world. Had they been in the van, maybe, who knows?" Brandt had figured out from the size of the van and the point of impact on the car that if Bruce had been in the van, he'd have been ten feet farther away from the point of impact. "I had that kind of a guilt to deal with, that I let them tell me that it was cheaper to buy gas for that little car. I should have said, 'Look, here's extra money. Put gas in the van and take the van.'"

"Did your feeling of guilt last long?" I asked.

"When I voiced that guilt," he said, "when I got it out to where I could look at it, then it wasn't a prolonged thing, three months or so. I analyzed it myself. There is no way I could have forced them without physical abuse to take that van. But I had to work that through in my own mind as to why I couldn't, I had to come up with a reason."

"And no general guilt about anything else?" I asked.

"No general guilt," he said, "other than things I would have done differently. The summer he died, he and I did the Scout troop canoe trip down the Potomac River. And I slept in with the adults and I could have spent that week in the tent with him. I just felt that the kids should be with the kids and the adults should be with the adults. I have that guilt, that he and I could have shared a tent. But then again, he may have enjoyed being with the kids rather than having his father in the tent with him. It's those kinds of things."

Elaine's husband, Walter, not only didn't begin by saying he felt no guilt, he also seems to have total recall of every possibly culpable moment. "Every once in a while I think about that," he said. "One time when we went to get chemotherapy, it was just too icy and I had to turn back. And I felt terrible about that. And then one time I remember I hit him and I think about that. And he always wanted a car and I didn't buy him a car. I could have taken him more places for even more treatments, gone to Europe. And I'm going to tell you something. When he was in elementary school, they had a show, and he was on first in a bear costume. He did his piece and I didn't applaud—I thought I should wait until the end of the show. And the next kid was a lion, and they applauded. So I *should* have applauded. And I regret that, that I didn't applaud him. But I hope he knew how much I loved him."

Nickie Copinger's ten-year-old son, Adam, died of a rare inherited immune deficiency. Adam had spent much of his short life in and out of hospitals with infections that his immune system couldn't throw off. "The thing was," Nickie said, "with every admission, night and day, I always was right by his side. But with the last admission, when he was in intensive care, I had a real hard time. I guess it was fear. I couldn't stay there for a long length of time. What I remember was the lights blinking for the heart beat, and the beeping, and that was one of the things I had trouble dealing with in therapy. It was guilt. I would say to the therapist, 'I never let my son down, for fifteen admissions I stood by his side. And the last admission he had when he was dying I couldn't handle.' I couldn't be in the room when the line went flat. I still feel, I can call it guilt a little bit. And there was another guilt thing. Was I right to have his coffin closed? I had it closed because he didn't look like my Adam when he died, he was so puffy. It's those little chunks of guilt in my mind: Should I have had it open? Should I have looked at him one more time? You can 'should' yourself until you're crazy. I try not to do that to myself any more, even when I'm thinking about it. What surprises me is how you're not even thinking about it and it's there."

Louise Lewis's son, Michael, was robbed and killed while he was inspecting a construction site for his father's business. A few days before, he had come to supper, "and I had a chicken and I think I had peas and mushrooms and a salad," she said. "And he looked at me and said, 'Next time I come, will you please have a baked potato?' And I remember that, he never got his baked potato. You can always find guilt, if you don't have guilt, you can always find guilt. Do I want to be guilty about not having given him a baked potato? Of course not. And maybe if we had not moved back to Baltimore, he wouldn't have been at that construction site. But it's so unrealistic, so I don't ever fool around with that. And I didn't want my husband to ever feel guilty, that Michael was in construction and he wasn't a lawyer or an engineer. You can just go back and dig up everything. What I really feel guilty about is, this young man had done all the hard things in life, by getting six years of college and a master's degree, he worked every summer, and, bingo, it's gone with one lousy bullet. It's just such a waste. I think I felt so bad, I didn't want any guilt. But I think we all feel guilty that we're living and they're not."

Louise's guilt because "we're living and they're not" is a result of what every parent knows: your job above everything is to come between your children and whatever might hurt them.

"It's somebody for whom you've been responsible," Leight Johnson explained. "Intellectually you know it isn't your fault that he got in a car accident, but you still feel, my kid and I wasn't able to take care of him. I can't imagine what it's like for people whose kid wanders out in the street after a ball and gets hit by a car, because they really weren't watching closely, even though it isn't physically possible to do that unless you keep them chained up."

Only one person I interviewed was in the situation that Leight didn't want to imagine—of not having watched closely enough—and the aftermath was appalling. This woman, whom I'm calling Nancy, was the only one of these parents with whom I truly felt uncomfortable. She hadn't been watching her three-year-old son, her husband's namesake, and he drowned in their pool. Her husband blamed her without saying so outright, and without acknowledging it, she took the blame. In the next two and a half years, she had two more children, she said, to replace the namesake her husband lost. Now, fifteen years after the drowning, the marriage had fallen apart. During the interview, she talked only rarely about her grief or her son, and answered most of the questions as though the interview were about the effects of divorce. Her divorce had made her feel that her husband had finally admitted that he blamed her, which was liberating for her. She had just gone to a therapy workshop to throw off the weight of her dead son, she said, and that, too, was liberating. After the therapy and the divorce, she said, "I can move on. I feel much better." She would trust the three-year-old again, she said, just as she had trusted him before.

I believe she meant what she said, but I don't believe what she said was true. No one trusts a three-year-old around a swimming pool. No other parent talked about throwing off the weight of their dead children; they spent their lives trying to do the opposite, keep their children with them. I'm sure she does feel better now, but I'd guess she's spent fifteen years trying to throw off her husband's blame and hasn't even begun on her own.

The reason for this guess is, when I asked if she had any way of making sense of her son's death, she answered: "I think I deserved this. The marriage was so bad it had to happen. We had all this pretty stuff—pool, home. It was taking over the spiritual. It was almost as though I understood it immediately, that his death was supposed to adjust that. It provided the opportunity for the bad marriage and the emphasis on material things to get straightened out. But then the guilt got going so bad, and I thought, 'I have to stay here; I'm too bad to leave; I've done the worst.'"

Back to Louise and Leight: "But I think we all feel guilty that we're living and they're not." Researchers and parents alike say that every-one expects parents to die before children do. Part of the reason is age, part is that the parent's role in life is to do everything possible to protect and preserve the child. So if the child is dead, then the parent must have died first. But if the parent is still alive, then something is as wrong as it gets. Either the parent is to blame, or the whole line of reasoning is wrong and the natural way of the world is wrong.

Of the two alternatives, the more sensible one to a human mind is that the parent is to blame: we're used to human error, we commit it all the time. So parents go through the litany: if Chris had been more aware of Mary; if Emily had reached Sue on the phone; if Sally hadn't gotten angry at Lisa. "Your whole mindset is that your kids are going to outlive you," Brandt said, "and then when something like this happens, you say, 'Maybe I should have done this different, and this wouldn't have happened.'"

But how obviously wrong these litanies are. If Chris had known Mary was going to commit suicide that night, he never would have left her alone. It doesn't need to be said: no one knowingly or even negligently allows a child to die. Even the parents know this. The next sentence after an explanation of what they should have done to avoid the death is usually, "But I know that would make no difference." The illogic of the whole argument is what they mean by saying "you can 'should' yourself until you're crazy" or "you're never going to know the 'why's'."

"At a Compassionate Friends meeting," Brandt said, "I said, 'One of my guilt feelings is that I didn't make them take the van.' And then I realized, that's been grating at me. And when I said it and got it out there, then I could sit back and analyze it. A couple people said, 'There's nothing you could have done about it.' But I had to work that through in my own mind as to why I couldn't. I had to come up with a reason."

These parents aren't to blame for their children's deaths, and even while they're blaming themselves, they know it. Then who is to blame? Why did the child die? When the parents talked about their "why's," they meant, "To what can this death be attributed?" This is a bigger question than it sounds.

A psychological theory called attribution theory says that people want to believe the world is controllable and predictable, and when the world isn't and terrible things happen, people need to know the cause. That is, parents need to have something to which they can attribute the death. The theory goes on to argue that the attributions people come up with should influence the way they adjust. Maybe people who blame themselves make better adjustments; maybe they make worse adjustments. The studies done over the last fifteen years contradict each other and support both possibilities. In fact, researchers still argue whether their initial premises are right, let alone who makes better adjustments.

I don't know about the adjustments, but every parent I interviewed supported those initial premises. They need to know to what they can attribute the child's death, who is to blame. As the sociologist Robert Weiss said, "It's hard to avoid finding agency."

If the parent isn't to blame, the only alternative is that their understanding of the world is to blame. That is, what people understand to be the natural order of the world isn't particularly natural after all. And this, of course, is the truth. Everyone dies. Parents die before their children, but only usually. Parents will intervene in their children's deaths, but only if intervention is physically possible. Our understanding of the world runs up against what it has always run up against: the limits of the physical and the fallacy of thinking the improbable won't happen. Usually when we have to face these things, the situation is unimportant: we can't avoid getting the flu, we hit five red lights in a row. But when a child dies, the importance is such that the parents' understanding of the world vanishes. In what kind of world do such things happen? Why did the child die?

Chapter 11

DELORES SHODA AND THE
UNCERTAINTY OF LIFE

∞

Delores Shoda's son, Larry, died of melanoma seven years ago. Delores was the only parent who said that neither she nor her husband felt guilt; nor did she follow up by saying what she did feel guilty about. I believed she felt no guilt, though not feeling guilt didn't mean she felt no responsibility for Larry; she did. It only meant she didn't blame herself for anything surrounding his death. But because she didn't, she had a problem. Who or what *was* to blame? Why did Larry die?

Answering that isn't easy. Is God to blame? Is life, or fate, or any other synonym for something that happens for no good reason? Finding someone to blame, even if that means blaming yourself, wrote Colin Murray Parkes, a psychiatrist specializing in the reactions of grief, "is a less disturbing alternative than accepting that life is uncertain." At the time of the interview, Delores hadn't answered those questions yet; she seemed to be in the process, subtly and indirectly, of facing uncertainty.

Delores is married, has one married daughter named Laura who lives out of state, and a granddaughter, Chelsea. Delores has a small, quick voice. She has an odd verbal habit: instead of saying "I," she

142

often said "you," as in "you have bad memories for three months." Sometimes she alternated between "you" and "I" in the same sentence: "when you're out playing golf, the butterfly lands on your ball, and I always think about him." This verbal habit made her sound as though she were keeping some distance from what she was talking about. She also talked as if I weren't there, as if she were reading notes from some internal screen, as if my questions triggered an interior monologue that required neither audience nor response. I don't mean to imply that I felt she was distant or closed-off. On the contrary, I felt like her diary.

Larry died on the day after he passed the bar examination to practice law. At the start of the interview, before I could ask Delores any questions, she began telling a series of stories about Larry's last days, how hard he had tried, and what she could or could not do for him—in short, how responsible she felt for him.

"I personally don't feel any guilt," Delores said. "Larry had a good life. He hadn't been at home since he was seventeen; he was an adult. We raised him, we were able to tell him how we felt about him, how he brightened our life.

"One time I told him—when his sickness all started and he said, 'What's the use?'—I said, 'You can't give up. You have to make yourself go on. You absolutely cannot give up.' Then when he was in the hospital, he looked at me and he said, 'Ma, I didn't give up.' And I just about fell apart.

"Another time in the hospital he was thinking about one of his coworkers who was arrested for petty theft. Larry had sat with this young man, and the police came and handcuffed the young man and took him to jail. And Larry was so upset because the young man's father wouldn't come down to the jail. And Larry kept saying he had to get this young man out of jail. And I said, 'Oh, Larry, don't you worry about that. Mom will take care of it.' And he said, 'Oh, Ma, you always take care of everything, and you haven't even been to law school.' I told him not to call me Ma, so that's what he always called me. Anyway, after he said that, the first thing that came to my mind was, here he's telling me I take care of everything and the one thing in the world that you would give your life to take care of, you can't do anything about.

"Later on, when he came home from the hospital, I laid on the bed and held his hand all night. It's hard to watch your child die and there's nothing you can do. You have bad memories about those three months, but you try to shut those out and not think about those. Neither my husband nor I feels guilty about anything we ever did or did not do. Because there's nothing that could be done that we didn't do.

"Larry wanted to finish what he'd started. He finished law school, passed the bar exam, and he died the next day. He finished what he set out to. And they had this ceremony on the first anniversary of his death in the courthouse downtown, and his picture is hanging in that legal museum. We got through the ceremony and it was hard, and to this day, I know where the picture is hanging but I have no idea what it says because it was just so hard for me to get through the ceremony. But they said that what he accomplished sitting through that exam for two days in so much pain, on medication, and he was determined to finish, and he passed it with such flying colors, it should be an inspiration for other people."

Delores seemed to be finished with her stories and had no more to say, so I began my questions: "Do you have a way of describing what the grief has been like?"

"People said to us, 'You handle this with such dignity,'" she said. "And I said, 'Larry handled his death with dignity and we can't do any less.' Still, I really have to work hard to keep my sanity, to not go over the edge. I think about that a lot, how easy it would be if you weren't a very strong person inside, to let yourself just go, just to say, I don't want the pain any more. Not committing suicide, that wouldn't be easy. It would be easy to retreat into your own little world and shut everybody out. You have to fight to keep your sanity.

"It's not like a physical pain like when he first died," she continued. Then she changed the subject. "I started working part-time in a day care center, partly because I had to be busy, partly to be with children. I like this part-time job. I don't feel I have to be there such-and-such a day. I can have the days off I want off, and I leave here at four-thirty and I *leave*. I don't want to work full-time because when I get ready to go somewhere, then I want to be able to go. If I have a full-time job, then you have to stay."

Because the physical pain when Larry first died seemed to lead into working part-time so she could *go,* I wondered if Delores somehow connected the two. So I asked, "Did you always feel like this?"

"No," she said.

"This is new?" I asked.

"Yes," she said. "I have trouble staying still that long, staying in one place five days a week, I just don't feel I can take it. I enjoyed working full-time until Larry died, and then it all changed. I don't want to be confined. There are days when I go in there, I think, I can't stay here all the time, I have to be somewhere else. But if I'm somewhere else, it's just that feeling like you have to run. I just don't feel that I could cope—that I even *want* to cope with a five-day-a-week job. If I'm having a bad day and want to get a cup of coffee and take a book somewhere and read, I can do it. I do stay busy. If I take needlework to my job, I'll go out and get a cup of coffee and sit in the car and work on it. I feel like I can't be still any more, like I have to run. And when I get there, I can't be there either, I have to be somewhere else."

Maybe Delores's pain was connected to her restlessness initially, but she'd implied that the pain was no longer as bad, and after seven years, she was still running. Quietly, and almost as though she were a little surprised, Delores said this over and over—"I have to run"—no matter what the question. She said it when I asked about her job, when I asked what she thought "get over it" means, when I asked if she felt more vulnerable, and when I asked if she has the same level of energy.

"I can't sit still. So many things come back to you, it seems like it was yesterday. It's in the back of my mind all the time, you've got to be doing something. And I don't want to be doing it at home. I want to be out and away from that house. I didn't used to mind doing things around the house; I don't want any part of it now. I make myself stay home to do the laundry. I have a lot of trouble sleeping at night, I do. I get up at three o'clock in the morning and iron, or wait for the paper. I just think, I want to be going. But I don't know where I'm going or what I'm going to do when I get there. That's gotten some better over time. It's just this feeling, that I have to be going."

Delores sounded as though she thought that repeating this feeling often enough would help her understand it. I certainly didn't understand it. Was she running away? From what? Other parents reported the same feeling of running or keeping busy, but to a much lesser degree. Maybe she was looking for something. Or maybe she had no purpose to her running at all, maybe she was just staying in motion. Whatever she's doing, she says, this restlessness disappears when she's visiting her daughter, Laura: "I can sit on the sofa and read a book, I can lay out by the pool, I can walk around her neighborhood, I don't have that restlessness, I sleep at night." So maybe she's also anxious; she was the parent who said in an earlier chapter, "You're always waiting for this other shoe to drop," for someone else to die.

I also wondered if her running had some connection with Larry, with either his death or his life. I asked indirectly: "Do you have anything that keeps Larry's memory going?"

"I guess I usually wear a butterfly," Delores answered.

Butterflies are Compassionate Friends' mascots, and for obvious reasons: because they emerge from cocoons, they symbolize some kind of transcendence over death. Compassionate Friends decorates its literature with butterflies and sells little butterfly pins; one parent snapped at me, "I *really* don't like butterflies." Delores went on to explain how, for her, butterflies keep Larry's memory going.

"Larry had a cousin that was a nun," Delores explained, "and he was talking to her about death. And she wrote him this letter that said, 'Death is like a caterpillar that goes into its cocoon for a little while, then it comes out to be this beautiful butterfly. And this is what death will be like for you.' And I guess that's always stuck in my mind. When I see a butterfly I think of Larry."

I didn't discount the butterfly's meaning for Delores, but the image was trite so I didn't take it too seriously either. As usual, I was wrong. Images become trite precisely because they refer to something universally felt. Delores said again, "I guess when I see a butterfly I always think about Larry." Then she started crying.

I missed the obvious, that butterflies were a sign to Delores that Larry was beautiful now and in some kind of afterlife. She didn't correct me. Instead I asked, "Because he's free?"

"I guess he isn't in pain any more," she said. "Because he went through a lot. Sometimes when you're out playing golf, the butterfly lands on your ball, and I always think about him. I do have butterflies in the house; Laura gave me some butterfly things to sit around. And at the cemetery they had butterflies in the flowers, and the man who did the flowers at the funeral took the butterflies out and gave them to me. Later when I took flowers to the cemetery, I took the butterflies back out there. It was because of what his cousin wrote in this letter."

Listening to Delores talk about butterflies, I was struck by the resemblance, not only between the butterflies and Larry, but also between the butterflies and Delores. So I said, "You've told me over and over you have to move around. Are you like those butterflies?"

"It could be," she said. "I just have to be free to go. I'm sitting at home at ten at night, and I feel the urge I want to get out of the house. I'll go down and get a cup of coffee and take a book and just sit down and read for a while, then I can go back home again. I have to be free to go. And I never used to be that way. But now, I can't, I don't want to be tied to anything."

Butterflies, I thought, are not only trite images of transcendence over death and an afterlife, they are also trite images of motion and irresolution. Butterflies are uncertainty incarnate. Was that what was going on with Delores? She'd said the one thing she'd give her life to take care of, she could do nothing about. Was the uncertainty of her running and the uncertainty of the butterflies, at bottom, an uncertainty about life? I think so. I know the equation of running, butterflies, and life uncertainty sounds a little pat, a little literary, and I know that human behavior rarely has any one explanation or interpretation. But I think Delores was making the equation, or at least she was preoccupied by uncertainty. The reason is the way she answered the questions about God.

"You think about all the prayers you said while he was ill," she said, "and you think, 'They didn't do any good. No one heard you.' That has something to do with your questioning your religion. I was raised up in the church. I always thought I had a lot of faith. But when Larry died, it was like, this is it. There's nothing else. You're never going to see him any more. There's nothing after this.

"There are a lot of questions now in your mind about why does this happen. I think it makes you either go one way or another—a religious fanatic almost, or you just quit believing. I'm not either one of those because I keep making myself go to church because there's always this question. There are still all these questions in your mind now that you never thought about before. Is there anything after this life here? Do I still believe that like I used to? My husband isn't really sure. He says, 'I know there has to be something out there, but I'm not really sure.' I never had that question in my mind, but now I do. I find I do. Is there anything else after this life? I wonder, why did this happen to Larry, when there are murderers walking around, or just useless people who contribute nothing to society. I know we can't make the judgment of who lives and who dies, and in my mind there had to be a God to make these—I can't say make these decisions, because I can't say He does make these decisions. There are just so many questions I never thought about before. Somebody had to create this, but was it really God that did it? I do think about it. Am I going to see Larry again?"

Delores asked these questions with the same surprise with which she talked about her need to stay in motion. Furthermore, Delores lumped together all these questions—Is there anything after life here? Do I still believe like I used to? Why did this happen to Larry?—apparently because they seemed to her to be different aspects of one single question.

Thinking now not only about Delores but all the parents, I took this to mean that the search for the answer to why the child died—

that is, the search for attribution—implicates not only the parents but also God. That is, if one possible answer to why the child died implies the parents' guilt, another possible answer implies God's negligence: "No one heard you," Delores said.

But Delores isn't blaming God and leaving the church. For Delores and other parents, when a child dies, faith in God now has a kicker: if you have faith, you believe in an afterlife and you'll see your child again; if you have none, you won't.

"If you keep yourself on an even plane," she said, "if you can keep yourself going to church, then maybe a little bit of it sinks in along the way. If I don't go to church for three or four weeks, I miss it, I feel like it's something I have to be doing. I think it's helping me. I don't think I'll ever find any answers to these questions in my mind. But maybe it just keeps in the back of my mind that, well, maybe I will see Larry again, maybe there is something to this, maybe I will see him again. If I quit going, this thought that you'll never see him again will keep creeping into your mind, into your mind. And I guess I'm not sure I could deal with that. So if I keep going, then maybe I can convince myself that I do believe. That's it—that I can convince myself that I'm going to believe all this again."

Chapter 12

JOB'S CHILDREN

Changes Toward God

∞

Parents feel guilt partly because they need to attribute the child's death to some cause, some explanation. The children died because the parents were argumentative or inattentive or elsewhere. If the parents were worthy of the name, they would be dead and their children alive. For the parents, guilt is one way to explain the death: I should have prevented it; I am to blame; I am guilty.

The guilt is deep and persistent but almost entirely unreasonable, and the parents know that. And knowing it, they need to find another reason, another way to make sense of the death. Maybe guilt persists partly because finding another way to make sense of the death is difficult. The first difficulty is making sense of any death.

I think people learn to make sense of death little by little. I learned about death, for instance, by growing up on a farm. We slaughtered chickens routinely and sheep every summer. We gutted them and our mother showed us what the hearts and lungs and intestines did; the animal was dead so these parts weren't operating any more.

The black cat disappeared during hay mowing one summer and our mother said the cat had been caught in the mower and had cer-

150

tainly gone off somewhere to die. The cat came back the next spring, walking bumpily on three legs.

When I was in college, a woman with multiple sclerosis for whom I helped keep house committed suicide; one day her husband called and said I wasn't to come to work any more, and I never saw her again.

Then my grandmother, with whom I'd been living, died. She used to ask me to read poems to her: "Grow old along with me / The best is yet to be." I read them badly. She'd been sick with pneumonia, and went to the hospital, and died there. I saw her dead and in her coffin, looking as though she were made of plastic. She was a little frightening like that, but she resembled so little the woman to whom I read poems that I didn't feel much. And a year later, her husband, my grandfather, died; same thing.

So ten years after that, when my father died, I could put together all those relatively smaller deaths and know more or less what to expect. My mother had called and asked me to come home, he was dying. I got there that night. He was in bed and I wasn't sure he knew I was there. My mother said she thought he was waiting for me to come, and I hoped she was right. I held his hand and even though he didn't normally like to be touched, he wouldn't let me pull my hand away. At one point, he sat up in bed alarmed, staring into the dark with more expression on his face than I'd ever seen. Later I went to bed, and a little after that, my mother woke me up and said, "He's gone, Ann. He's died." He looked dark and uninhabited. We called the funeral director, who came and put a sheet over him and wheeled him out on a convertible stretcher, while we sat in the living room in our nightgowns, quiet and stupid.

From the point of view of those still living, death is a strange state. Death first reduces people entirely to the physical: like the chickens, people's bodies stop. And then even worse, death makes people not physical at all. Like the woman I worked for, you don't see them again; and unlike the cat, they don't come back. Most things in our experience that disappear are either retrievable or replaceable. For a person to be gone, never to come back, and to be nowhere you can go to, doesn't make sense. "Every once in a while I get strange thoughts," said Julia Marcus, "about how can you be alive and then how can you be just so dead? That's just a gap I can't close."

But over the years, piece by piece, you learn to close the gap and make sense of it. One central fact of our universe is time. Stars, worlds, people, animals, and plants all age, die, and make room for young ones. I hated my father dying, but I knew to grow up and take his place and do whatever I was going to do in the world before I died too and made room. What I'm saying is, death seems inexplicable, but little by little, we find an explanation. Death is the natural way of the world; things have their time. The story ends sadly but is, on the whole, a good story, and one that makes sense.

A child's death, however, remains inexplicable. Children are the reason that death makes sense; they are the young ones the rest of us die to make room for. Their deaths are unnatural, senseless, and wrong. I can't explain that more fully, nor could the parents, though I asked until they got impatient: "What do you think people mean when they say a child's death is unnatural?" "What effect do you think this unnaturalness has on you?" "And why should unnatural-ness have any effect at all?" These questions were sincere but unanswerable. That is, a child's death is unattributable. When you try to make sense of these deaths, you hit a wall. All the parents could do is repeat: a child's death is unnatural, senseless, and wrong.

"In my way of thinking, when it's your child, it's totally out of the question, it's totally unnatural," said Diana Moores. "My whole world is upside down. When other people die, it shakes you but you stay right side up. When a child dies, somebody who's little and down here and younger, it flips your world over completely."

"The death of a child isn't in the order of things," said Emily Miller. "This is *real* unnaturalness. To think you'll never speak to them or hear their voice, never touch them again, I mean, it's more than you can imagine. How can you understand the depth of that? Your child is part of you. Physically. She came from my body. When you brought them into this world and you're not going to see them again, it's just *unfathomable*."

152

"There's no words you can describe about it," said Elaine Levin. "I don't think there are words that you can describe. I really don't. Because I think it has to do with, it's out of the order of things. It's just the wrong—" Elaine paused, apparently trying to finish the sentence with the right word—"the wrong order."

I also asked the question about attribution in another way: "Do you have some way that your child's death makes sense to you?" To be honest, I wasn't sure what I meant by the question. The parents, however, did seem to know what I meant. Making sense of death turns out to be a larger variant of naturalness. A death that makes sense is one that was just or right in some way. Perhaps the person who died had lived a long, good life. Perhaps the person had done something wrong, or was a bad person, or lived dangerously. Perhaps the person hadn't wanted to live. Or perhaps the person's death had been offset by some greater good: the person died saving someone else, or other people became better because of the death, or some good to society resulted. For the parents, without exception, not one of these reasons worked. Some parents dismissed the question.

"Do you have some way your child's death makes sense?" I asked.

Diana: "No. Not even close."

Elaine: "No. No. I wonder who has answered yes. That's ridiculous. How could it make sense? It makes no sense. It makes no sense, no sense."

Delores Shoda: "No. Other questions, you have to think about. This one is cut and dried. No. No sense."

Sally Lambert: "No. Does anybody say yes to that?"

For some parents, making sense of the death was not a big problem; they said they didn't have to make sense of life, either. I'm not sure I believe them, but the question clearly wasn't keeping them up nights. Or perhaps, like me, they didn't really know what the question meant.

"I can't make sense of it," said Anne Perkins, "and it doesn't bother me that I can't. I don't care whether it makes sense or doesn't. I've never had to make sense out of life, to have it add up to whatever. None of that matters to me."

"It just doesn't make any sense," said Joan Gresser, "but I don't ponder it, I don't sit and think about it."

I said, "I guess the big question is, why it happened."

"Well why not?" Joan said. "I finally got to a point where, dead is dead. That's it. They're dead. They're not 'gone over' somewhere, they're *dead*. That word, dead."

"The loss doesn't make sense," said Emily. "But it *is*. Does reality have to make sense?"

For the majority of the parents, however, their lives had made some sense, they had faith in rightness, justice, and order, and so they expected sense in their children's deaths; and they couldn't find it. One research study done four to seven years after the child's death found three-quarters of the parents "unable to make any sense or find any meaning in their loss."

Marge Ford: "I can't imagine. I'm not going to say it taught a lesson to anybody else or—no. It doesn't make any sense at all to me."

Walter Levin: "Absolutely not. I've tried to find a way that his death would make sense and I can't think of any way. This is a terrible thing to say, but because I work downtown, I see people his age doing some terrible things here and I say to God, 'Why couldn't you take them, not him?' I could not comprehend, if there *is* a pattern or something, why this was done. It saddened my and my wife's life. And the *world,* the world was deprived of a kid who could have discovered a cure for something. So absolutely not. I can find no reason whatsoever for this."

Mitch Dudnikov: "My wife thinks sometimes maybe she was *meant* to give one child up to help a lot of other people. Because on the phone for Compassionate Friends she has helped hundreds of people. I'm selfish, I can't see it. To me, Marc is worth all of them. He's worth the whole world. It's not a nice thing to say, but it's the way I feel. I can't, I just can't, make any meaning or sense out of any of this. I can't make any sense really out of *any* of the youth dying. It doesn't fit. It just to me *shouldn't* be this way."

Louise Lewis, in the years after Michael was murdered, became partially responsible for passage of Maryland's handgun-control laws:

"I cannot turn this thing around, that I was *supposed* to do this handgun-control work. I would hate to think that that was why. I may have put my energy there, but it's just what people do. His death was senseless. Wrong place at the wrong time, that's all. Just fate."

Notice that "fate" and "wrong place at the wrong time" go a step further than "no sense." Some parents had a way of attributing the death whether or not they understood it: I don't understand it, they're saying, but it happened because someone made a bad mistake, because living creatures get diseases, because things like this happen. Attribution is at least some sort of sense. Attributing the death even to the random probabilities of the universe, wrote Dennis Klass, is "philosophically the opposite of the religious sense of divine providence—but as solace, they function in the same ways in the life of the bereaved parent."

Julia is a long-time social worker in pediatric oncology: "I haven't found that these deaths make sense. I think about that periodically. I have not decided that it makes sense. I hear people say that sometimes, that there is a reason. I'm stubborn about that one. I don't think it makes sense. It doesn't make any sense at all to me. No, I don't think it makes sense. I mean, I looked for all kinds of reasons for why the children died of cancer. I don't see good results coming from it that couldn't have come about without a child dying. So I've decided that's not why children die, to make good sense. I think it's just the hard physical world. Whatever makes people get sick. I have really become nonreligious about that. It certainly hasn't brought me any closer to God."

Brandt Jones: "No. It makes no sense whatsoever, it never has. I don't believe in 'God did it for some reason.' Some people are super into 'God only takes those who have done all their work on earth.' That drives me up a wall. It was a mistake that was made and it happened; there's no sense to his death in the great hierarchy of things. That's a damn difficult question when it comes down to it."

Notice also that religion and God have entered the equation. And now the question becomes, as Brandt said, damn difficult. This is the parents' reasoning. Why did the child die? I can think of no reason good enough. Maybe these things happen for no reason. Maybe it was just a mistake, fate, a fact. Or maybe God had a reason.

This reasoning is precisely the plot of the Book of Job, which biblical scholars call the most troubling book in the Bible. Job was a devout man who was also rich in sheep, camels, oxen, and donkeys and was blessed with ten children and a great household. When God bragged to Satan—who hadn't fallen yet but was still an archangel and a sort of prosecuting attorney—about Job's devotion, Satan replied that being devout is easy when you're rich.

"But put forth thine hand now, and touch all that he hath," said Satan, "and he will curse thee to thy face."

Go ahead, said God, but don't touch Job himself. So Satan destroyed Job's house and killed all of his animals and his children besides. Job tore his clothes, then fell down on the ground and said, "Naked came I out of my mother's womb and naked shall I return thither; the Lord gave, and the Lord hath taken away; blessed be the name of the Lord."

Back in Heaven, God pointed out to Satan how Job held on to his faith, and Satan said "Skin for skin, yea, all that a man hath will he give for his life."

Touch his skin then, said God, but don't kill him. So Satan covered Job's body with sores and boils, and Job sat down in the ashes of his estate and scratched himself with a broken pot. Job's wife, devastated and bitter, told Job, "Curse God and die." Job replied that she was foolish and asked her, "What? Shall we receive good at the hand of God and shall we not receive evil?"

Meanwhile, Job's friends came by to commiserate. They sat quietly with him for seven days and nights, and by that time Job could see how terrible his condition was and wanted to explain it to them. "Let the day perish wherein I was born," he began, and went on from there.

The friends told him he must have done something wrong to deserve such punishment. Job said he hadn't. The friends told him that God doesn't do these things for no reason. Job said that if he's a good man, and he's sure that he is, then what's God's reason? The friends just repeated themselves. Eventually Job asked his question of God directly: "Then call thou and I will answer: or let me speak and answer thou me. How many are mine iniquities and sins? Make me to know my transgression and my sin."

Out of a whirlwind, God answered Job with violence and unparalleled eloquence that the universe is beautiful and unknowable, and God isn't answerable to man. Job said he understood now and repented in dust and ashes, and God gave all Job's riches back.

Except for the last-minute happy ending, which takes six one-sentence verses at the end of Chapter 42, it's a harsh story. Biblical and literary scholars have been trying to make sense of it for centuries. I think the parents are having the same problem. The parents' questions are Job's questions about God's gratuitous cruelty, and their reasoning is the friends' reasoning about personal blame. And though God's answer is all anyone will ever know about the answer, it is no answer at all.

Octavia Pompey repeated this reasoning almost exactly. "I went through one of those things where I questioned God," she said. "Is there a God? There can't possibly be a God and Him let me go through the things that I'm going through and my family, and all this pain and hurt. There can't possibly be a God. But I changed. I know there is a God and I try not to question what He does. Sometimes it's hard. It really is. I was never a overreligious person, I didn't go to church every Sunday. But I always believed in God and said my prayers and read my Bible. And I don't now disown God. I don't know how to explain it, I just accepted it. Some things you can't change and you leave it alone. Because it just makes you sick and crazy."

Research on the effect of such faith on grief finds bereaved parents with religious faith are better off. One study, done in 1991, found that up to eighteen months after a child's death, the parents who attended church more regularly had lower levels of such grief reactions as guilt, anger, loss of control, and despair than did parents who attended less regularly. Another, more recent study found that although parents whose infants had died two months earlier were not necessarily consoled by their religions, the more religious parents nonetheless were less anxious and depressed. I wonder if both these studies weren't done too soon after the child's death to be able to comment with any certainty on the parents' faith. Nevertheless, some of the parents I interviewed agreed with the research, and with Job and Octavia: even though they didn't understand why their children died, they believe that God had His reasons.

Ginny Mitchell: "As far as religion goes, I have my faith. But I don't know why Joel died. And that's just one of the things that's a mystery. I don't guess I'll ever find the answer to why it happened or why it happens obviously to lots of people. But we did not lose our religion. We have a very deep religious background. Both of our families have been very religious, so we were completely immensed in it."

Ginny means "immersed," but "immensed" does seem a better word. "I read the Bible more," she went on. "I pray more, I guess. And it makes me feel better. My feeling about God, I guess, has gotten deeper."

Chris Reed had to accept that he'll never understand why Mary wanted to die, and in the end, he decided that God allowed her that choice, and so Chris had to allow it too. In his ten-year process of answering why Mary died, Chris changed: "I'm more willing to listen to people's cares and concerns," he had said. "In some way I think maybe I'm even closer in my religion to God. I think I really have become a better person. I think I've become a better person because of my relations with things outside myself. Get the connection?"

I have no interest in being religious and never have had, and though I believed Octavia, Ginny, and Chris, I didn't understand them until I listened to Mary Norris. Mary had a period of doubting, but it was short. I had asked her if she had a way of making sense of her son's death, and she didn't: "I can't make sense. I don't know whether it makes sense or don't make sense. There was a reason, that's the only thing I know. And if you say anything, that's questioning God. I can't be doing that."

If Mary couldn't be questioning God, I had nothing further to ask, and so I changed the subject. "Do you still think about your son?" I asked. But Mary hadn't finished the subject.

"Oh yeah, I still think about him. I still think about him. But it's not as hard. I don't get really deep into the hardness any more after I talked to the pastor. The pastor explained things to me. I know my son is in peace. I know he is OK. So it's much better."

"Have you let go of your son," I asked, "or is he still with you?" I was asking these questions because I wanted to know whether Mary felt she had some sort of continuing relationship with her son. Mary repeated what I was missing, that her son wasn't gone, his soul was still alive, both in another world and in her heart.

"I let go," she said, "because I know he's taken care of. I know he's in good hands. So I have let him go."

"What does that mean, to let him go?" I asked. "It's not that you don't still love him."

"Oh no, it don't mean that," Mary said. "It really don't have to be that way. You could still be close with him and still let go. I had a long talk with my pastor right after, you know. Because the same day that I buried my son, and that night it started raining. That's when I got on the phone with this girlfriend of mine. I said, 'Oh, this *rain*,' I was crying, saying, 'He's laying out there in all this rain.' She said, 'I'll be there in a minute.' She called a cab, she came over to my house that night and stayed the night. That night I did question God a little bit you know, 'Why?' And that weekend, I went and talked to my pastor and he sat down and explained everything to me about death. And that's when I started making changes with my son's death. The pastor say, 'He is gone but he's still here. His body is just gone but he's still there in your heart. Don't remember him in the pain. Always re-member him in the happy times. And that will ease your heart.' And I did that. It took me a while, but I did, I did. That's when I start re-membering my son always pat me on my shoulder and call me, 'Old

Lady.' I used to start thinking about that. He was a very sweet kid. The pastor say, 'Always think about him in happy times. He is peaceful. He's taken care of now. He's not gone, just his body's gone, and he's still there in your heart.'"

Later on, I asked Mary if she felt the same about her own death.

"As far as myself is concerned, I'm not afraid of dying," she said. "I am ready to accept it. When the pastor talked to me about my son, it look like he put me prepared. I am really not afraid of dying."

"How did what your pastor said help you?" I asked.

"Because I know that my son's at peace," she said, "I know that. I really know that."

According to Dennis Klass, Mary is not alone in this. Other parents who are also believers turn over their parental responsibilities to God. They feel that God gave them the child to begin with and they must now give the child back. They trust that God will be as loving a parent as they were themselves. Klass says that the "bond with the Holy" these parents feel is "to them, indistinguishable from the bond with the dead child," and that this leaves the parents with a sense of peace; Mary says the same.

Several other parents also said that their faith in God eased their pain, but they were more pointed in how their pain was eased. Like Delores, they want to see their children again.

Walter Farnandis: "I've heard a lot of people say, 'There isn't a God to take a nice child like that.' Well, I don't believe that way. I think there's some reason for it. I sometimes try to think, 'Well maybe they need some young good-looking guys up in heaven.' That's a crazy thought, but you can't have all old people up there. I do believe in God and a life hereafter. It gives me a great consolation that James will be with me again in the future. Without that, to think that you'll never see him again, is terrible. And if a person is an atheist, I don't see how they get through this situation. I think if you do believe in God, if you believe in the life hereafter, it gives you the knowledge that you will be with your son again. Which is a *big* boost, big boost. I find a lot of solace, it gives me strength. It has helped me tremendously, *tremendously,* tremendously."

160

The desire to see the child again is so strong that even a relatively nonreligious person like Anne Perkins can contemplate an afterlife. "I have fuzzy unstructured feelings that there is something out there," she said, "but that's as far as it goes. I do have a real strong feeling of spiritual existence after Robert's death that just seemed so strong at times. I read a number of books, and I've been tempted to go to those people who talk to the dead—those things are very tempting to me and never would have been before. So I don't know what all that says. Have I come to any conclusions? No. Maybe the immortal spirit that continues on into some transcendental thing, I don't know I really believe that, but it's appealing."

Klass and other researchers find that bereaved parents almost cannot *not* believe in an afterlife. "The sense that the child is in heaven is a widely held belief among bereaved parents," he writes, "even those for whom other aspects of their former faith have been unhelpful." In my own life, I agree. I have no belief whatever in heaven, hell, purgatory, or an afterlife of any kind. But I find T.C.'s death so unbelievable and I want so much to see him again that I truly think that when I die, he might be there.

Janet Wright goes a step further and faces what I won't: "I think all those good Christian people, they think we're all going to meet one day and the people who died are all going to have little wings on them and we're all going to say, 'Good to see you again.' And it's not going to be like that. I don't want Bill to come back like that. I want *my* Bill again. And that's never going to be. But I guess people who have this hope, it's wonderful. But you have it or you don't. You can't just go out and say, I want it. It's like saying you want to be smart. Not everyone can believe it."

To be honest, the issue of believing in God because you'll see your child again is a digression. If the question is why children die, then belief in an afterlife is incentive to trust God's reasons but it is not the trust itself. The question still stands, and only some parents, like Octavia, Ginny, Chris, and Mary, answer it with trust in God. Other parents, like Ruth Banick, don't understand why the children died

161

and have their doubts about God's interest in the matter. According to Klass, this, too, is a common reaction. "It is difficult for some to reconcile the death of their child with their belief in God as an omnipotent protector," he writes. "For others, the simple faith they knew before has been challenged by the tragedy of their child's death." Ruth, for one, is thoroughly angry about it.

"People say to you, 'One day you'll know the answer and it'll all make sense,'" she said. "That may well be, but I truly resent the thirty years that I may have to live here not knowing. And I can't understand how this could *ever* have made me a better person. I think a lot of hardships in life I was able to accept—I realized I had some input into those things. This one, I felt like came out of the blue, and I didn't do anything to deserve it. And I do resent it. I resent having to live life without Leslie. And I talked to many parents at Compassionate Friends, and instead of adding any understanding, it just added more misunderstanding. I *don't* understand at *all* why these children had to die. I spoke to a parent whose son loved motorcycles. He was fifteen, he did something stupid; he brought some motorcycle parts down to the basement and was cleaning them with gasoline, and the fumes and the furnace started a fire. He was badly burned, he went to the Francis Scott Key Burn Center, endured horrible pain and suffering for three months, and then died."

At this point, Ruth, who usually talks gently and ingratiatingly, was in tears and shouting. "I think to myself, 'If he was going to die, why couldn't he have just *died*? Why did he have to *suffer* like that for three months?' Not only *he* had to endure that but you know his mother and father endured every step with him. *I* don't know. Now there's a thousand more unanswered questions because now I'm not looking at it from just my 'why,' but I'm looking at it from a thousand 'why's.' I know a woman whose daughter graduated with Leslie and was murdered. And they had to go through the trial and at least they did catch him, but he killed three people and he tortured her daughter for three hours before he shot her in the head and killed her. The father found the daughter and was taken into custody by the police because he was the first one to be there. Her son was taken into custody because he was the last one to be with her. And then the trial and listening to how he had tortured her, and they weren't allowed to show any emotion in court because it could prejudice the jury and he could get off with a mistrial. How could you say there was ever a reason for something like this to happen? There *wasn't*. There is *no* explanation. When people try to give me explanations, I just tell them very bluntly, 'You cannot give me an explanation that would be acceptable. So I'd appreciate it if you wouldn't try.' I have learned to live with the unanswered questions. But there *is* no explanation. There's *no* reason good enough."

I asked Ruth whether Leslie's death had changed her feelings about God, and I got a concise, quieter earful.

"Yes," she said. "I think I have retained my faith. But I no longer— I guess I no longer have the—the words are hard to find. I no longer think that God is necessarily looking out for my best interests."

Leight Johnson came to the same conclusion but with less intensity. "Shirley and I had gone to church, not regularly," he said, "but we belonged to Towson Presbyterian Church and we had the funeral service there. I haven't been back there since. We both did a lot of thinking at that time. You hear people say, 'It was God's will that he died.' You hear people say that about a little girl who's been raped and murdered, 'It was God's will.' It was just at that point we decided we really don't believe any of that stuff. I guess we both felt that this religion, so much of it is just a lot of mythology. I'm not here to say, there is no God, He doesn't exist. But I personally am not convinced that He does. I can't believe that He controls our lives to the degree that a lot of people seem to like to think so."

"Back when you were still going to church," I asked, "did you believe more that God was in charge?"

"I don't think so," he said.

"Why did you stop going to church then?" I asked.

"I don't know," he said, sounding sincerely puzzled. "I even taught Sunday school for a couple of years. I was a trustee of the church there. I don't know, I just sort of lost interest. I guess I felt, why am I doing it when I don't really believe it? Because we stopped going right when this happened. And yet you know, I have a feeling now that there's something missing. Because if Shirley died tomorrow, I would want to have a memorial service. Where else would you have it? In the church—you don't want to do it at the town hall."

Leight seemed to be having trouble delineating what he does and doesn't believe, but this apparently was as far as he had gone in his reasoning or as much as he wanted to say, because he abruptly changed the subject: "This is a nice chair, by the way," he said. "I think I might take it home."

Other parents also followed Leight's and Ruth's reasoning and agreed with their conclusions: God's sphere of influence is limited or God doesn't make decisions about individual lives.

"It's just that we're all raised in the belief that your parents will die before you and you'll die before your children," said Walter Levin. "That's the normal order. A child's death takes it out of order. It's just something we were not brought up to understand."

I'd already heard this almost verbatim from Walter's wife, Elaine, and I interrupted: "So if this disrupts the order of things, do you lose faith in that order?" I wasn't sure what I meant by that.

"I think you're right," he said, "less faith in controllable order, in the ability of anybody, including the Almighty—though I shouldn't say that—to control the order of things. I read that book by that rabbi, *When Bad Things Happen to Good People,* that basically says, God can't control that."

Walter repeated what the rabbi's book said a few more times, then seemed to lose interest in the question.

"Has your feeling about God changed?" I asked.

"I must say that immediately after the loss I really felt very resentful of God," he said. "But the answer is, I have regained my faith in God; I mean, I pray to God, I think there's an Almighty presence. Although, and possibly as a result of reading that book, I think that maybe it was outside His power, that He really couldn't control this thing. The big order of things He can control, but some of these things He can't."

Walter added kindly, "I'm giving Him the benefit of the doubt."

Other parents also seem to believe that God's influence is limited or that God simply doesn't make those decisions, He wasn't part of the children's deaths.

Janet, before she talked about the good Christians meeting in heaven with their little wings, said, "I was mad. I stopped going to church. But now I go back sometimes. I don't think God does things like that, kills those little babies in the cancer ward at Hopkins."

"I felt very angry with God," said Sally, whose daughter's needs seemed to be so unfillable that she committed suicide, "that He put all that He did on her. Because she suffered a lot that we didn't know. I thought, just a poor young kid to have to carry all this. But that's past. I'm not angry with Him now. I'm not pleased with what He did. He didn't do it though."

"I don't think it was God's fault," said Tom. "I don't blame it on God." But because Tom shares Marge's worry that David is in purgatory, I suspect Tom's thinking is more complicated than he wanted to tell me.

"I believe in God and I believe that there was something that caused all this stuff to be here," said Brandt, after he said he didn't "believe in 'God did it for some reason.'" He went on: "But I don't believe that God is omnipotent as people think He is. We cause a lot of our own problems. I don't think it's changed my feeling about Him. I didn't get mad. Betty got mad at God because it was somebody she could get mad at. She's still angry."

Notice that many of these people were angry, as Ruth has been, but have now settled the anger and seem to have little to say on the subject. Brandt is right about Betty, however; she is indeed still angry.

Betty has retired from the day care center where she worked, and now volunteers for the Red Cross and an animal-rights organization, plays in several bridge groups, and runs her local chapter of Compassionate Friends. Betty presents Job's whole argument, but comes to the opposite conclusion.

"I'm one of the rare people who has no guilt," she said. "My husband built up a guilt trip because the automobile they took on this trip was my mother's little car, a Fiesta, instead of our bigger van. But when it's 9 A.M. on a Monday morning and your son is sitting next to his grandmother, you have nothing to feel guilty about. My husband manufactured guilt because somebody has to be blamed. I fortunately didn't manufacture guilt. There was nothing I could do to prevent this accident. When Bruce was growing up, we spent as much time together as a mother and son could ever have. I was there when he left in the morning, there when he came home from school, active in his Scout troop, active in his DeMolay, active in his youth fellowship, school, PTA. He had a good seventeen years, he did a lot of neat things. When he was in tenth grade, his German class was going to Switzerland. I thought it was something you do when you're a senior, not tenth grade, and I wasn't in favor of it. But he said he would save the money, and he did; he put off getting his driver's license. Now I'm so glad he had it. I'm just so glad he went."

For Betty, guilt is a result of worrying that you should have done something differently, maybe even prevented the death. She knows she not only couldn't have prevented the death, but she also did everything she could to ensure that he lived a good life. So in her terms, she feels no guilt. She still, however, has trouble with attribution. Why did Bruce die? In particular, she has trouble with Job's version of the question, Why did God *let* Bruce die?

"When Bruce died, it was hard going back to work, to the day care center," she said. "One child was very low IQ. I'd look at him and think, 'Why are you alive and you'll never amount to anything? And my child is dead. Why not you? Why my healthy, bright child?' Though I was very careful not to show those feelings or treat him any different. But it shouldn't have been my good, wholesome child, who would have been a contribution to society. Should have been the murderer, should have been the bad kid. Not only is it my loss, but some woman was deprived of a good husband, good children would have been born, he would have given to the world, and the world has lost as well as I."

"So how do you make sense of Bruce's death?" I asked.

"Before my son's death," she said, "I would hear of great tragedies, terrible tragedies, where people lost their husbands, all their children. And always in the back of my mind, I thought, 'Well, there had to have been a *reason.*'" Betty began imitating the little thoughts in the back of her mind, which whispered: "They were *bad people.* Maybe nobody knew it, but there was some good reason for what happened to that person. Maybe that person had been a bad person *and nobody knew it,* but maybe he *was. Always* there was some reason."

Then she returned to her normal voice. "There was some reason until it happened to me. Then I realized, this can happen and there is no reason. I was a good person. My child was a good child. After he died, about six months later, I went through his room with a fine-tooth comb. I figured I was going to find something in this room that would prove to me that my child was a *bad child* in some way. You know what I found? Half a pack of Salem cigarettes. He was seventeen years old and *that's all I found.* I mean I searched every nook and cranny. There *had* to have been a reason. The reason had to be in his room and I would find it. So I realized, this *does* happen to people for no reason whatsoever. It just happens."

By now, the hair was standing up on the back of my neck. But Betty had just gotten started.

"Here's another thing we need to touch on," she continued, "and that's religion. I found at Compassionate Friends that either people get a lot of support from their religion because God is helping them through this, or God has turned away from them and they don't care about God. I'm one of those ones that God has turned his back on. Our family was very involved with church and religion. My son's Eagle Scout project was an outdoor chapel for the church. Church was a big part of our family life, *big* part, very active, always with the church, taught Sunday school, active in women's association, active in church affairs, very, very involved in church. Kids always went to Sunday school, always went to youth fellowship. A lot of ministers in my family over the generations."

After that setup, Betty took a deep breath. "And I feel, where were you, God, when we needed you? I've come to the thoughts now that if there is a God, it is either not a loving God and I want nothing to do with Him, or once we are born and are on earth, God has no control over our lives. If He has no control over our lives, why bother to pray to Him? And I have not been to church except twice when I had to go to a baptism and a wedding. I'm not interested in religion. If I'm somewhere and people say the Lord's Prayer, if I can get by without even saying it, I'd rather not. I don't go to church and I don't miss it and I don't care to go again and I want nothing to do with God. I wouldn't actually call myself an atheist because I can't say there is no God. I just don't know that. But my feelings are, if there is, it's not the kind of God I'm interested in. I feel like, shit on you, God. You shit on me, the hell with you, God. I'm still feeling that way after fourteen years, and that was one big definite change in my life."

Betty wasn't in charge of Bruce's life and death, God was. Despite my lack of religiousness, Betty's anger at God makes perfect sense to me: Betty trusted God to have good reasons, and Bruce died for no good reason. Other parents agree with Betty, though without quite her vehemence.

Nickie Copinger: "Why did this happen to my child? Who else took him? It had to be God. The priest said, 'God takes your children back because He needs them.' I remember, at Adam's funeral service, I remember sitting in that pew thinking, 'Not any more than I do.' My belief didn't change except for that questioning. But Beau, my husband, said, 'I'd rather not believe in God than hate the one I'm supposed to believe in.'"

Loretta Marsh said that when she goes to the cemetery to visit Mike's grave, she, like Job, talks to God. "I say to God, 'Why do I deserve this, what did I do?' I don't know of anything I ever did. I don't know how I could have. No, I don't think I did either."

So I asked, "Has your feeling about God changed?

"Yes," she said. "Oh yes. Yes. We were brought up religious. My feeling has changed because I don't understand why He let a thing like that happen. I don't understand it. I say a lot of times, 'Why, why,

why, did He take somebody who is good as they can be?' I know kids who's on drugs, who's alcoholics, not that I wish anything would happen to them, but why does it happen to the good ones? I'll tell you what the minister told me the day that we put Mike away, he said, 'Mrs. Marsh, if you went out to pick flowers, would you pick a live one, a pretty one, or would you pick a dead one?' I said, 'I'd pick the live one, the pretty one.' He said, 'That's what God does.'

"Now, was he right?" Loretta continued. "Was that minister right or was he trying to comfort me? My mother's real religious, and she thinks I'm terrible. I don't go to church, I don't think I'd ever get religious any more. I've cursed God and I probably always will. And maybe I'm wrong. I don't think God did me justice. I don't think I had justice."

A story illustrates all this. Estelle Lemaitre's thirty-two-year-old son, Robby, drowned eight years ago: "Five young people had gone out on a boat and it was in October, and it was a very hot day and they decided to go for a swim. So they just jumped off the boat and the current got him. Robby was the only one, and it took the Coast Guard three hours to find his body, at Magothy River. And he was an excellent swimmer in excellent physical condition, so I don't believe there was anything he did or didn't do. It was just one of those things. And we were in Florida at the time that we got word that this had happened. So of course we had to fly right back."

Estelle was the original bad interview, that is, she gave short answers, didn't elaborate, and then sat silent for as long as I could stand the silence. She didn't seem to be hiding or withholding anything, just answering as economically as possible. On this subject, however, and without being asked, she got down to business. "You know," she said. "You question everything. I still do. Maybe I'm looking to blame somebody. At the time my son died I was thinking, if his wife had not divorced him, maybe he would have been home with her."

Then Estelle's search for somebody to blame moved higher. "When we were in Florida we had out-of-town guests, and we all had gone to Tarpon Springs and went to a church there. And we went in and my cousin and I were lighting a candle. And at the time we were doing this, I found out later, that's the time our son was drowning. So I felt, sometimes I still feel like God deserted us."

Estelle stopped talking, and after a long silence, I prompted her: "When you say you question everything . . . ?"

"I even think, October is not swimming weather, but it was so hot that day and I keep thinking, this was God's way of allowing him to go swimming that day. If God hadn't let the weather be so warm, this wouldn't have happened."

She stopped again, and after another silence, I said, "You talk about God as though you have a lot of faith in Him."

"I *have* to," she said.

"Do you still?" I asked.

"Yes, to a sense," she said. "I strongly believe."

"But that's changed in some way?" I said.

"Yeah," she said.

"How would you say it's changed?" I said.

"I don't understand why these things happen," she said. "Not only our situation, anybody's. Why there's so much grief in this world."

Another long silence, after which I went on with my list of questions: "What was your career before?" I asked.

"I was a housewife," she said.

"Is that still what you do?" I asked.

"I'm into crafts now," she said, "I make crafts. When we lost our son, I guess I was trying to find something to do to occupy my mind, to keep my sanity. So I started making crafts and selling them. And it's kind of gotten to be a little business now."

I went on with the interview, during which I learned that she runs her crafts business not for her own profit, but for the church's. "How does this work fit into your life?" I asked.

"I think in the beginning I was looking for answers," she said, and looked directly at me. "I'm still looking for answers, Ann."

"How does working for the church help?" I asked.

"The church makes money so they can run their charity projects.

I show other women how to do crafts. And gifts, soliciting gifts to give as prizes. It's a big involvement."

"So even though you aren't as sure about God—" I began.

She interrupted: "I'm sure about God. But I feel He deserted me."

"If God deserted you," I asked, "why are you so nice to the church?"

"I don't know," she said. "I really don't know. Actually it's three churches that I help. It's two here and one in Florida."

"Can you describe why you like doing something for the churches?" I asked.

"I don't know that it has anything to do with Robby's death any more. It's just that they need money, and I'm available."

I decided she was giving me the answer she had to give, and went on with the interview. "Is there any way your child's death makes sense?" I asked.

"No," she said.

"And you've looked for that?" I said.

"Yes, I sure have," she said. "For about a year after Robby died, I couldn't go to church. I would go to church every Sunday, I would be in there maybe ten minutes, fifteen minutes, and I would get hysterical and I would go sit in my car and wait two hours for my granddaughter to get out of Sunday school. And about a year later, I spoke with our priest, since I was looking for answers. The priest said that since I was lighting the candle when Robby died and asking God to take care of the children, maybe this was God's way of taking care of Robby. That had he stayed here, maybe something worse could have happened to him."

"What do you think?" I asked.

"Sometimes I think there's nothing worse than death," she said.

The parents have answered Job's questions with the entire range of possible answers. Like Job, no one knows God's reasons. No one knows why the child died. Some people are content with no reason, some are angry about it. Some trust God's purposes, some don't. Most people have God implicated in their reasoning. Most people settle for not knowing.

Elaine: "I always thought it would happen to the next guy, that I was going to sail through life; you got married, you had kids. I think after Hilary was born, I realized that's not true. Hilary is a retarded child and nobody could find out the reason why. I felt sorry about that for a little bit, but then I said, 'Let's pull ourselves up by the boot-straps and see what can we do for this child.' And it proved marvelous. This girl works as an aide in the kindergarten. That didn't come overnight, that took a lot of effort. My thing is, if something is bad, I wallow in it for a little bit, and then start doing something about it. But that didn't work with Merrill. There *are* no answers. I was never a great believer in God to begin with. I remember saying to my husband when Merrill got sick, my husband was praying to God, and I said, 'I think you better pray to the doctors.' It's just the luck of the draw. There isn't a why."

Nickie: "Why does anything happen to anybody? I say to myself, 'Look, nobody's going to answer you.' It's one of those questions you don't get an answer to."

Chapter 13

DIANA MOORES' WORLD

∞

In the last chapter, I didn't include what Diana Moores said about religion.

"I did have my own religion," she said, "all built in and came with the package. But when Mindy died, that was all totally worthless. I have to rebuild now by what my own thoughts create. It's a real slow process because now belief has to be constructed with evidence. Those pieces of evidence are few and far between. And in the meantime you have to have some sort of structure, but the structure is made of your wishes and thoughts, and it's not real strong. It's not a sure thing. I'll only believe sure things now, absolutely sure things."

Not many things are sure, of course. So for Diana, limiting belief to absolutely sure things dictates a bare, pure world.

The circumstances of Mindy's death were unusually bad. Six years earlier, Diana's husband, Jack, had taken Mindy to her first day of school. He was fooling with the radio—as he often did, Diana said—went off the road, and hit a parked flatbed trailer carrying steel I-beams. One of the beams came through the windshield and went through Mindy's head. Jack was trapped in the car with Mindy's body

173

for maybe half an hour. During that time, a friend of Diana's, driving to work, happened on the accident, then called Diana. Diana got in her car, hit the traffic jam caused by the accident, parked by the side of the road and ran to the accident, but the police wouldn't allow her near it. Finally, a state trooper told her, "I'm not supposed to be the one to tell you this, but I can't put you through it any more. There's no more life left in your child." Later, at the hospital, the doctor advised her not to look at Mindy. Diana explained bluntly, "Her brain exploded."

The story was so terrible I could think of nothing to say. I started my list of questions. Did she have any guilt or self-blame?

She said she sure did, "a deep dose of it." Just before the accident, she said, "was a period of time I was working ten, twelve hours a day, and I wasn't attentive to Mindy's needs. I turned her over to Jack; he was her primary parent. I didn't even take her to the first day of school. I was spending time out socially and spending time at work. I learned from Mindy that she was having problems with it, and I had just begun to stop the socialization and I told Mindy that I'd tell my boss the next day, Monday, that I couldn't any longer work so much. I spent the day with her Sunday, just the two of us. Yeah, I feel a lot of guilt. Sometimes I feel that's why she was taken away, because I didn't cherish her enough. I was neglectful. It had to do with my marriage; it was all aimed at Jack. It didn't occur to me she was in the middle of it. I try to ignore the guilt, but there's such a lot of it."

Diana wasn't functioning well during the funeral arrangements, and a friend deputized for her. "She became me for the things I couldn't do," said Diana. "I asked her to go the funeral home and come back to tell me what Mindy looked like, things I needed to know but couldn't do. She placed my birthstone ring on her, placed my cross on her, she kissed her. She was able to do these things for me—I don't know how but she did—things I needed to have done. She was my proxy. But I have a tremendous guilt for not doing these things myself. I feel like Mindy was waiting for me and I never went to her."

By the time her husband returned from the hospital a month later,

Diana was alternating between rage and no emotions whatever, mostly the latter. After another month, on the advice of her psychologist, she checked herself into a local psychiatric hospital, where she was diagnosed, she said, with "major depression" and "complete dissociation" and kept for a year and a half. When she came back out, she couldn't go back to the house she had lived in, so she moved into a rented apartment in a large complex. She lives alone. She didn't want to divorce her husband but she had to, she said; she can't live with him. "We're best, *best* friends," she said, "and we're both so careful and so gentle. But how can I forgive him?"

Diana now works as a dispatcher in a police department. When she interviewed for her job, the interviewer asked her if she could handle the rough parts of being around a police department. "I thought, 'Be nice, Diana,'" she said. "And I said, very respectfully, 'Sir, after you've gone through what I have and landed back up on your feet, there really isn't anything on earth that particularly bothers you.'" She likes the dispatcher's job; she says the police department is like family, and the work keeps her structured. She doesn't miss a day of work.

I went on with my list: "Do you still have pain from this?"

"The horrible thoughts are truly horrible," she said. "But sometimes it's the thoughts that are beautiful, the memories, that are much harder. That's something people don't understand—they say, 'Don't you have good thoughts and good memories?' Yes, I do. They *hurt*."

My own good thoughts and memories hurt too, and I wanted to know if she had some way of understanding this.

"The word 'compassion' keeps flashing in my mind; the answer is related in an *enormous* way to the word 'compassion.' She's missing and never will be again, and to see this smiling face and this happy memory and know what became of it, the horror, the gore, the violence, all of that attached to this innocent little being. It just takes your heart and just wrenches it, just grabs it and pulls it right out."

"When are other times that are particularly painful?" I asked.

Diana answered the way all parents did: birthdays, anniversaries of the death, holidays, and all the random times some small reminder appears.

"With Mindy, her birthday and death are days apart," she said, "so we really get a good dose of it in August. My husband and my other daughter, we put our notes together and we realized that as soon as the hot weather, June-July hits, we go downhill real fast. And going to the cemetery is difficult. Sometimes it doesn't affect me until I drive away. The cemetery is very hard to leave—this is a little child, a tiny little girl who's not able to take care of herself, how can you leave her? She needs me. She must be looking for me."

Diana looks like a model, and her voice is quiet and matter-of-fact, with a little tough edge. Because of the horror of her story and her blunt eloquence, I was quieter than usual. I was also confused by her. She seemed to be withholding no part of her story or her reaction to it, but she was so self-possessed she seemed almost remote. She seemed to be talking about someone other than herself. But I also noticed that she talked a lot about other people's feelings and used the word "compassion" often—neither of which seems characteristic of an emotionally remote person.

While I sat there confused, Diana was telling me about her other daughter, Kristin, who had gone through periods of needing her and how Diana didn't want to take care of anybody anymore, so she'd push Kristin back on her feet and out on her own.

But now things are better, she said. "My daughter has a baby now. It's funny, when he was born, people kept saying, 'This is going to make things so much easier for you.' And I thought, 'Yeah, I know, wipe the slate clean.' But when the baby was born, I thought a sun, not Mindy's sun, but another sun is going to rise and set on this child. And I will *love* him so dearly. But you know, I think he's cute as a button and I *love* to watch my daughter love him, but I don't have a strong connection to him. It's scary because you think you're supposed to bond to them, and you're not a very nice person."

Diana went on to tell a number of stories with a similar structure: she felt close to someone or great compassion for someone, then she pulled back from them. For instance, one friend, with whom Diana had been close for thirty years, had never met Mindy. "About two, three months ago," Diana said, "after thinking about it, I said to her that if she saw a videotape I had of Mindy, she might know Mindy a little more. I had a need for her to know Mindy more. She thought about it and called me back and she said, 'I don't think that's a good idea. I don't believe I could bear to see her.' I was infuriated. I'd offered to show her my child. She rejected it because she didn't think she could take it. *You don't want to see my child?* Wrong answer. Wrong answer."

Another story: "There was this friend of my sister's whose six-year-old also died just going off to school—his father ran over him with a tractor. It finally ended up that the mother and father have been in contact with me and Jack. I had such an enormous need to take this horrible mess and help somebody, at least to listen to them. So we've been doing that. This little boy was born just after Mindy died, and he lived his six years, and he was killed. Phenomenal. We got real strongly enmeshed in that, but we're trying to back off a little bit. The little boy didn't die long ago, so they haven't really felt anything yet, and you don't want to tell them that. They're going to know soon enough. You have to be careful what you share—there's so much stuff, and it's so thick, and so murky and heavy. And it doesn't get easier. You just learn to be a better actor for people."

And another: "I think that the only thing I can get out of life is to be helpful; it's all I really have to offer. I want people to open up, but there would still be distance. But when you do that and don't have a license, you get in trouble. I stopped with this one guy at work. He's real sweet and we have a wonderful working relationship. We're right where I need for us to be. I backed off real quick at one point, because he said, 'You know, it's so wonderful to talk to you.' And I thought, 'Uh-ooh!' Little warning went off. So I'm not quite as available."

Granted that the reason for her pulling away was different for each one of these people, the pattern is still the same: she wants to be close or to help, then she backs off. I'm sure everyone alive feels the same tension between closeness and distance, but for Diana, the tension seemed omnipresent. On the one hand, she said that since Mindy

died, she has developed more "people skill": "Perceiving other people's thoughts and feelings—I have more skill at that now than I ever
did. I'm so tuned in to people, at times I feel like I can almost read
minds. People are the most important thing in the world; you need to
be tuned in to each other. I have no patience for people who aren't,
no patience. If you can't do that, what are we *here* for?"

On the other hand, she says she's much more remote. "You said
that you can understand other people," I said. "Does other people's
understanding also feed back to you?"

"No," she said. "No, it goes out, goes out to other people."

"So you're more distant from other people?" I asked.

"Oh, very much so," she said. "I used to be quietly social. But now
I really haven't any use for any of it at all. I'd really rather spend time
isolated. It takes too much energy to socialize with people and be
where they want you to be. I'd rather be by myself."

"Who in particular are you more distant from?" I asked.

"Anybody that wants to come into my world," she said. "Anybody, man or woman, that wants to get better acquainted, it's like,
wait a minute, nobody comes into my world. This is where I live. It'll
never work out because you'll never understand what I've been
through and how I live now."

So Diana thinks people are the most important thing in the world,
feels she is unusually empathic, and won't let anyone else into her
world. As contradictory as this sounds, I understand it a little. I feel as
though I often know what other people want and need, and occasionally enjoy helping them out, but I have few hopes that they can
return the favor. T.C.'s death so drastically changed my world that,
though I am content to live in it, I worry that it's bad news to other
people. As with Diana, communication between the worlds is only
one way, from my world out. During the whole interview, Diana said
only twice that she'd like to be understood. Once was with the old
friend, who in the end couldn't face Mindy's reality. The other time
was when she answered a question about what she liked to do best: "I
like to write," she said. "I like to write things from my head. The

things I write are constant attempts at explaining what goes on in my head, so that somebody someday can say, '*Oh!* I get it! *That's* what you're talking about.'"

Otherwise, Diana is, in her word, encapsulated.

"The world that I had before, it's totally ruined," she said, "it's no use to me. I've had to build another world. I didn't choose to, but out of functioning in life, I've had to build a new type of world. And yet I have to pretend at times that I'm living in this world that other people live in because it's expected of me and because I care about them. But when I'm released from them and come back to my own surroundings, I'm back in my world again. Which is quite different, you know. Since my child died, I have around me an atmosphere that I live in. It's hard to describe. I live encapsulated in it. People in the other world, my previous world, have this free, fresh air. Everything's normal, natural, expected. My world is unreasonable. I guess sometimes my capsule and I have to go into this other world. I have to use energy and forethought to get through and communicate with them so they're not concerned about me. And say to them, 'Oh dear what a problem,' when what you want to say is, 'Be real!'"

"How do you think this encapsulating world of yours is different from the one you used to have?" I asked.

"It's a *lot* smaller. It's gray—though it used to be black. It's very small because I'm the only one that lives in it. It's a *very* small world."

"You don't seem unhappy in it," I said.

"No, it's just where I belong," she said. "There are times when I'm very unhappy, very depressed, but it's not because of the world I'm in. It's mine, it's tailor-made only for me. It's very cozy. I have no desire to be in a larger world at all. I'm encapsulated in my own world. It can be compared to being underwater. And nothing ever penetrates it. Nothing can. The only thing that could ever penetrate that world would be the true voice of my child. That could do it. That could get right through."

The way Diana talks is almost frightening. Possibly, because she spent time talking to a psychiatrist, she's unusually practiced in describing how things seem to her. Possibly she's a natural poet, so her descriptions are unusually vivid: she's encapsulated in a world, in an atmosphere, underwater. Possibly she's not altogether cured of dissociation. Possibly she has found a way to mimic Mindy's small, gray world of death.

I have nothing to say about those possibilities, and prefer instead just to take her literally: because of Mindy's death, Diana now lives in a world that is incommensurate with anyone else's world and from which communication goes outward, rarely inward. The only inward communication, "the only thing that could ever penetrate that world," is Mindy's voice, "the true voice of my child." Mindy's true voice is Mindy's voice if she were alive again. And of course that's impossible. So Diana, like all the parents, does the next best thing, and has Mindy inhabit Diana's world with her.

"It's really hard, you know, with a little child like that—it's really hard to make her last," Diana said. "I remember a feeling in the beginning of not letting go, not letting go. I'd get angry at times that time would try to take me away farther, and I'd hold on harder. But I don't feel her going away now. She's with me all the time. When I'm not concentrating just on her, perhaps she goes and does what she needs to do. But as soon as I turn around and I need her, she's right there. She's never not there."

When I wrote that for me, communication goes one way, from my world out, I meant a social isolation that is fundamental but only occasionally noticeable. Was Diana talking about an isolation greater than that? Is the literal truth that Mindy's death obliterated Diana's world completely, and that she has constructed a new one that includes Mindy and from which she can reach out but cannot herself be reached? I don't know. But if she's constructing her new world only out of sure things, then so far the only sure things seem to be herself and Mindy.

I asked, "Do you think you don't have hope of life?"

Diana got sarcastic: "Words here—*life?* I have no need for hope of life. Life was Mindy. What I have is existence, I function. I have no hope and no need for life. Why would I want life? Mindy's not here.

Why would I want that? I have no need for it."

"Do you think you feel differently about your own death?" I asked.

"Oh *yes,*" she said. "Definitely. I used to have a great fear of death. But I think, 'Mindy's been through it, she's done it, she's there. And she was little when she did it.' So I have no fear. I can think, maybe I'll get hit by a bus and that'll be great. I want to go where she went. I have no fear of death. I would welcome it. If I don't have the opportunity to die before I'm old, I would like to age very rapidly. I want to do it. I've lived my life in this world. What I'm going to do here I've already done. I am so tired. I'm ready to quit."

Chapter 14

THE ZERO POINT

Changes in Perspective

∞

Diana is unusual in her ability to detail every aspect of what in her world has changed. One aspect was the horror of Mindy's mutilated body, her brains and blood. Diana never saw Mindy dead, but a friend did. Diana's friend, who deputized for her at Mindy's funeral, was also a doctor, and Diana had asked her for all the details of the injury and the findings of the autopsy. "Mindy was mine," Diana said, "and every detail belonged to me."

Like Diana, all the parents have had to face either in imagination or in person the concrete details of their children's deaths. An unlucky few of the parents see their children's bodies at the scene of an accident. Many parents see the bodies at a hospital or in a morgue. The sight, and later the memories of the sight, are literally unspeakable and, unlike Diana, most parents talked around the subject.

Ruth Banick's daughter, Leslie, was driving a new four-wheel drive truck. "She was going too fast," said Ruth, "and she lost control of the truck and left the beltway on a curve. And she ran into a tree, and the truck turned over, and she died. These things are imprinted in your mind forever. Of course, in the beginning, that's *all* you can think about. Because I did go to the morgue to see Leslie and for the longest time I tortured myself about that. That's a horrible image for a parent to remember."

The parents who did not see their children's bodies instead imagined their children's last moments. Sally Lambert's daughter, Lisa, hanged herself on New Year's Eve. Lisa had gone out on a date, and her date called Sally at 3 A.M., saying that Lisa had taken his car and had she come home yet? "I was on the sofa waiting for her," Sally said, "and while I was there, around four, I had a feeling that was almost as if"—Sally hesitated for a minute—"she was on her way and stopped by here. It was like a presence, like she was with me. And I thought, 'She's *died*.' Her date had rope in his car, and she had gone up to Cockeysville Junior High and hung herself. I think the suicide itself was bad, but to think she went out in the middle of the night. What state of mind she had to be in. And to drive up to that school and get out and go do that. She had to be in such torture. It took me a long time to get over just that part."

"And that has stayed with me," said Nickie Copinger, whose ten-year-old son died in the hospital, "that I feel in my heart that I think he must have been awake a little bit while they were preparing him for the intensive care room, that I could have stayed. His breathing was so shallow they had to put him on a respirator, so they had to put something in his mouth, so he was knowing what was going on. But I—this is the part that's hard to live with—I still feel, six and a half years later, that I could have had another minute, five minutes with him. I don't know. It seems that you'll never forget. You don't dwell on it every day, but it does come up, it doesn't—it's not forgotten."

"Michael was superintendent of a townhouse project in Baltimore County," said Louise Lewis. "And on a Monday morning he went to inspect a broken window on a townhouse. On a February morning, cold, getting ready to snow, and he went in and he was confronted by an escaped convict who must have been hiding out to maybe rob the shopping center across the street. And he robbed Michael of the little bit of money he must have had on him, and took the keys to his car, but before he left, he shot him in the back of the head. And he was brain-dead."

Then Louise stopped remembering and addressed me: "Did your son—did he stay alive for a little while?"

Then she went back to remembering: "They didn't find Michael until the next day. The fact that he was alone, dead, all that time. You imagine the holdup, the scare. He had to go through a communication with this person, 'Here's my money and here's the keys to my car, now leave me.' You just always wonder what transpired. What conversation. I still wonder about that. I get hooked into it."

The answer to Louise's question to me was, yes, T.C. did stay alive for a while, because the autopsy report said he died of trauma and smoke inhalation, and if he was breathing, he must have been alive. I hope he was unconscious. A few weeks after he died, I tried verifying that hope by calling the doctor who did the autopsy, but the doctor was busy and didn't return the call. I didn't try again because I'm no Diana; I used up all my courage calling once. I didn't see T.C. dead because the detectives and priest who notified me of his death said that he was burned and advised against seeing him. I was scared of the image of T.C. burned and I didn't have the courage to argue. I went through a period when I thought pretty constantly about T.C. staying alive for a while and maybe wanting me there. What a coward: he could go through dying, but I couldn't even look at him dead. I don't think about it much any more, but like Louise, I can get hooked into it.

All the parents have gone through this or worse. They call thinking about these memories or images, "dwelling on it," and they avoid dwelling on it.

These memories and images are terrible. I mention them because they are hard facts; they can't be softened or explained away. They can be ignored, but they are never far away and resurface easily. These memories and images seem to me to embody what the parents now know: that the children are dead, that the deaths are senseless, and that the parents could do nothing about it. And because the memories and images don't go away, this knowledge doesn't either. Years after the child's death, this knowledge translates into a changed outlook, a new perspective on life.

Perspective is a subtle word. In a painting, perspective means the way the elements in the picture appear larger or smaller or skewed in shape, depending on where the painter stands. In normal conversation, perspective means the same: if you stand in a different place, or if you stand back emotionally or intellectually, or if you learn something new about a person or a situation, then you see things differently. The parents now know firsthand about life's hard facts and so they see life differently. Their perspectives on life have changed.

But exactly what is the change? A few parents described the change as a visible difference in the world. Diana said her new world was smaller; she was encapsulated in a gray world, in a different atmosphere, or underwater. Others described a feeling of having a wider view of the world or of living in a grayer, dimmer world. Otherwise, parents described their changes in perspective as differences in their own selves.

"I just was pretty confident that if you did things right and tried hard, that you could succeed at what you did," said Julia Marcus, echoing Job, then taking the reasoning the next step. "I look at everything differently now, a total turnaround. I think you should try hard and be positive. But I'm just not sure that things are within our control. My son would say I'm grim but I think I'm more rational. I'm a lot more mistrusting of the future. I anticipate that *anything* can happen. We *know* it can. I used to not worry about—how can I say this?—I was really a carefree kind of person that wasn't afraid of much. But now, unless you're someone who pulls the curtain down, it becomes clear to you that everyone around you is going to die. You can't ever again become naive or protected about what the outcome is. It seems normal that every now and then you panic."

Lydia Frasca: "When we got married, we wanted to have children, buy a house, all those things. And those things seemed to come so easily to other people. But all of a sudden the world isn't as safe as you thought. Your plans don't happen and you're not going to be guaranteed. It changes your outlook. When you read about all these murders and accidents and you think they never would happen to you—now things like that are closer. I don't plan too many big things now. I really do not. I honestly do not plan."

Julia and Lydia both begin by saying that they'd expected normal lives. Then Lydia says that now she knows the world isn't safe, and Julia says that knowing the outcome of this child's life means knowing the outcome of everyone's life. So for Julia and Lydia, the knowledge increased their sense that life is unpredictable and dangerous. Julia knows that *anything* can happen; Lydia knows she's not guaranteed. Julia now mistrusts the future and finds occasional panic reasonable; Lydia doesn't bother to plan.

I came to the same conclusion as Julia and Lydia by a route only slightly different. I have a good friend named Jean, also a writer, with whom I talk about the usual: what happened to her, to me, and to people we both know. When Jean is doing the talking, all these happenstances become stories; she presents the events in their most effective order and the characters by their most telling details. When she is done with a story, I know what sort of people the characters are and why some event happened the way it did. Jean makes reality into a story that is coherent and often pleasing. She is the author, she is in charge; otherwise, there would be no story. Her stories make reality make sense.

After years of being trained by Jean, I learned to see stories everywhere. We're surrounded by stories—in newspapers, magazines, television, songs, books, movies, and every day's conversations. We say, "What's new?" to our friends and colleagues, and they tell us a story. Stories are entertainment, information about life, and moral education, all of which people like. I also think people like telling stories for the same reason Jean does—they become the authors of their own lives. They encounter difficulties, turn the difficulties into stories, and take charge of the shape of the story and its ending. So in general, stories do two things: they make reality orderly, coherent, and sometimes beautiful; and they make life controllable. I'll bet we're born wired for stories.

Anyway, right after T.C. died, I told Jean, "No more stories." I felt this strongly. Jean said I was wrong, and I didn't argue because I wasn't sure what I meant. In retrospect, I see I meant that because T.C. died, I can believe neither that reality is coherent or beautiful nor that we write our own stories. My life is not a story, or if it is, it's not me writing it. I can't believe anyone would write a story like this.

That said, Jean is now telling me stories again, I continue acting as though life is beautiful and coherent and I'm in charge. I act this way because I don't know how else to live. But the fact is, life is not pretty and not coherent, and I'm not in charge and I know it. I can't believe I ever thought anything else.

In short, if you're looking for sense, rightness, order, or answers about God's reasons, you're out of luck. This is another hard fact. All the parents said this in one way or another: you're on your own, life isn't safe, anything can happen, you're not guaranteed, you're not in control.

This hard new perspective ought to cause anxiety. Psychologists say that one effect of not feeling in control is increased anxiety, and researchers do find that bereaved parents score high grades on tests of anxiety. When I asked the parents whether they felt more anxious or vulnerable in life, a few said they were more anxious in general or had attacks of anxiety or were on anxiety medication. For the most part, however, and with the near-universal exception of worrying about risks to their other children, their answers were cursory.

That is, the parents were more aware that they weren't in control; they just didn't seem interested in it. Those parents who seemed most aware of their vulnerability talked about its inverse, greater self-protection. I asked Diana if she felt more vulnerable in life. No, she said, "I don't think so. I really have such a protected covering I really don't think so."

Sally said, similarly, "I guess I close a lot of things off. To protect myself. The doors creep open every now and then. But it's a way of protecting yourself and you have to do it."

Emily Miller: "I think you're more defensive, putting the wall up to protect your vulnerability. Because you can't stand too much hurt any more. You never expected this kind of hurt."

Delores Shoda: "I think it's hard to let yourself really care about anything any more, to let your emotions be to the point where you might get hurt again."

None of these four were talking about protecting themselves from grief, as Tom Ford was when he said, "I didn't dwell on it that much. It was like, protect yourself more." They were talking about protecting themselves against life, whatever that means. Otherwise, none of the parents—not even those who noticed a change, not even Julia and Lydia—seemed interested in their own vulnerability.

Walter Levin is a good example. I asked him if he felt more vulnerable. "Me personally?" he asked, then repeated the parents' usual exception. "Not really. I feel my loved ones more vulnerable rather than I. I don't really feel any more vulnerable. As a matter of fact, recently I was diagnosed as having prostate cancer. But for some reason I don't feel vulnerable myself. I had a radical prostatectomy, whatever it's called, and it was all confined. But even at that time of the diagnosis, I didn't feel any vulnerability."

If the parents do see vulnerability and lack of control as facts of life with no great emotional content, one reason must be that such facts aren't news. Life isn't fair and anything can happen; you do your best and sooner or later, you and everyone you know will die. Everybody says so. I think, however, the parents now know more about lack of control than most people, the way a heart patient now knows more about the body's fragility than someone who's never been sick.

"I know that I'm here," said Mary Norris. "Don't know how long I'm going to be here. So you live your life to the fullest while you are here."

"Do you think you understood that before your son died?" I asked.

"I probably would have said it in my mind," she said. "But after he had died, I think that it stick in my heart."

Maybe another reason for the parents' lack of interest might be this depth of knowledge. Maybe knowledge that sticks in your heart becomes basic or second-nature. You get used to it; it's like breathing and it's no longer impressive.

If the hard facts of life, the harsh new perspective doesn't seem to cause a sense of vulnerability, it does seem to cause disconnectedness, disengagement. The parents are, at some fundamental level, less interested in life. This makes sense to me. When I was a teenager living in my parents' house, I didn't want to clean my room: it wasn't *my* room. The fundamental circumstances are out of my hands, so why invest?

When researchers talk about this, they say that the parents have lost a sense of purpose, a sense of the meaning in life. One study found this loss to be long-term: parents two years after their children's deaths reported less meaning in life, as did parents eleven years after. Another study found parents reporting an improvement over time, at first feeling life was not worth living, but later more or less reinvesting in life. Parents also reported that their children's deaths changed what they had once believed to be the purpose in life. I don't know whether these studies contradict each other or not; they weren't asking the same questions and their terms are vague. The researchers seemed to be implying that children give their parents a purpose for living, and of course children do. I'm unclear whether the researchers also implied that losing a child therefore means losing a reason to live.

For whatever reasons, in various ways, and to varying extents, the parents have disengaged. I suspect they'd agree with that early metaphor of mine: that I had expected to pay for my good life with my own death, not T.C.'s; that life is in that way a bad bargain—I've paid a fortune for dime-store junk. Diana, for instance, expects little from life or from other people. She doesn't care whether she has a reason to live, and she's not interested in her own death. Most of the parents, like moderate versions of Diana, became a little more remote. The parents noticed this disengagement in their jobs, or in their feelings about other people, or in the amount of interest they had in life.

Julia: "I think we've just gone day to day a lot of this time. I think energy comes from enthusiasm, and I think I lost a lot of basic enthusiasm for life. I don't think it'll all ever come back. In order to do what I want to do, I have to dredge up enthusiasm, and I mean, why bother? I have felt very, very old since she died. I'm serious. I didn't feel old the day before. Now, just very, very old, a hundred years old."

"Why do you think that is?" I asked.

"I don't enjoy life as much, not ever fully," she said. "I don't expect as much out of life. That feeling seems to me to make sense; I mean, I can understand it. And I don't agitate about it because I don't think it's going to change. I mean, life is not going to be whole again. I think it's just a fact."

Louise: "Have you ever reached the point where you hear terrible stories of wrecks or murders or death or illness, and you totally tune out and you have no feeling? I found that scary, not to have any compassionate feeling. It was like, so what? Another one? I don't think it touches—do you know what I'm trying to say? It just doesn't trigger. I used to get upset when I heard wonderful music, a sentimental song, but it doesn't even turn me on any more. I don't mean to be unkind but I don't have those deep sensitive feelings any more."

Ruth: "One of the life changes for me was, the year Leslie died, I was registered at Towson State. I was going to go back to school and be a teacher. That was my life's dream, to be a teacher. I was thirty-nine years old, and it was going to be an eight-year struggle, but I thought, 'I'm going to be fifty years old some day and this is what I want to do.' But you know, when Leslie died, that dream died. I don't have that commitment to get through that. I think I had that commitment when Leslie was here because then I thought I could do anything. Then. If you could say one expression that describes me, it would be that Leslie's death broke my spirit. I still cope, I go to work, I go to church. I hate to say it, but my heart isn't in it. I just don't think I have the heart for it any more."

Delores: "The biggest change in my life was maybe that I was always a happy type person, and content. And I don't feel that I'm a happy, content person any more. Larry was just a part of my life. When he died, this part died with him. It's part of my heart that's dead. It's just gone. You can't *ever* have it back. Some capability of being able to care so deeply about anything or anyone again. Life just sort of goes on. I'm still doing the same things, but I don't feel the same. We just—you know—tomorrow comes and tomorrow comes."

Loretta Marsh helps her brother at his job. I asked her if she was still doing the same job she had done when Mike died. "Yes, but not like I did. And my brother that I help out, he could tell you I used to be a go-getter. I tell him now, 'I'm sorry, I don't care.' I guess for the first two, maybe three years, I would go to work, come home, fix dinner, do the least housework, I didn't care. I still really don't care. I don't *care*. My friends tell me I'm withdrawing from people more than I ever did since I lost Mike. I don't really answer them directly, but I could look right at them and say, 'I don't care.' Maybe it's wrong, I don't know. It's wrong he was taken. Is it wrong for me to withdraw from people? I don't know."

Loretta's "I don't know's" have exactly the same inflection as her "I don't care's." Later, she added, "I look at my husband and think, 'If you're all right and Eddie's all right, I don't even care what happens to me.' It just don't bother me. I used to fear death. I don't."

After the first few interviews with parents, and hearing them say things like "tomorrow comes and tomorrow comes," and "I don't care what happens to me," I began asking an additional question: Do you feel differently about your own death?

A few parents seemed never to have been concerned about the issue and weren't now. "I think Shirley and I both have started to realize that we're not going to be together forever," said Leight Johnson. "But I don't think it has to do with Johnny's death. Just the stage of life."

"Do you feel the same about your own death?" I asked.

Though Leight volunteers for hospice work and spends a lot of time around dying people, he apparently hadn't thought about it: "I don't know quite how to answer it. I can't really say yes. I don't know that I do."

When I interviewed Brandt Jones, he had recently been diagnosed with prostate cancer; a year or so later, he died. "I know that I'm going to die," he said, then paused for a long time. "I guess I have reached the stage where I think that it's not going to be that far off. I don't think too much about my own death or what it's going to do. I hopefully have done preparation for making sure that Betty's financially OK. But I don't know of anything else that would be there as far as my own death is concerned."

I believed both Leight and Brandt because they knew what they were talking about. I suspect neither one thinks about his death much because they've more or less settled how they feel about it and are willing to let nature take care of the rest. Ruth wasn't dealing with death face-on, but she got the information that Leight and Brandt had in her own way.

"It's easy to say I don't fear death," she said. "But I wondered how accurate that was because I'm not faced with death. So I spoke to a friend at Compassionate Friends when she was first diagnosed with lung cancer. I said, 'We always think that facing death would be no problem now. Now that you're actually facing death, can you still say that?' And she said yes, she could. She said losing her son was much worse than the problems she was facing now. That confirmed it for me. And I don't believe I *do* mind dying, because I think, to me, with having two girls, and if I stayed here I could be with Laura and if I died tomorrow I could be with Leslie. I would hate to leave Laura, but then I hate to miss Leslie."

Some parents agree with Ruth and don't mind the idea of their deaths because they think they'll be with their children.

"I don't fear dying, and I think I'll see Lisa," said Sally. "And that's one thing to look forward to. I feel right now, not that I want to die, but it's not such a bad thing."

Walter Farnandis, at age seventy-two, has his gravestone already set out. "You're going to go sometime," he said, "and I'm going to be with James, though I'm not in any hurry to get there. Before, I had some fear of it. I'm not afraid at all of death. I think, suppose I'm wrong about being with James in heaven, at least I'm laying next to him at the Greenmount Cemetery. Close to him. I already have my stone up right next to his. The people out there couldn't believe I had a stone up already."

Louise agreed that death wouldn't be so bad with Michael there, but added a reservation she must have felt because of the way Michael died.

"I think I used to be more scared of what death would be like," she said. "That part of the fear has almost gone now. It's true that nobody's come back to say being dead is bad, but if Michael's there, what difference does it make? I only think about the *manner* in which I might die. *That's* what the gloomy thing is now. Because I visualize a lot, somebody standing there and holding a gun to the back of my head. And that is terrifying. Oh, I used to be afraid of flying—the plane might crash—and I'm still not mad for it, but what's the worst thing that can happen? The plane's going to crash and I'm going to die, and so what? I have a real so-what attitude about it."

Like Leight and Brandt, Julia as a social worker in pediatric oncology has had direct experience with death. Working with dying children, she said, has helped her "*really* grasp early on what is mortality, your own mortality. The fact that everyone's going to die, including me, I think I'm comfortable with that." Because of this, Julia said, Simone's death didn't change her view of her own death. Then she added, "But I'll *never* be comfortable with my child dying. I guess the only thing that's changed about my feelings about my death, I wish I had died instead of her. I still think about that. I wish I had gotten something terrible and died."

I still daydream scenarios where I am allowed to trade my death for T.C.'s, and in my daydreams I am all business: "Let me see him just when he gets on that train, and I'll get right on it instead." So I laughed and asked Julia if she also worked out scenarios in which she makes the trade.

"Absolutely," she said, laughing too, "absolutely. I think that's how most people must feel. I don't express this to people, but I'm sure there've been times when I'm not only comfortable with my death, I wouldn't even be real upset at all."

The parents were saying, in different ways and in so many words, that their children's inexplicable deaths made life seem relatively less interesting, less worth the investment, a bad bargain. And as a bad bargain, life won't be all that hard to give up.

These thoughts sound depressing. I think any right-minded psychotherapist hearing what these parents say—they can't be bothered to dredge up enthusiasm, they don't have deep, sensitive feelings any more, their hearts just aren't in it, they have a real so-what attitude about death, they wouldn't be real upset to be dying—would diagnose depression. Depression is, after all, one of the symptoms of grief. People expect to be depressed when they're grieving, and researchers expect the same. For the last thirty years, studies have found depression a normal part of grief. Though most of these studies were done within the first two years after the child's death, one study done in 1991, of parents whose children died of cancer, found the parents were as depressed seven years later as they had been two years later.

Nevertheless, ever since Freud wrote "Mourning and Melancholia," researchers have been trying to differentiate depression from grief without clear-cut, universally acknowledged success. In other words, they cannot with confidence tell the difference between the symptoms of depression and the effects of grief. Some researchers interpret the parents' thoughts and symptoms not as depression but as the change in attitude that inevitably accompanies such a loss.

I'm unsure what this latter means, but I agree that these parents aren't particularly depressed. When they were saying those depressing thoughts, most of them didn't sound as though they also felt the helplessness or hopelessness that are the foundations of depression. Instead they sound matter-of-fact, this-is-not-news. Occasionally they even talk about the depressing thoughts almost light-heartedly, as though a lesser investment in life were almost a relief. They talk with the same verbal shrugs with which they talked about their vulnerability. As Julia said, because she knows life isn't going to be whole again, she understands having these thoughts and doesn't agitate about them; they're just facts of life.

For myself, life might be a bad bargain, but I have no impulse to act on these depressing facts of life and do myself in, either physically or psychologically. And if I'm not going to act on the facts, I see little point in thinking about them. I can live with and around these facts; I can take pleasure and find interests, and I'm certain the other parents can too. I think the parents came to the interviews, answered my questions about their changed perspectives honestly and accurately, and then went home and ignored the whole business.

The knowledge of the facts, nevertheless, remains. I suspect it accounts for an odd phenomenon, another issue I hadn't known to ask about until the parents repeatedly brought it up. The parents seem subject to a kind of jumpiness, both a general distractability and a desire for distraction. One parent after another said they needed to keep busy, or they just can't be still, or they had trouble sleeping, or they could no longer concentrate. Delores Shoda's "I have to run" is an extreme example. Walter Farnandis said the secret in life was to keep busy so "you don't have your mind on what happened." Emily said free time is not good for her. Betty Jones said she reads books in bed or while riding in the car, because "I *want* to keep my mind busy, not dwelling on it."

One explanation for the jumpiness might be that the parents need distraction from the harshness of their memories and new perspectives. Another—because these symptoms are also the classic symptoms of anxiety—might be that the parents are acting out the anxiety that they otherwise deny.

Louise: "I always either have the television on and I'm not watching it, or I have the radio on and I'm not listening, from the time I walk into the house until I leave, because I just like the sound of the noise rather than me getting into my own inner thoughts. Do you experience that? Do you have trouble concentrating? I still have, I find that my concentration before Michael was murdered has never come full-speed ahead."

Estelle Lemaitre: "I have very bad sleeping habits. I wake up very early and I become hyper to get started. And I guess I'm hyper all day long. I can go to sleep very, very easily in the evening, but I don't stay asleep. I feel sometimes like I wake up ten times a night."

Estelle is the person who gives short answers followed by long silences. After one of these silences, I said, "Sounds like your mind is going."

"Yeah, constantly," she said.

"Any idea what that's about?" I asked.

"No," she said. "I went to the doctor's one time after Robby died—I guess it was a year afterwards—because of the bad sleeping habits. I was just totally worn out. Even now, if I'm watching TV I have to jump up and just go to another room, maybe clear the kitchen sink, I don't know, take the trash out, and then I can go back and sit again. Even if I'm in the car, I remove my seat belt, I open the window, I just do *something*. It may last two minutes, and it passes."

Ginny Mitchell: "I can't read. I used to love to read and now I find myself rereading the same thing fifty times. And I'm unorganized. I don't know whether I was *that* unorganized before Joel died, that I'll start on something and then before I realize, I'm on to something else. I just can't seem to do as much in the home as I used to. I don't know, maybe I'm running, getting away from the home. I had always been active outside and I think maybe I do more so. So that I wouldn't be *there*."

Julia: "I'm a lot more easily distracted by inner thoughts. I have more trouble really sticking with something. Also, my job is the kind where you get in earlier and earlier and you leave later and later. And I'm sure that I've used that as a way of avoiding difficult things, of not thinking. I mean, there are some days—a lot of days—where you really have to think about everything and everybody else."

They sound as if they're talking about quicksand or some irresistible magnetic field whose force they evade. They're not getting into their inner thoughts, not having their minds on what happened, not dwelling. Truly, even though everything looks different, they don't think about it.

Besides disengagement and distractibility, the biggest change caused by the parents' new perspective is a changed set of priorities. Mitch Dudnikov explained this change like the scientist he is: "Everything started over—the zero point was Marc's death—with, did a thing mean more or less?"

The zero point is the child's death and is embodied in the images of the child's death. The parents' registers have been reset to zero, and in Mitch's words, everything starts over. Stand at the zero point, and everything looks different.

"Most of us," said Sally, "we don't think it'll ever happen to us. And when it does, you just have different priorities. It changes you totally. You're a different person. I'm not saying you're a better person or a worse person. To put it into specifics? I can't. It's just that I *feel* like a different person."

I'd asked Sally what her definition of recovery was.

"It's just little things," she said, "little things, to enjoy them. People say, 'Did you have a good summer? What did you do?' Well, come to think of it, I didn't do a thing interesting. But I had a *great* summer. The weather was delightful. Nothing bad happened."

Sally started laughing at her new definition of a great summer: "Nothing bad happened."

Chapter 15

ANNE PERKINS' PRIORITIES

❦

Eight years ago, Anne Perkins was a state legislator. Her son, Robert, had just finished college and was working so he could take a year off and travel around the world; he was going to start in Asia. Meanwhile, he took a short trip with a friend, drove too late, got tired, and drove off the road and hit a parked tractor-trailer. Anne was not forthcoming with details, except to say that Robert wasn't wearing his seat belt, and "I was one of the sponsors of seat belt legislation. And dammit, the last thing I said to him when he left in that car was 'Put your seat belt on.'"

Other than that, she blames no one: "Yes, he was driving too late and he should have pulled over and slept. But I drive too late, everybody does, he was just being human. I never had any interest in finding out whether the truck driver had parked too close to the highway—it just didn't make any difference."

Shortly after Robert died, Anne and her husband, who had been having marriage difficulties for years, divorced. She has two daughters, both grown and married.

Anne is a lawyer. When I first interviewed her, two years ago, she was still a state legislator, but that didn't last. Within a year of the interview, she had resigned her office to teach English for a year in China. When she returned from China, she took an interim job, then a year later, resigned that job to advise provincial legislatures in South Africa on setting up new governments. I interviewed her again on a trip home from South Africa.

She began by saying that she could tell me only how she had changed since Robert's death, but not why. Perhaps, she said, the changes were not because of Robert's death, but because of her divorce, or her age, or living alone, or any other of her life's circumstances. "Fair enough," I said, and began my questions.

Few people answer questions directly, but Anne's answers were unusually indirect. She was smart and perceptive, but her logic was seldom obvious. Her answers branched from one subject to the next, as though answers were not isolated entities but connected to all other answers. Each answer seemed to be a small piece of a mosaic, and to understand what she was saying, I had to put together the whole mosaic. Probably she talks like this because this is how her mind works. But the effects of grief are subtle and complicated, and what she was trying to say was also pushing the limitations of the language.

"People say having a child die is unnatural," I began. "Do you know what that means?"

"There's nothing in my mind about the natural process of birth and death and order," she said, contradicting what many other parents had said. "I don't care. Unnatural doesn't register with me. What does register is this physical, spiritual attachment to a child. They're so much part of your total being."

"Can you describe the feeling of loss?" I asked.

"It changes over time," she said. "The pain was at first almost physical. It was something almost physically taken out of you. And then the feeling of loss changed. Close to his death, his spiritual presence was very present in friends and things he did and places he'd been. It's kind of like a recipe, if you put A, B, and C together—there's a combination of people and things that can make it exactly like Robert, and over time that has faded and not been therefore as painful. Over time I did feel that spiritual presence of Robert passing away. It seemed like it drifted away."

Understanding what people mean is always more difficult on the printed page than in person, and during the interview I thought I was more or less following her. I think she was saying that what impressed her about Robert's death was the extent to which he was a part of her, both physically and spiritually. And as a result, the feeling of loss was also both physical—"something almost physically taken out of you"—and spiritual. By spiritual, Anne seems to mean "of the spirit"; she's talking about her sense of Robert's spirit, of his presence. When Robert's physical presence was gone, his spiritual presence stayed for a while in people with whom he had been associated: certain combinations of people and things had the power to evoke Robert's presence exactly. But those associations became painful. And in any case, Robert's presence in the associations began drifting away.

To make sure I was getting it, I asked, "Your sense of Robert's presence is also fading?"

"Yes," she said. "I think of it as how dandelion seeds, when you blow them close to the ground, they'll cling to things and then float off, cling to little pieces of grass and then they'll blow away. I feel like part of Robert's being clings to things. But eventually it blows away. That image is not a violent, angry thing, which his death was. It's more a gentle, flowing, natural thing."

This wasn't the first time I heard Anne say something like this. I know her because she lives across the street from me, and one night, just after a rainstorm and just before dark, she was out sitting on the ground planting flowers, up to her elbows in mud. I walked over to see what she was up to, and the conversation came around to grief. She told me she felt that with time, Robert's presence was pulling away. She said it felt like Michelangelo's painting of the creation of Adam—God's arm outstretched to Adam, Adam reaching back to God but pulling away. Anne sat there in the dark, slapping mosquitoes with muddy hands; we were both crying.

I didn't know then whether she meant that she feels more distant from Robert, and I'm still not sure. If that's what she meant, she was the only parent to say so. Maybe she means that those things that were associated with Robert are not now as associated, don't evoke his presence as strongly. She clearly misses Robert's presence, whatever makes him recognizable even without his body. So what to do about that?

"I remember the day after he died," she went on. "I went for a walk by myself and everybody got all upset and went out to find me. I remember at the time, worrying about will there ever be joy again, worrying about the feeling that joy is just going to pass. I found even in the months after Robert died, to survive, I had to take time out from just falling apart all the time. I'd wipe out everything in my mind about being sad and grieving. I've heard talk from psychiatrists saying it's a good thing to focus your grief, and maybe on the grave. I felt like I almost focused on my need for happiness.

"That has continued in different ways," she went on. "That feeling, sort of an abandonment, just free, just carefree enjoying, I find very difficult to have with people with whom the association with Robert is so strong. When I am most happy, it's not in situations where this sadness is just, just too much. I don't feel like it's avoidance. The word I use is 'managing.' There are things I don't need to torture myself with, and I shouldn't."

So, one way of keeping joy from passing was to manage her involvement with those people and things that evoked Robert too strongly. In fact, like other parents, Anne has disengaged. The word she uses is "disconnected": "The disconnectedness is interesting," she said.

Part of doing her legislative job well, she said, was "being out and around and having people feel you're available. I used to enjoy this, but there was a real clear point when that stopped. Now if I go to a political thing, I do what I have to do, and I leave. I feel much more disconnected. For a year, that was fine; then it wasn't fine any more. I should go out to community meetings much more than I do. I think my feeling is, I really don't care about being there. It doesn't bother me in the least that I felt that way. And now, I find much more than I did in the past, going into a room with people I know, and just feeling disconnected. When I do connect, it's when the conversation is most objective. Men like to talk to me about politics—I'm a curiosity, a woman politician—and they like that gossip. So that will be where I connect, not necessarily talking to the women in ways I used to talk to the women. Women talk about family, how are you feeling. Sometimes that's harder than others. It's a very objective conversation now. I do feel that disconnected, isolated feeling.

Then she made one of her logic jumps. "The disconnectedness goes along with life priority stuff," she said, "what is and isn't important. This kind of horrible thing can set the priorities up real straight. It happens real quick. It puts into perspective what's important. I find what's important real clear; you've seen the ultimate and it just makes everything else just line up. It's not just what's bad and what's really bad. It's also what's good and what's really good. And there is a peace that comes with that."

In short, her new perspective disconnected her from other people, made her feel that she stood apart from them. And standing in a different place, having a new perspective, clarified her priorities.

"If you go through something like this, you have an edge on people," she explained. "I've done something that, no matter what someone's life has been, they've *never* done. I didn't want to do it, but I did, and here I am. I find being able to sort out what's important real easy. It makes decisions easy. In my job, there are lots of pressures to do certain things, but it's real clear to me. I just do what I think's right and I don't worry about whether some legislative leader likes me or whether I get some appointment. I find it easier to know how I want to be, and that's it. It does sometimes give me a feeling of—I can put it really crassly—'to hell with you, I don't give a shit,'" she quoted herself telling some invisible legislative leader. "'I know things you don't know and this doesn't matter. Push me, I don't care.'"

She started laughing at her tough talk. "You can say it in a lot of ways other than the way I just said it. Or you can just *be* that way and people know what you're saying to them. It makes people nervous. I was always independent to begin with, but there's another ingredient here. I put it back to being able to sort out what's important."

She lumped all these effects of Robert's death—her disconnection, her changed perspective, her newly lined-up priorities—together, as though they were a single effect. Another effect, she said, was one particular priority.

"The other thing is," she said, "when you have something like this, you appreciate, you value life more. When children die right at the edge of adulthood, like our children did, there's no other time when life is so exuberant and promising and on the threshold. Life is with capital letters. Life was poured into them and now at this age is the time for them to pour back out. If you give up living, give up life, and I can't say this . . ."

Anne, who had been talking fast, suddenly began to cry. A minute later, she collected herself and went on.

"There's something *wrong* about that. Because they lost life and you should value it. And if you value *their* life . . ." Anne began crying again, stopped again, and continued.

"If you value their life, you should value your own. It's not that I feel like I have to live a life that he would have lived. It's just that he was so *full* of life. It brings home so vividly the value of life. And then you make the next step: the value of their life has got to be the value of everybody's life, and particularly, it's got to be your own. And you should *live* it. And in a way that isn't halfway living it. I mean, you can't just fold up. I felt like if I just folded up I would not be valuing life. It's important to live it well and figure out how to try and do that."

Anne had said that immediately after Robert died, she'd worried about joy passing, and that "just carefree enjoying, I find very difficult to have with people with whom the association is so strong." This is not to say that Anne then leapt up out of her grief: "There's always this sadness," she said at one point. "Even when you're happy, you've still got this sadness. I'm just dragging around this little bit that's sad. In a way, it's a handicap that we've got. It's there, and I think it always will be." But Anne put together her desire for joy and her lined-up priorities and figured out how to live well.

"It would have been two and a half years after Robert died," she said. "During the legislative session that year, I think I was depressed, and this must have been noticed by a couple friends because I remember two of them taking me out to dinner, and tears and all this stuff."

During the dinner, the friends mentioned that their daughter was in a cultural exchange program in China that summer.

"I'd heard about the program before," Anne said, "so I just called, and had the interview, and got into it. I operate this way, on my gut instincts."

"What about it appealed to you?" I asked.

"It was," she began, then hesitated before going on, "an adventure. And I like doing things to help people. It was completely different from anything I'd ever done. Maybe instinctively it was just that there was no pain attached to it. Anyway, I didn't have anybody needing me or depending on me, so I could go away for five weeks. Not many people can, so uniquely I can do something like this."

So that summer when the legislative session was in recess, Anne went to China, returning that fall. "It was real clear to me after I came back, I just felt better about everything. Things kind of took off—I was happier and I could cope with things better. Until I felt better, I wasn't able to see how bad I'd been. It's a funny thing to me, because whereas right after Robert died, these associations of people who were close was comforting. Now it's more like the people I've met doing the China job, I can have more fun with and they don't have the memories attached to them that remind me of my sadness."

So the following summer, she went back to China. "I took nine high school kids who have been studying Chinese, and we had two classes of Chinese middle school students. We taught them English, they taught us songs and martial arts, and we got to be friends. Cultural exchange. It went for four weeks. It was new and intellectually interesting to me, and I have enjoyed the people I've done it with.

It's not associated with anything that's sad. It made a break with un-happiness."

So Anne saved up her money, and the next summer she quit the legislature, rented out her house, and went to China to teach. She came back a year later.

"When I came back from China," she said, "I had to get a new job. I could have run for reelection, but I had been through four campaigns; I just didn't have the energy. One thing is real clear, that there was a difference in the energy level for that job before and after Robert died. I just couldn't get myself up to—you know how a sports person visualizes himself doing this perfect dive?—I couldn't visualize myself knocking on doors eight hours a day. I loved that work, but it was like I would be going back and doing the same thing. So. So I came back, looked different places for different jobs."

She told how she met someone who worked for a Washington, D.C., institute that advised emerging democracies on setting up governments, how that seemed interesting to her, how she interviewed for a short-term assignment and got sent to Namibia for three weeks, came back again, and continued to look for jobs. When she got tired of looking, she said, she took a job with people she liked, though she found the job "a little bit boring." So when the Washington institute called her back with a longer-term assignment in South Africa, "obviously that was a good fit, so that was it." And once again, in the space of two weeks, she quit her job, left her house in the hands of a boarder, said good-bye, and went to Africa.

"Are you the kind of person who picks up with two weeks' notice and goes to China and South Africa?" I asked.

"I think I've always done things a little bit out of the mold," she said. "I think I always have had a little bit of the adventurer in me."

Anne does not present the usual picture of an adventurer. She's calm, a little diffident, and always seems comfortable where she is. She says so too: "I've always taken time to sit and stare. I can work in my office all day or read a book or watch television, unenergetic kinds of things. But I do get bored. I don't particularily like routine."

"I'm impressed with how unusual these jobs are," I said. "You know, most people of our age, middle-age, are settling in."

"I do feel ambivalent," she said, "like I should be finding a job and staying here and putting roots down. But on the other hand, I'm choosing a job that is more interesting. All the people in this job," and she began laughing, "they're all twenty-year-olds. It's not that I want to be with twenty-years-olds. But that kind of—just really having fun with new experiences—I was missing that. When your kids are in their early twenties, they can be a lot of fun. It's like you finally can relate to them on a mature, adult level, and you can just have fun. I used to have *fun* with Robert. We would go to the movies, go out to a Japanese restaurant, eat sushi, he loved that. Robert was a lot of fun. So in some ways, the things I'm doing are a generation younger than what I am."

"Do you feel closer to Robert in these new jobs, when you're having these new experiences?" I asked.

"It's clear to me that Robert's presence is there, but it's hard to explain it. I think, 'This is something Robert would have loved to do; wouldn't he have had fun with this.' It's just hard to explain. There is a presence connected to this."

"When do you feel his presence?" I asked.

"That's very interesting," she said. "In a way, that's the most—that's very interesting. I think that's where he's most present."

"Where?" I asked.

"In things he would have liked to have been doing," she said.

"Like what?"

"Like some of the things I'm doing," she said slowly. "It's true. I'll be doing some weird thing in Africa and I'll think, 'Hey, Robert would like this.' He liked to have fun. He liked to do adventures."

She went on, talking about China and Africa, and when the interview ended, she walked me to the door. She said that only at these ends of the earth was she "separated from things that had too much reminder clinging to them, too many things that made it too difficult." Only there, she said, could she "flourish."

206

Chapter 16

SURFACE DITTIES AND CARPE DIEM

Changes in Priorities

∞

When the parents' perspectives changed, so did their priorities. Nearly every parent said this, and in nearly those words. "This kind of horrible thing can set the priorities up real straight," Anne Perkins had said. "It happens real quick. It puts into perspective what's important. I find what's important real clear; you've seen the ultimate and it just makes everything else just line up."

Anne's ultimate view is the same as Mitch Dudnikov's "zero point." Mitch, before he retired, was an industrial chemist: "Great, I'm grinding limestone, I'm helping customers with little petty little *stupid* questions. I *liked* chemistry. But I felt, what the *hell* am I doing? I got the self-satisfaction of making a better product, but so what? The meetings, they were all jockeying for position. That to me is trivial and a pain in the neck. I'd just say to myself, 'Young people are dying, not only Marc, wonderful kids are dying, and these guys are worrying about stupid little things.' Everything started over—the zero point was Marc's death—did a thing mean more or less? Very few things after Marc's death meant more."

The child's death becomes the zero point, the reference point, against which everything else is compared. As a result, priorities are recomputed. Or change the metaphor slightly: the zero point works something like the center of a yardstick, where half the yardstick is less than zero, and half, more. Those things on the plus side of zero mean more, and those on the minus side, less.

The parents all said that, in general, their priorities had changed, then talked about specific cases of those changes. They mixed the cases together, talked about both sides of the zero point at once. They agreed with Mitch that compared to a child's death, most things meant less, so they were particularly articulate about the minus side.

Moreover, like Mitch, they often talked about their recalculated priorities in terms of changes in their feelings about other people. I think this particular change differs from the changes toward other people talked about in an earlier chapter. In both kinds of changes, the parents feel closer to some people and more distant from others. But where the change talked about earlier was imposed by the loss of common ground, by the parents' hypersensitivity, and by other people's fears, this particular change is a result of the parents' new zero point.

Specifically, the parents feel more distant from those people whose priorities seem now to be, in the parents' words, trivial, petty, and inconsequential: Ruth Banick's phrase is "surface little ditties." In fact, the lack of shared priorities becomes just one more piece of common ground now lost. This is what Anne meant by saying, "The disconnectedness goes along with life priority stuff."

Brandt Jones: "I stayed with the Scout troop for three or four years after Bruce passed away. But it was hard dealing with the kids. Because I could see where they were getting an opportunity that my son would have loved, and they didn't appreciate what they had. And some of the fathers didn't appreciate what *they* had. And those things grated on me. You don't want to say, 'Look, stupid, that boy may not *be* here. You'd better take advantage of it that he is.' So you say to yourself, 'This guy is stupid, but I'm not going to change his outlook.' It takes a disaster to change somebody's outlook."

Then Brandt switched subjects, from people who didn't know

what was important, to his discomfort with people because he does know what's important. "When you've gone through this experience and other people are talking about mundane things, you don't say anything but you think, 'Why are they so worried about this, when *these* things could happen?' But they have no knowledge that these things happen—*we* didn't have any knowledge of it before it happened. But now you're the odd man out because you're sitting in a group of people and they're talking about things that—" and Brandt pantomimed his own reaction, throwing his hands out—"Who cares? *Who cares?* I get the feeling that some people are just not looking at the big picture. I experienced a similar thing when I first went in the navy, went overseas, and came back, and saw my friends who had not left Baltimore. And they're talking York Road, Hampden, the bar. And I want to talk about Oslo and Lisbon and the World's Fair in Brussels. This is a similar situation. You've been away and you have this knowledge in your head that says what's important. You've become worldly and they're dealing with Baltimore."

Emily said that at athletics and games, she'd lost her "killer instinct," her "competitive edge," because she no longer felt winning was important. "You've lost a lot more than anything you might be losing now," she said. "You put one against the other, there's no comparison. Your perspective changes drastically, and that alters what's important to you. It's not the same as it was."

"How are you different?" I asked, and she gave me an answer that must set a new record for internal contradiction.

"I overlook things I wouldn't before," she said. "I'm a kinder person than I was before. I don't put up with a lot of bullcrap. I see things more on a long-term basis than on an immediate basis. I try and enjoy life as much as I can. That's not to say I always enjoy it that much. You're on cocaine if you're happy all the time. You can't live in this world and make believe."

I didn't try to impose logic on what she said and assumed she meant all of it, contradictory or not. Instead, I went on with my list of questions: "Do you feel more distant toward other people?"

"Yes," she said immediately. "Did you notice how long it took me to answer that? I'm definitely more distant from people. I love our friends, but sometimes I care less what's going on."

"Why is that?" I asked.

"Well, you know," she said, "different things are important. We have one couple we're friendly with, we've known them for a hundred years, *nice* people, and yet I don't enjoy going out with them terribly much, because conversation is always about the past, who's going out with whom from high school. There's nothing *wrong* with it—I don't want to go out and discuss Nietzsche—but I don't bother with pettiness or a lot of bull. I haven't the patience for it."

Later, Emily went on to say that, since her daugher's death, some things were also more important.

"Life can be snuffed out in an instant," she said. "Chapter one is closed, chapter two begins. I think that if we're smart, we learn to live with that in mind. You keep your connections so that if anything happens to you or your connected person, there's no regrets. I mean, living life keeping death in mind. That's the type of thing, when I say I'm a changed person, that's what I've learned."

Ruth Banick: "I don't care as much. And maybe that removed a lot of inhibitions. I always say to myself when I get to a tough situation—like I'm going on a new job interview—I'll say, 'Ruth, what could this do to you that hasn't already been done?' Well, then I *plunge* ahead and do the best I can do. It removed a lot of junk from my life. I hear a lot of people at work saying this and that, and I want to say, 'Now stop and think. What does that really matter?'"

Then Ruth explained more about the people at work. "I feel like there's distance between other people and me, because I don't feel like they've faced the same threatening things in life. And I'm glad they haven't. But . . . I think a lot of things are such surface little ditties. I work with a woman—I'm not making any moral judgments; I wouldn't be in any position to do that—but she's living with a guy and he's an absolute dirtball. And I said one day, 'Jane, you're an attractive woman, you're educated, you have a wonderful son and he married a girl you love. You have one negative in your life and it's this dirtball. Why don't you think of all the things you have and get rid of him?'"

"So do you feel like you know some things other people don't?" I asked.

"Of course, I always feel like I do," she said. "I feel like a lot of surface diddley things have been removed from me. And I feel like I'm dealing more with life basics."

"And what are those life basics?" I asked.

"I think I value people. There is *so* much need out there, people who are hurting. And I think, when I leave this life, I want to leave it with no regrets. That I helped where I could help, and then when I go, I'm not looking back."

"What kind of help?" I asked.

"My daughter, Laura, is an attorney for abused and neglected children," said Ruth. "She told me about this little girl at Spring Grove State Hospital who was thirteen. And this girl has no family. I can't go see her, because by Laura representing her, anything she says to me I might have to say in court. So I can't see her, but I send her things. Christmas and her birthday, holidays, and sometimes on anniversaries for *me* that are hard—I think about how she has no family and I don't feel as sorry for myself on that day. She doesn't know me. She probably never will. I am a secret pal."

"Did the hospital set this up?" I asked.

"No, no, I wish they would," she said. "It's hard sometimes to think of things I *can* send her, because I can't send her anything she could hurt herself with. Books, and she likes hair things so I send her a lot of hair things, and bubble gum. I think in a way she's as much in prison as I am. She can't control what's happened to her and I can't either. I'm not a wealthy person and never will be, but that seemed to turn the occasion around from one of total devastation to 'Well, what can I do with this?' I think that's the only real peace of heart you get."

Leight Johnson: "It changes your sense of what's important and what isn't. I remember maybe six months after Johnny died, a friend of mine was moving out of town and I wanted to take some pictures

211

of him and his family. I went over to his house, his phone rang, his son had a fender-bender with the car and called to tell his father everybody's OK. This guy was so upset about it: 'Oh my God, there's been an accident.' The first thing I said was, 'Was anybody hurt?' 'No, but good Lord, the fender.' And he went on in this way for a while, and then said, 'Oh, I can't do this picture session, I'm just too upset about it.' I thought, 'I had a son killed six months ago, and he's having hysterics because his fender got bent.' I got so mad at him. Never did take his picture. It irritates me when people make so much of inconsequential things."

"What sorts of things are not inconsequential?" I asked.

"Life and death," he said, "not much else really. Unless you're hungry."

Leight's irritation was not so much at the man's insensitivity as at his short-sightedness, his myopic inability to see that his car was less important than his son. This is what I think Leight, Ruth, and Emily and all the rest of the parents are saying: if the zero point divides what's less important from what's more, and if the zero point is the child's death, then what's important is whatever is related to life, death, and love. Anything less, the parents say, is trivial.

This division of priorities into only two categories, "life-death-and-love" and "trivial," is a little radical. I feel the same radicalness about my own priorities: any given thing is either worth dying for or it's not on the list. With time, I've become more moderate and expanded my categories to include "fairly important," but I do this consciously. Still, when I find myself interested in when my editor is going to bother printing the article he commissioned, I also find myself easily losing interest. The radical division is still there, and I am as irritated at other writers complaining about editorial delays as Leight was with his friend's myopia.

This irritation with which Leight and I and the other parents talk about other people's surface ditties seems to shade easily into anger: "stupid," "dirtball," "bullcrap." Leight went on to say that if he did take his friend's picture, he would light his friend's face like a horror movie bad guy, from below. This particular anger didn't seem related to the parents' anger at what they saw as other people's insensitivity, which seemed to be over some sort of social contract they felt that other people had broken. In fact, I doubt that this anger is at other people at all. It is more general; it sounds more like the parents' anger toward God. I think the anger is at variants of God—at life, at fate, at the way things are—and just spills over onto the ordinarily imperfect people who don't know what the parents now know.

Delores Shoda: "Our family doctor that helped us when Larry died, we don't see him any more." Delores went on to tell about their doctor and his family who were "like part of our family," and the doctor decided to leave his wife and children. "He had some problems and put his family through a lot of hurt. I look at him and I think how good he was with us, and then I saw his children crying—his daughter was talking about suicide. They had to put her in therapy, and his wife had to see somebody too. But he said he had to do these things. I said, 'You don't put anybody through pain like that just for your own self-ego. If you bring children into this world, you're not to hurt them. They're your responsibility first. You come second.'"

"I get angry," said Octavia Pompey, "especially when I ride down the street and see these young people hanging on a corner doing absolutely nothing constructive, selling their drugs and doing their drugs. And I get angry. I say, 'Why are they still alive?' They are contributing absolutely nothing to society. But then I say, 'Somewhere these kids have mothers too and they would be just as devastated if something happened to them as I was.' And I try, I really try to believe that."

Mitch said, almost identically, "I have my little moments that I get angry. Every time I read about another drunk driver who was let out on probation or they revoked his license and he continued to drive, I say, 'Why does something like that have to live?' I'm not looking for the good in him. I say, 'Why did he live and my son die? Why?' I get these little anger spurts, then it goes away. I just let the anger abate."

I've listened to parents at meetings of Compassionate Friends, who, years after their child's death, can talk of nothing except their anger at the iniquity of the judicial system or of the police force or of the medical profession. I don't know if they talk like this only in the safety of Compassionate Friends, or if their lives are truly full of anger. For the parents I interviewed, however, this general anger didn't seem to dominate their lives; it came and went. It was rarely more than, as Mitch said, little anger spurts. Still, the anger did seem readily available, just below the surface, as though the spurts came from an underlying ocean.

For the parents, talking about priorities almost always evoked anger. I feel this same underlying anger about my own new priorities and don't know why. Maybe the parents' priorities had been their children, and the parents are angry about the deaths of those child/priorities. Maybe the parents think what's important is now so clear, they get angry when it isn't equally clear to everyone else. Maybe relatively unreligious people don't get angry at God for injustice, but they had similar faith in life, and therefore get angry at life.

Sometimes I suspect, for no good reason, that the anger is a permutation of the parents' continuing love for their children. Maybe the love, frustrated because it can't be expressed, turns to anger. Sometimes I think I could fill every atom in the universe with anger, then the anger seems to turn into pain, then the pain into love. So maybe I suspect that anger and love are the same because they feel similarly infinite.

The intensity that sounds like anger when the parents talk about the minus side of the zero point, sounds like excitement when they talk about the plus side.

Leight had said that the only things important were life and death. He added hunger, but it, too, is life and death; I added love. The parents agreed on this, of course, but each parent had a slightly different definition of life, death, and love. For Ruth, it was her secret pal; for Emily, it was her connected people. For some parents, their other children and their spouses became even more important; for others, people who need help or people who have been kind.

The definition of life, death, and love about which the parents were most excited was a certain attitude toward life that Walter Levin called his "carpe diem philosophy." "I'm adopting more of a carpe diem philosophy," he said, "that's 'seize the day,' 'live for the moment.'" For Anne Perkins, a carpe diem philosophy meant living adventurously, "flourishing." For Ruth, it meant leaving life with no regrets. For Emily, it meant living life while keeping death in mind. I wondered what Walter meant, and asked him indirectly: did he spend money differently?

"Well, I'll tell you," he said, "it's a funny thing you should ask that question."

And at this point he started talking so fast, I couldn't understand him. Whatever he was saying, however, it wasn't about money. I think he was talking about eating sensibly and watching his cholesterol. At any rate, he ended a string of blurred words by shouting, "Peanut butter. Crackers, sandwiches. I say, the hell with it. I say, 'I want it, damn it, I'm going to eat it, peanut butter. And that's it.'"

Walter calmed down a little: "I assume that attitude translates into the financial too. Things were tight when Merrill was growing up. I always, in myself, feel bad that he couldn't go to some of the places that I can now afford to go to. Or cars, that type thing. Yes, I've spent money more, even aside from the fact that I earn more. There's no question about that."

"Is that related to Merrill's death, or just getting older?" I asked.

"I think it may have some relevance to his death," he said. "Again, using that example of the peanut butter. I mean, if I want something, I basically say, 'What the hell.' I say, 'Who cares?'"

I think all the parents were aware of a carpe diem philosophy, though they meant slightly different things by it. "Whatever I have, I seem to appreciate more, let's put it that way," said Walter's wife, Elaine. "I don't think I ever was before. I was a 'gimme, I want' person. I still am, certainly. But not as much as I used to be. I'm sort of grateful for whatever it is."

"This sounds like a cliché," said Lydia Frasca, "but I think I appreciate simple things in life more. At nighttime, Tommy, my thirteen-year-old son, still wants me to walk him upstairs, say a few things before he goes to bed. I treasure the time. Because life's too short. My daughter had twenty-two hours of life, that's it. And when I think of Tommy, he's not promised to me forever. So I want to take time."

I asked Joan Gresser, "Do you have the same energy for every-day life?"

"I'm fifty-five years old, no, I don't," she said.

"So if you've lost energy, it's for natural, age-related reasons, not because of Stephen's and Teddy's deaths?"

"Yeah, absolutely," she said.

"Is there anything you have more energy for?" I asked.

"Tap dancing," she said. "I *love* tap dancing. I love to dance and I love tap dancing the most, and every Wednesday night our tap class is at six-fifteen, and I come home from work and drive in that horrible rush hour traffic on I-695. I get there and I'm dead I'm dead I'm dead, I'm going through menopause, and man, I get my leotard on and I am ten years old. I'm one of the oldest in the class, and these youngsters, they cannot keep up with me. Life is today, and that's it."

Nickie Copinger: "You learn to cherish minutes and hours and days more than you did before. And if you feel like you want to do something, you know now you might not know what to expect the next day, so you do it, you do it now."

Julia Marcus's son, Phil, is grown up and away from home. "I truly do value more my son and my husband, Jake. We don't take *anything* for granted. I'll tell you one thing—we never, never, never, even if somebody's going around the corner to the grocery store, not a one of us doesn't say, 'I love you.' I mean, we never got to tell Simone that before she died. Phil does the same thing, which always amazes me. I felt kind of funny at first doing it, but I'll do it no matter how many people are in the room. So does Jake, so does Phil."

"What do you think you appreciate most now?" I asked.

"I think what I have I fully appreciate, a lot more than I ever did," she said. "And I think that I have become able to really think about things more thoroughly than before."

"Do you have an example?" I asked.

"I'm not good about putting things into words," she said. "I just feel like I got another layer of understanding of things."

"What kinds of things?" I asked.

"*Anything,*" she said. "I enjoy art a lot more than I used to. I've always enjoyed going to art museums but I never *really fully* appreciated it. I think I have a better understanding of what I'm looking at than I did before. I just think everything is more *rich.*"

"Isn't that odd, that one of the effects of your daughter's death is that life is richer?" I asked.

"Isn't it," she answered. "Some of the things I say sound crazy. You just don't treat life as lightly, and if you don't treat things lightly, they do become richer."

Julia was the person who also said, "I don't enjoy life as much, not ever fully. I don't expect as much out of life. I don't like it as much." She doesn't expect much of life and life is richer? I doubt that Julia is contradicting herself. Not expecting much of life, not liking it, is not the same as treating life lightly. Not treating life lightly is the full meaning of "carpe diem": pay as much attention to each day as you would to your last day.

Julia figured out how to see life, or parts of it anyway, as rich. She appreciates things more; Elaine, Nickie, and Lydia said the same, and so did other parents.

I think they've found a way, as have the other parents, of seeing what in life is good. Everyone wants to believe that life is, on the whole, good, that things work out, that everything's going to be all right. The death of a child makes that belief seem silly; the new perspective is harsh and cold. Those things on the plus side of the zero point, the things in life that are good, also seem to be an antidote for the new perspective.

That is, I don't deny the hard facts of life for a minute. So finding the good parts of life seems comforting, a relief. I feel as though I can relax a little and trust something. I feel as though I can find some direction in which all this love can move. For me, finding the good parts of life does not feel like a Pollyannaish looking on the bright side; it feels like being able to breathe. I think that's what Anne meant when she said that she knows what's good and what's really good, and there's a peace that comes with that. It's why Ruth said helping other people is the only real peace of heart you get. And Emily said, out of the blue, in no context whatever, that peace is the best thing you can wish a parent who's lost a child.

The priorities on the plus side of the zero point must be a way of recovering faith. The child's death was senseless and life is no bargain, but not everything is bad. Maybe the good things in life become associated with, or a conduit for, the child's goodness and the goodness of what the parent felt about the child.

If a zero point means starting your priorities from scratch so that anything less than life, death, and love is trivial, and if finding the plus side of the zero point is the only peace of heart you get, and if all these are the effects of a child's death, then I'm also impressed by the magnitude of those effects. As I said in the introduction, one of my reactions to T.C.'s death was surprise: I simply had no idea how much he meant to me. I'm still surprised. These parents' lives have been swept clean, and the parents are reconstructing them using whatever works. What are children, that their deaths have such an effect?

Chapter 17

WALTER LEVIN

∞

Walter Levin, a lawyer for a state union organization, is nearing retirement. I interviewed him because when I interviewed his wife, Elaine, she talked nearly as much about Walter as she did about herself. According to Elaine, sixteen years after their son's death, Walter is still fundamentally damped down, disengaged. "As much as he does," she said, "and he does a great deal, he's not 100 percent there. He was *never* 100 percent after that." She told me I ought to interview him, so I asked Walter, and Walter agreed.

Walter fidgeted through the whole interview, playing with paperclips and rubber bands, sorting through his desk drawer, looking out the window of his office, scrooching around in his squeaky desk chair. He could have been nervous because he didn't want to be interviewed, but he seemed happy to talk, so I think probably he just fidgets.

He also cried, off and on, through the whole interview. The only other person who cried in that way was Marge Ford. Neither seemed to be crying from some catastrophic release of emotion; they just cried quietly while they talked.

As you would expect of a lawyer, Walter talked both fluently and carefully. He answered questions with the completeness of a prepared statement. He told me, however, that answering completely was difficult for him: "I want to tell you something; it's very hard for a lawyer to talk. We train witnesses to only answer the question and not to elaborate. We'd say, 'Do you know the color of that wall?' And they'd say, 'White.' That's the wrong answer. The answer is, 'Yes, I know the color of that wall.' You're supposed to answer the question directly—you don't volunteer anything."

But he overcame the difficulty so well, I didn't have to ask too many questions.

"Merrill was our first child—we had two girls after Merrill—and he was an exceptional child; he was quick, he learned everything. I really wasn't with him at home, my wife was. Later in life, very frankly, he developed into the kind of person I hoped to have been. Just a marvelous personality, great in sports—which I never was—good sense of humor, smart, well-liked by his peers, just an all-around exceptional child. I considered myself very close to him. I would say he was probably my best friend.

"He died at seventeen. He was playing basketball in his sophomore year. He felt he had an injury in his shoulder, went to the doctor to have it x-rayed. The doctor, I remember, called me out of a meeting, said he didn't like what he saw."

Now Walter began talking slowly, with long pauses between words. "I guess I went back home. The doctor felt it could be a malignant tumor and indeed it was. They tried to treat it at Johns Hopkins Hospital with chemotherapy and they thought they were reducing the tumor, and then the very bad news: it was not being reduced by these treatments. And then the doctor said, 'The chance we have is to amputate the arm, the right arm.' And the kid was just so brave."

By now, Walter was crying silently. His crying had a pattern to it. He'd cry, wipe his eyes on his sleeve or cradle his eyes in the crook of his arm, then look out the window or at a picture. Then he'd sigh, blow his nose, clear his throat, and pick up where he left off. He was matter-of-fact about this pattern of regaining composure, as though he were used to it.

"When I went to see him after the operation, I broke down," Walter continued. "He was just courageous. He learned to do with his left hand. He went back to the team; they made him manager. He learned to drive with his left hand. For six months or so. Then it spread further and he had a number of operations, and then they said it was a matter of time. We wanted him home and he stayed with us. Until the time."

After Walter blew his nose and cleared his throat again, I asked him how long Merrill had lived after he'd been diagnosed.

"Exactly a year," he said, "a little over a year, from the time he was first diagnosed to the time he passed away. A lot of nice things."

Walter abruptly changed the subject, as all parents did when what they were saying was painful, to the nice things that happened to Merrill and the niceness of Merrill himself. He told how a team member from the Orioles came to visit Merrill, how Merrill's basketball coach gave him a team letter, how Merrill would play music he knew his father liked.

"He was just a nice kid," Walter said. "And I remember one incident—I tried to tell the people at the funeral but I couldn't get it out—my daughter had taken the dog out to the pond, and the dog fell through the ice. And my daughter came back hysterical, and we all ran, and I tried to get the dog and I couldn't do it. My son laid himself down on the ice and brought the dog in. And another thing—he had friends who were cutups, as well as the tops. He passed in all those cultures. I remember one time he was very proud. He was in the men's room after a game and a black player said, 'What do you say, blood?' He was very proud of that, they called him blood. And piano, played the piano by ear, ukelele, he could pick up anything and play it. He had great musical ability. Academic ability. Sports ability. Great personality.

"Just a golden child," Walter whispered, "just a golden child."

"So that's that part of it," he went on. "When he died, I was with a law firm and of course I really couldn't do much work at all, several months at least. But fortunately I had a wonderful woman who works with me who just covered all my bases. So when I was able to resume,

I remember the first case I tried, before the Court of Appeals—the highest court in Maryland—I did a terrible job, I know I did. Actually, I think I won the case, but nothing that I did, did it. But thereafter I became more my old self and able to think straight, resume my career.

"But one of the things the loss did, I lost the desire to really make a lot of money. For example, I knew my girls—though I love them dearly—really weren't going to college. Whereas I really wanted a marvelous career for Merrill. I wanted him to go to an Ivy League school and hopefully become a lawyer like I was and my father. But that wasn't—. If I had that pressure behind me to make sure I could send him to a $30,000-a-year school, I really lost that urge. But I do OK."

"So your career leveled off then, after Merrill died," I said.

Walter corrected me. "Probably my urge to *succeed* leveled off." Then he corrected himself. "I shouldn't say succeed. I should say to do more, to become a judge. I enjoyed what I did. But when I put everything in perspective after I lost my son, nothing meant a whole hell of a lot—very frankly, nothing. Win a big case? Big deal. Who am I going to show it to? I really wanted to show it to him. I'm sure Elaine would take pleasure in it, and the girls. But he was really who I wanted to show. I do enough to get by, but I'm not on fire. That's right. My fire is dimmed by that loss, my fire."

I asked him what he thought the reason for that was.

"I'll tell you the truth," he said. "Very frankly, I lost that reason to live."

"Why was that?" I said.

Walter repeated what he'd said at the beginning of the interview, that Merrill had grown up to be the kind of person Walter wished he had been. "See, I saw myself in his eyes," he explained. "When he was scoring a basket, I would have the vicarious sensation. That would be my living again. And now I'm not going to live again. I have no name, no heir."

I started saying, "It sounds like you're saying he was almost—" but Walter interrupted excitedly.

"An extension of me," he said.

I interrupted back: "Or an incarnation of you?"

"Yeah, yeah," he said, "sure, yeah."

"And he was the part of you that was going to go on," I said.

"Absolutely, absolutely," he said. "Absolutely."

"How do you mean that?" I asked.

"I'd be able to see myself in him," Walter said, talking more slowly now, "in his actions, in his words, in his life. And I would gain pleasure by him. Living his life would be the greatest thing that could happen to me. To see him happy and doing well, from the bottom of my heart, that would just be the greatest pleasure. He was like somebody saying to me, 'Here's a million dollars.'"

By now, I was nearly crying myself. "Because he turned out to be the way he was, a million-dollar gift?" I asked.

"Yes," he said. "I had no idea I could be so close to a child. All I can say is, he was my best friend. He was my best friend. I lost my best friend. The person I hoped would perpetuate my life by living his life."

"Is there anything you're doing that carries on Merrill's name?" I asked.

"Every year we give money for a scholarship in his name at the high school he went to. But I wish I could do more. Very frankly, in fact, I'm looking at the gifts, whatever it's called, where you give a dying child a gift. And the Ronald MacDonald home that when a kid is sick, it enables the parents to stay with them and be with them. Because I really want to perpetuate that name while I'm living. Somewhere inscribed, in perpetuity, the name Merrill Jon Levin."

I went on with my questions. "Are there any particularly bad times?" I asked.

"Periods I become morose and I don't know why," he said, "just periods or seasons or times. Sometimes I talk to the family but usually I just handle it myself internally. I think Compassionate Friends helped me a great deal. At that time, I realized that people mourn in their own ways. And if my way was to go visit the grave frequently, that's not wrong. And so I've done that. My wife does not do that, my daughters don't. They go a couple times of year, that's fine. But I go when I can. I go on Sundays.

223

"The reason I picked Sunday, very frankly, was that Sunday morning was always my favorite time. I remember I loved that time even when I was a kid. I'd stay in bed and read the funnies. And so now I get up early and I go to the cemetery and I talk, briefly, to his grave, and then I sit in the car and read, in sight of the stone so I can keep an eye on it, and then I come back and say a few more words, and then I leave—an hour or so. I feel good about doing it."

"It sounds comforting," I said.

"Comforting, that's correct," he said. "I think it's comforting to me. I want to share that time with him. Except when it's really cold, I spend an hour. I go out there to talk to him, then I sit in my car and read the paper."

"Are you sad when you do that?" I asked.

"No, oh no," he said. "Really. There are times when I feel sad. But usually I just casually make a report, the things that happened that week. Then I put a little stone there."

"Why a stone?" I asked.

"I think it's more a New York- or Boston-type of Jewish custom, actually Baltimore too, to put a little stone by the grave that indicates that you were there. They usually do it in the Jewish New Year. But I've been there so many times, the whole tombstone is filled with all those stones. And then I started picking up little stones in the places I go, from the beach on Ocean City or from California, and I've put those stones there."

"When you do that, do you feel like you're giving something to Merrill?" I asked.

"Oh no, no," he said. "The custom originated just to indicate you were there during this year. So I just use it and every Sunday I put a little stone. But I'm not giving, oh no, not at all—it's just in case somebody comes by and they would know that I had been there quite a bit. Let me say this to you. At one point, either Merrill said to me or maybe a book that I read indicated that people are afraid they'll be forgotten. And so also I say, 'I'll always love you.'"

Walter, who had been crying again, blew his nose. "So that's it," he said. "I just say my report and also by the way, recite in English the prayer for visiting a grave of a child. I say that."

"How does it go?" I asked.

Walter began reciting fast, with no inflections, just reciting. "'In thee, oh Lord, have I taken refuge. Be thou to me a rock of refuge.'"

After a few lines, he began forgetting this prayer, maybe because he usually said it in such different circumstances. He skipped around in it.

"'It is a tender and deep love for my dear child that has brought me hither. Oh merciful Father, have mercy upon me. Send the healing balm of consolation to my grieving spirit.'"

And then he bogged down again and paraphrased the rest: "You gave the life, you took the life, and I have to remember that you gave the life."

I said, "Some people say they feel more distant from their child now, others closer."

"That's a tough thing for me to say," he said. "Obviously I realize that my child is no longer here. But I must say that Merrill is with me at all times. I think that—I hope that—he is aware of what I'm doing. And I hope that he is not in any pain. Because he was in pain. And now I read this article where doctors are saying you really should give pain pills to cancer patients. And I say, those dumb sons of bitches; he was obviously in pain and now they're saying there's no reason not to give pain pills to cancer patients. The answer is yes, I don't think he's in the past. I hope his soul is in another life and doing great."

My last question is always, "Have we covered everything?"

"I think you've covered everything," he said. "I thank you for taking an interest in it. It probably isn't going to make you happy. You're going to say, 'Sixteen years later and he's still—' you know. But I imagine you'll be the same."

"I imagine I will," I said.

"They say the Second Coming," he said, "everybody comes back, and maybe that'll be soon. And we'll see our sons again."

I thought, Walter is Jewish; maybe he's being polite to me, a Christian. I got up to leave and said, "I would love that."

He repeated in a whisper, "I would love that," and got up to show me to the door. He said, "I can't wait until Sunday to mention this."

Chapter 18

THE NATURE OF THE BOND

∞

Walter Levin's wife, Elaine, said she remembered Merrill differently: "I once said to Walter, 'Who is this person you're describing, the saint? Who *is* this person? Don't you remember the night they went out with the tent in the back and did these terrible things, and the neighbors complained? You don't remember those things.'"

Then Elaine described the Merrill she remembered: "Merrill never sat still until he got to be eight or nine. Then he could channel himself, and he had the sports and the music and the this and the that. On the whole, I didn't know how terrific he was. We expected of him and he produced, and anything less, then we would have something to say. But he never gave us less."

"Can you describe what Merrill meant to you?" I asked.

"It wouldn't only be Merrill," Elaine said, "it would be any child. There's no words you can describe about it—I don't think there are words that you can describe. He meant everything. He meant everything. He was everything."

How Elaine and Walter both feel about Merrill is nearly palpable, even printed on the page. "To see him happy and doing well, from the bottom of my heart, that would just be the greatest pleasure," Walter had said. "He was everything," Elaine said, any child is everything.

What is "everything?" What is this bond between parents and children? One way to understand the nature of any bond is to look at what happens when it breaks. That is, to understand what children mean to parents, look at what happens to parents when children die. So far, this book has described just that, the effects on parents of their children's deaths, and those effects, whatever else they are, are wide and deep. If the breadth and depth of these effects are any measure of the bond between parents and children, then that bond must be great indeed.

Much of the research into the nature of the bond is based on this same reasoning, studying what happens when the bond breaks. Experiments to test this reasoning by separating children from their parents are immoral and illegal, and no one does them. Researchers do separate animal parents and infants, which, though hard on the animals, is more palatable to the researchers. Research on humans, however, must be contrived by nature or necessity. That is, researchers study parents and children who have been separated by war, economics, emotional problems, or death.

Unfortunately, much of this research, both on humans and animals, focuses on the reaction of the child, not on the reaction of the parent. The child's reaction to a broken bond says little about the parents' because the bond between parents and children is not symmetric. That is, children's feelings about their parents are not the same as parents' feelings about their children.

For instance, the psychological theory about human bonds, called attachment theory, was first proposed by a British psychoanalyst who studied children evacuated from wartime London and no longer living with their parents. The psychoanalyst John Bowlby found that these children went through a period of protest, then despair, and finally detachment and rejection of any comfort, even when reunited with their parents. Bowlby's theory helped describe the bond between parents and children, and by extension, between the parents themselves and within the family in general. Other researchers used attachment theory to understand the grief of widowed spouses. But attachment theory describes these bonds only from the point of view of the children and perhaps of the spouses. No research based on attachment theory accounts for parents' grief. "We know little about what triggers attachment to children," wrote Robert Weiss. "Nor do we understand fully why parental grieving so regularly persists indefinitely."

The research on parents' reactions comes from studying both animals and humans and suggests several principles. One: the bond gets set up early. Animals seldom nurse infants that are not their own. Hamsters whose pups are taken away one hour after birth, then returned, nurse those pups briefly then stop; hamsters whose pups are taken away forty-eight hours after birth nurse the pups much longer. Dairy cows whose calves are removed a day after birth, then returned, will resume nursing as though the separation had not occurred. Goats that spent anywhere from two to twelve hours with their kids could recognize their own kids and reject a kid not their own.

Two: the bond in humans, whether or not it is set up at birth, seems to persist. Earlier research suggested that like animals, humans needed immediate contact to cement the bond. Recent research on the subject refutes that. For example, mothers who, for reasons of health, had little contact with their premature newborns were no more likely to abuse or mistreat their children later on. This would not surprise anyone who knows a father or an adoptive parent.

And three: the bond, in mothers anyway, seems hard-wired. Before the birth of a lamb, the ewe rejects the smell of, or even an approach by, another lamb. In fact, if a ewe smells a lamb before the ewe gives birth, the nerve cells in the olfactory part of her brain simply don't respond. After birth, however, the same odor increases the activity of those cells dramatically. In other words, the birth process changes the ewe's brain so that afterward, the ewe not only accepts the lamb, but accepts hers and no other.

The notion that the bond is immediate, persistent, and hard-wired isn't news. This notion is ingrained in our culture's definitions of parents; we think parents who do not meet this definition are unnatural.

Our culture's definition of the bond, however, isn't the last word. During much of human history and in large parts of the present world, nature has run a larger-scale experiment whose results suggest a different definition.

In other words, before about 1850 and in much of the modern Third World, children died and still die in terrible numbers. In ancient Greece and Rome, 30 to 40 percent of the children died before they were a year old. In France in the 1640s, 20 percent of the children died before a year (deaths before a year went unrecorded, so that percentage is certainly much higher). In England in the 1640s, between 25 and 33 percent of all children, regardless of social class, died before reaching a year. In England two centuries later, in the mid-1800s, between 15 and 25 percent of children died before age fifteen. In America during the 1800s, nearly half of all deaths were children under five. In a present-day shantytown in northeast Brazil, the average mother has 4.5 living children and 3.5 children who have died; their mothers call those who die, "angel babies."

The reasons for such rates of death are mostly obvious: appalling sanitation, inadequate nutrition, ineffective medicine. Historically, medicine was ineffective partly from lack of knowledge, partly from lack of concern. Obstetrics was practiced by midwives and not by trained physicians until the mid-1700s. Pediatrics was not a specialty until the early 1900s and even then, physicians saw infancy like old age, as a time of extreme fragility. The effect was a sort of feedback loop: because children were likely to die, medical expertise was more usefully applied to adults, so children were more likely to die. In short, what with families of usually more than five children and mortality rates of roughly one in five, most parents had a child die.

With this kind of wholesale mortality, parents' grief should surely be celebrated in song and story; after all, lovers' grief certainly is. Parents' grief, however, is not. Records of everyday life—letters, journals, stories, autobiographies, songs, folktales, paintings—rarely mention either children's deaths or parents' grief. Death and grief are notable—notable to us anyway—by their absence. The reason is that anything as frequent as children's deaths is normal, not noteworthy.

In these other places and times, newly born babies are seen as transients. In the Brazilian shantytown, mothers say their babies are like little birds likely to fly away, or like flames likely to go out. In ancient Greece, babies weren't named until a week or more after birth. Greek epitaphs of people of all ages commonly used the word for "untimely," *aôros;* the word was used only rarely in the epitaphs of children under two. In Europe and America, for several centuries, babies under a year old were neither named nor baptized.

The result, according to most historians, was that these parents kept and keep a certain distance from these children. The high death rates, wrote the historian Lawrence Stone, "made it folly to invest too much emotional capital in such ephemeral beings." And in the same feedback loop as the medical ineffectiveness, the parents' lower investment also allowed babies to die of neglect. In ancient Greece and Rome, and for centuries in Europe, babies were commonly handed over to wet nurses under whose careless attention they were twice as likely to die. Some arguable evidence exists that the ancient Greeks exposed their weak babies in fields to die. In the Brazilian shantytown, weak or sick babies are simply not fed; they starve to death.

Nor, when babies died, did parents fuss overmuch with the funerals. The parents in the Brazilian shantytown rarely go to the funerals. The baby is simply put in a cardboard box and the neighborhood children carry the box to the graveyard. In ancient Greece and Rome, children were buried cheaply in plain clay pots, and in one case, in a beehive; "It is difficult to resist the impression," wrote Robert Garland, a historian, "that any serviceable container was acceptable for the body of a child."

If so many parents apparently invested so little in their children, what does that mean about the bond between parents and children? Are we wrong to think that the bond is wide and deep? Is the bond, instead, fundamentally casual, depending only on the probability of the child's living?

Historians do not argue this. Stone points out that much of the evidence of the parental bond is in personal writing—journals, autobiographies, and letters. And because few men of the lower classes and fewer woman of any class were literate, much of the evidence depends on whatever a relatively small group of educated, well-off men happened to write down and keep.

Some historians also argue against stating the bond in economic terms, in terms of the probability of return on an investment. They doubt that parents are wholly free to manage the investment of their love based on their assessment of risk. Historians acknowledge the shortage of records expressing love for and grief over children. But even Stone points out that expressions of love for children come and go in history, and not necessarily in synchrony with periods of high infant mortality. In England, what Stone calls "affective relationships" improve between 1650 and 1750 when, he writes, "morality was at a peculiarly high level." In America in the early 1800s, mortality rates were high at the time when mothers first began recording in their diaries their feelings about their children.

The most striking example of this latter is Fanny Longfellow. In 1844, Fanny, who had kept a diary her whole life, wrote about the birth of her first child: "With this day my Journal ends, for I now have a living one to keep faithfully." By 1847, Fanny had three children and began her diary again. In 1848, her eighteen-month-old daughter died: "I seem to have lost all interest in the future and can enjoy my children only from hour to hour," she wrote. "As I controlled her life before birth, so does she me now."

In short, maybe parents felt the grief but didn't record or otherwise express it. Stone suggests that the scarcity of recorded grief might say less about the bond than about cultural rules about expressing emotions. This is apparently true for the mothers in the Brazilian shantytown. Where a historian must rely on whatever records were made and still survive, the anthropologist Nancy Scheper-Hughes could go to Brazil and ask the mothers questions. She found that Brazilian culture does indeed frown on expressing grief. She also found that the mothers truly seemed not to grieve. Pointed questions to the mothers confirmed, she wrote, "that one does not really miss a very young baby."

Scheper-Hughes doesn't believe this means the bond is casual, however, because mothers who lost older children "grieve for those children for months and years on end." Stone says the same thing, and quotes a wealthy Englishman who lost three infants and then, in 1636, a son, nearly two: "We both found the sorrow for the loss of this child," he wrote, "whose delicate favour and bright grey eye was so deeply imprinted on our heart, far to surpass our grief for the decease of his three elder brothers, who dying almost as soon as they were born, were not so endeared to us as this was." The same Greeks who buried their infants in clay pots, buried their older children with toys and gifts—in one case, a gold necklace, in another, a pet piglet—and wrote epitaphs for their older children praising them. The epitaph of one woman, Xenokleia, says she died of grief for her eight-year-old son.

So probably this near-universal lack of grief over fragile infants says less about the bond and more about our culture. For us, expressing grief is not discouraged and is sometimes actively encouraged. More important, however, we live in a special place at a special time.

In the first place, we are unusually distant from our religions. One reason that parents didn't grieve their infants is because they believed in a literal heaven. Scheper-Hughes says that the Brazilian mothers tell each other not to mourn because tears will wet the angel-baby's wings and the baby can't fly to heaven. One early New England mother who lost eight of her eleven children wrote, "So it pleased God to take away one after another of my dear children, I hope, to himself." The ancient Roman, Plutarch, wrote in his *Moralia,* "For the laws forbid us to mourn for infants, holding it impiety to mourn for those who have departed to a dispensation and a region too, that is better and more divine. And since this is harder to disbelieve than believe, let us keep our outward conduct as the laws command." "Grief at the death of an angel is not only inappropriate," writes Scheper-Hughes, it also shows "a profound lack of faith."

In the second place, we have an unusual distance from life's harshness and from death itself. In the Brazilian shantytown, Scheper-Hughes wrote, life "resembles nothing so much as a battlefield or an emergency room in an overcrowded inner-city public hospital." A medieval child's primer in an exhibition in a Paris library has these lines for children learning to read: "Are you a student?" "Yes, I am a student." "Are you a leper?" "No, I am not a leper." The most striking feature about early European families, Stone writes, "was the constant presence of death. Death was at the center of life as the cemetery was at the center of the village."

In other words, in places and at times when children die readily, parents see death as benevolent partly because it opens the way to God and partly because life is malign. Life is a struggle, Brazilian mothers say; their word is *luto.* A baby has little attachment to life, and some have less than others. These unattached babies simply don't have the strength for the *luto,* and they should be allowed to return to God. An American mother in 1800 wrote much the same thing: "I will bless God who has taken thee to Himself before thou couldst offend him and has saved thee from life of sickness, sorrow, and woe." Plutarch, writing a fairly pompous letter to his wife after the death of their two-year-old daughter, quoted a Greek expression: "The most fortunate soul is the one which is able, in the poet's words, 'to pass as swiftly as possible through Hades' portals' before a strong love of the things of this world has been engendered in it." In the Greek play, *Oedipus at Colonus,* Sophocles wrote something similar: "Not to be born is best of all; when life is there, the second best is to go hence where you came with the best speed you may."

We don't talk about life like this any more. Life is good, we say, and our newborns are robust. We grieve as much for infants as the ancient and unfortunate parents did and do for older children. I doubt that the bond has ever been casual. The parents of fragile, transient infants sound harshly pragmatic, but they don't sound unloving.

The parents I interviewed are, of course, another experiment in the nature of the bond. The questions I asked the parents about the bond were what do you think you miss most? and do you have any way to describe what your child must have been to you? The questions are, of course, unanswerable. I asked just to hear what the parents might come up with. Their answers were as short as Elaine's and more or less the same: I don't know, children are part of you, they're everything.

Chris Reed: "After Mary died, I felt that a part of me had died with her. I don't know how else to describe that. I'm not sure what I mean by 'a part of me died.' I guess I mean that I'll never be quite the same again. Because an important part of my life is gone. I can't put that into words; I don't know what else to say about that."

"What do you miss about her?" I asked.

"Everything," Chris said. "Everything. I don't know, I don't know. I really can't focus on any one thing. So much. I guess I miss everything."

From the first interview on, I was interested in the nature of the bond, and so I listened especially carefully when the parents talked about what they missed. I think the bond has two aspects, and one aspect is obvious.

The parents missed the whole catalog of what could be called the bond's selfish aspects, that is, those aspects that gratify their own egos: feeling needed, knowing they have brought up their children successfully, knowing their children as adults, having grandchildren, being looked after themselves. That some part of a bond is selfish and ego-gratifying is only reasonable; any human relationship has such rewards. In the historian's metaphor, part of the bond is economic: the parents made an investment in time, energy, and love, and their return on the investment is in pride, reliability, friendship, and grandchildren. Moreover, the parent has a self-image as someone's parent—as a competent, important, good person—and doesn't want to give it up. Researchers say, too, that one part of the bond is the parents' desire for competence, a desire to protect the child effectively and to live up to what society expects of parents. When a child dies, researchers say, parents must face feelings of incompetence, which some of them handle by substituting other competencies—for instance, by working with Compassionate Friends or Mothers Against Drunk Driving.

When I asked Mitch Dudnikov what he missed most about Marc, Mitch was ready with the entire catalog.

"I miss having his children to spoil," he said. "I could have made them handmade toys that would be different from the general run of things. Besides, everybody would like to have grandchildren to show them off."

Then Mitch digressed into a story about how his father and mother and their children all had dark eyes and dark hair, but all the grandchildren had blue eyes and blond hair, and how his father loved to show off these unlikely-looking grandchildren. "I wanted that too," Mitch said. "Marc was going out with a Japanese girl, and if my grandchildren were Jap-Jews or Jew-Japs, I would have taken the kids around and said, 'I don't know why they look oriental, but they do.' That's what I miss, that's what I miss. You would like to see your line continue. That's a selfish thing. It's a continuation. Marc would have been the one that kept the family name alive.

"What I miss, probably more than anything else," he went on, "is that he died just at this transition from father-to-son to friend-to-friend. It was just beginning a friendship on an equal basis, neither one is over the other. I think I could have really had a good friend, somebody that I could unload my problems with, knowing that if anything happened to me, he would have been there to help his mother.

"I also missed, what would he have been? At the time I was in my fifties, I had a little niche in industry, but nothing to speak of. He would have done so much more. I was a grind, I had to sit and grind everything out. And for him, everything came easily. He would have had one hell of a good time. I could have gone walking around the neighborhood saying, 'That's *my* son, that's *my* son.' That's what I missed out on."

Mitch went on to talk about how, in his little niche in industry, he had developed a manufacturing process that would make cars lighter and therefore use less gas. "If Marc were alive, I would have been very proud of that," he said, sounding now like Walter. "I would have said, 'Look what I've done, I've helped this country save thousands, maybe millions.' But after Marc's death, I'd say, 'So we use more gasoline, so what?' See, I was interested in doing the chemistry and becoming a winner because—which I've never said before—I wanted to go up the line. I wanted to be technical director of a company, or vice president; I don't think I'd ever made vice president. But after Marc's death, I'd say, 'What difference does it make whether I'm technical director or chief chemist?' The satisfaction, the taste of the fruit was not as good."

Marc's death, he said, using a metaphor researchers note and parents use, was an amputation. "What makes me so hurtful," he said, meaning full of hurt, "is I've been amputated. It's like some surgeon went crazy and decided to amputate."

Notice that as Mitch talks, every item in his catalog of personal, selfish losses changes to a larger, different kind of loss. Mitch misses Marc's children, misses his grandchildren. He also misses being able to continue what his own father started, goofing around with exotic-looking grandchildren. In fact, he misses being the link between his father and his son, between the past and future of his own family.

Likewise, he misses Marc as an adult, misses being able to rely on him in need, misses having a friendship between equals, misses being able to brag about how splendidly Marc turned out, better than Mitch. He also misses having a reason to do well himself, to go up the line professionally. He misses the sweet taste of the fruit. He was amputated, he lost part of his own self.

This is true for every parent. Losses that are personal and selfish always seem to merge into losses that are more generally human and almost altruistic. So the bond seems to have two aspects, one personal and obvious, the other more general and subtle. I think this more general aspect of the bond is the aspect the parents could describe only by saying children are part of you, they are everything.

"I lost the chance to enjoy a lot of grandchildren," said Lydia Frasca, who, after two miscarriages and the deaths of two infants, had a son named Tommy. "Children are an extension of me. When Tommy was little, I could dress him the way I liked, comb his hair the way I liked. And people would say, 'Look how well he's doing.' It's a pride thing, your child makes you prideful. Then when they get a personality, it's like you release that pride to them, and they're doing

236

all this on their own. You're in the background behind this little guy, helping him become a whole nother person. I think motherhood's probably the best career in the whole world. So what do you do with that now? Your career is now shattered. Your legacy to leave on is gone. It's like this whole nother person all next to you, connected to you somehow—no, connected to you, period—is dead. That lifeline is gone, it's cut."

Again, like Mitch, each of Lydia's personal losses resonates with a larger loss. Her loss of grandchildren to enjoy also means loss of a legacy to leave on. Her loss of the children to be proud of also means losing children who are proud of themselves and individuals in their own right. The lifeline that's cut is not only between her children and herself, but between herself and the future.

In the personal, selfish part of the bond, the child is someone to give to and get from, and seems separate from the parent, external to the parent. In the larger, more mysterious part of the bond, the parent seems to merge with the child in some fundamental way. The parent and child seem to be indistinguishable, or at least inseparable. "It does get complicated when you get to thinking about what all you have lost," said Julia Marcus. "They're with you and inside of you and just a part of you."

Researchers also say that from the parent's point of view, children are merged with the parent. The child can seem to be the parent's best self or the parent's not-so-good self. Or the child can seem to be the same as the parent. Or children can represent the parents' own childhood, with all the virtues and drawbacks that implies. Or children can be a chance for the parents to replay or to rectify their own childhoods. If the child who died somehow represents the parent's bad self or unhappy childhood—and therefore the parent's relationship with the child has been ambivalent—some research suggests that the parents are left with more psychiatric symptoms, more health problems, and more generally negative feelings. In all cases, when the child dies, the parents must face the death of some part of their own selves, whether good or bad, which often leaves them with feelings of amputation.

Even though both researchers and parents use that metaphor about amputation, I think the part of the parent that is the child is not detachable or expendable.

None of this—that children are a central part of parents, are the link between the parent's past and future, are tied up with the parent's own self-image—is surprising. In fact, this is all said so often, it's a cliché. What is surprising is that it's true. We're not used to this sort of merger with another person. We're used to thinking of ourselves as separate individuals; we fall in love, we make alliances, we have obligations, but we do all this as free agents. We choose our own lives and die our own deaths. But we don't choose our love of, alliance with, or obligations to our children. Our children are much more central; they're something like our own humanness or our reasons for being on earth. If children are part of parents, they are not arms or legs but bones and breath.

One reason I believe in this centrality is that the parents said it even when they weren't talking about it. That is, the most convincing evidence of the centrality was that the parents weren't especially conscious of it. I noticed it when they would appear to change the subject for no reason, talking in apparent non sequiturs. When I filled in the gaps, connected the first subject with the next, the connection seemed to be this unity between parent and child. Perhaps I filled in wrongly and these non sequiturs are coincidence. But I heard many of them, and I think the connection is real.

Sally Lambert, for instance, was talking about getting through the first year after Lisa's suicide. She read a book, she said, that advised her, "'When you feel this horrible pain, just remember it's not going to last forever, it will go away.'" Then she explained the book's advice: "I think the book was trying to keep a person from doing any harm to themselves by saying to wait, this feeling will pass. Like Lisa that night. 'Wait, this feeling will pass. It won't last forever.'"

But Sally never mentioned wanting to harm herself; only Lisa did that. Sally's interpretation of the book makes sense only if Sally and Lisa are nearly the same person. Telling Sally the pain will go away was the same as keeping Lisa from harming herself. What Sally reads, Lisa hears: the feeling will pass, don't hurt yourself, wait.

I asked Octavia Pompey, "What gives you your greatest satisfaction in life?" Octavia's greatest satisfactions turned out to be Erin's. "I guess a couple of things," she said. "One was I knew how important it was to him to finish school and he did that. He was looking forward to his prom and he did that. I mean, he could have been killed two weeks before and he would have missed out on graduation and his prom. And he got to do those two things. He got to do what he liked to do best, and that was playing ball. His trophies are there to show he was good at it. I know that he knew that I loved him. And he knew that his father loved him, and his brothers. And I guess that's about it."

When I asked Tom Ford what had been the biggest changes in his life, he first said that his life hadn't changed. Then with no break, he wondered how David's life would have continued. "Well, other than periods of sadness," he said, "I don't think there are any changes in my life. I sometimes wonder—he'd be twenty-four years old now, twenty-five—what would he have been? A lawyer, a soldier, or a bum, who knows? You'd like to think he'd have done a lot better than you did. What the hell would he have been—twenty-five, twenty-six years old, maybe have three kids by now, maybe he wouldn't have any. I think what I miss most about him is knowing what he would have been."

Tom is answering a question about his own life by imagining David's future. Brandt Jones did the same when he explained replanning his future as changing "all these brilliant plans where Bruce was going to get through four years of college, he was going to marry this girl down the street, they were going to have these kids." This same unity between the parent's future and the child's future is probably what Walter was talking about when he said Merrill was "the person I hoped would perpetuate my life by living his life," and "living his life would be the greatest thing that could happen to me." The unity might be part of the reason that the fire was dimmed in Walter's own life, that Ruth didn't go back to school to become a teacher, and that Mitch didn't bother to go up the line professionally.

The parents all talk as though the parent's life and the child's future, and the parent's future and the child's life are all the same thing. But saying that this bond is a unity between the parents' and the children's futures is still too narrow. The parents talk as though their lives and their children's lives are segments in one long line that goes back through the parents' parents and beyond, and goes forward through the parents, the children, and on into the future.

The nicest example of this is Leight Johnson: "I have to tell you this, it tickles me. My father was Leight Johnson and Johnny was Leight Junior. And they both died, and I was the only Leight Johnson left. Last summer, one of my twin sons who got married and had twins, a boy and a girl, and he named the boy Leight. It just tickled me. It's not for my sake but for my son's, more than anything. I'm just pleased to see there'll be another Leight Johnson."

Later, I asked Leight whether he had any memorials set up for Johnny, and he said no, but went on to talk about "the closest thing I have to a memorial."

"I had him cremated," he said. "I told you we had a house in Vermont with thirty acres of land. When my father died in the early seventies we had him cremated and I scattered his ashes back in the woods under three maple trees, three big old maple trees. And then when Johnny died, we decided to do the same thing. And now whenever I go up to Vermont, the first thing I do the first day is walk back—it's back in the woods, a good hundred yards back—and I talk to them. Leight the first, that was my father, and then me, and then Johnny, the three Leights back there, I go and I talk to them—'How you guys doing? You keeping an eye on the woods for me?' I remember one day—it must have been ten years ago now—we were up there late March, and had a very warm day. I went back there alone and sat down on the ground right there under these trees, with the warm sun coming in—the first warm day of spring—and I fell asleep, just lying on the ground there. And when I woke up a few minutes later, I remember having the most terrifically peaceful feeling. *Just*— I don't know how to describe it—just to say, so completely peaceful."

"Why do you think that was?" I asked.

"Because of the warm sunshine, you know how that affects everybody. And just that association with my father and my son, just everything came together at that moment. I'm kind of an agnostic, but that's as close as I come to believing in an afterlife."

I think this merged, mysterious aspect of the bond is that both parent and child are links in a chain that connects the past with the future. And the chain isn't just any chain. It's family, it's one's own kind, it's a definition of you that goes beyond your own self.

My grandmother and her sister, my great-aunt Thyra, grew up and settled down in the prairies of Illinois. They'd drive my grandmother's Jeep down those straight, bare dirt roads, passing farms now and then, me in the back seat listening, and they'd talk about the people who lived on the farms. "Junie Kuhn lives there now, he's John and Clara Kuhn's son. Wasn't Clara a Miller, cousin to Paulie Miller, old Charlie's youngest?" I learned fast: you knew who someone was by knowing who they were kin to.

Of course, that's old-fashioned now, and with a few exceptions like Brandt and his family "feeding down to the fifth and sixth generations," families are scattered all over. But even in small families, we define ourselves by who our parents and our brothers and sisters are and are not. My mother was a librarian; I began my career as a librarian. She kept a messy house; I keep a neat one. My father loved Bach's music, and so do I. My sister could bake pies, so I specialized in cakes. But the definition that families provide goes beyond careers, tastes, and specialties.

"My family was a small family," said Julia, meaning the family in which she had grown up. "They were not close; they all kind of lost each other. So I was very slow in really grasping what my friends seemed to realize just naturally—that what children mean to you, when you talk about meaning overall, in the big sense of meaning, is all these different generations on down. It's really a *part* of you. I never really thought much about grandchildren, I could take it or leave it. But as I think of Simone and I think of children she might have had—your children, whether they're biological or not, just are such an extension of yourself. Talk about mortality, they're your immortality. In some kind of common everyday kind of language, that has to be a part of all these strong, strong, strong ties."

The tie, the bond, is indeed strong. But its exact nature is still unclear, and saying that the parent and child are somehow merged doesn't clarify it much; the parents unconsciously described it by identifying their children, their own futures, and their own kind.

Anne Perkins had another way of describing it. She began in her usual roundabout way. "I can see how you might say a part of you has died." Then as though she were continuing the same subject, she said, "Even with my kids older, I'm always thinking creatively about them. I remember thinking before Robert died, I'll buy those sheets for Robert, or at Christmas he looked like he needed a new pair of socks, or I wonder if he forgot to get his hair cut again. Children are always present. Then suddenly, they're not there and you can't have the same kind of presence. You can't think, what are they going to be like on the job? or should they be calling so-and-so? You're creatively engaged in their lives. But they die and that changes, and the change is, they're on your mind but in another way."

I thought I knew what she meant by "thinking creatively" and "creatively engaged": that parents create their children's lives the same way they create their own—new socks? haircut? job? I said, "I used to daydream about T.C.'s job options the same way I did about my own."

"Exactly," she said, "It's part of being a parent, that you're always a parent. They're so much part of your total being."

Another reason I believe the centrality of the bond is much simpler: I just listened to the parents talk about their children.

Estelle: "I have to tell you about an experience. For many many years, I used to say, after he died, 'If I could just hug him one more time.' That was constantly in my mind. About three or four years ago, my sister-in-law was visiting from Chicago and she's a very religious person. And way into the night we were talking about religion— saints and angels and the devil and God. And we finally turned in about 2 A.M. And I went upstairs, and I was sitting on the side of the bed—I was not asleep—and all of a sudden, I saw my son in front of me. And I stood up and he came into my arms and I hugged him."

Estelle's voice got high and shakey: "And then it's as if I hugged so tight that I lost him. And since then I can't say, 'Dear God, let me hug him one more time,' because I feel He let me do it. And I think if I told this to the wrong people they would think I was crazy. But I *felt* him that night."

I am unable to believe such things. I do believe Estelle believed it. Whichever belief is right is irrelevant. Anyway, which is harder to believe, that Estelle's son would come back from being dead and hug her, or that Estelle would want him back so much that her brain would reconstruct his body for her?

Loretta Marsh: "I think people are telling me that I should let go of Mike. I wouldn't have let go if he was still here, so why let go if he's not here? He was my son, I raised him. I'd had different people say to me, 'Would you rather that he'd lived but been crippled?' Oh, I've told them—'No hands, no arms, no legs. I would have took care of him the rest of my life.' I went one night to the cemetery at twelve midnight, got out of bed and went up there and screamed and screamed and screamed. And I thought, 'If you could just come back, five minutes.' And then I thought, 'Loretta, it's been six *years*.' But I guess at fifty years I'll still feel the same."

Julia: "Most people have no reason to think about all the layers that children mean to you. I mean, you just *love* them so much, that I don't think you ever really think about how much they mean to you until—I mean, you just love them so much."

Whatever this bond is, it doesn't break. "Something happens during the establishment of the parent-child bond," Robert Weiss said, "so that the child's well-being is the same as your own, and it doesn't even feel like altruism. We don't fully understand it, maybe we don't understand it very much at all, but we do know that it is as powerful a bond as it is in people's capacity to establish. The bonding is what you're about."

Chapter 19

ONE PERSON NOW

The Continuing Trajectory

∞

The main reason I believe that children are central to parents is that when the children die, the bond doesn't break. What does that mean, the bond doesn't break? What do parents do about that?

The parents face two mutually exclusive facts. The child is gone and not coming back, and the bond is, as Robert Weiss said, "as powerful a bonding as people have in their abilities." Somehow, in their day-to-day lives, the parents have to balance these facts. Do I let the child go, or do I continue as though the child were still part of my life?

I doubt that the parents are aware of this as a problem. Or rather, they seem to be aware of it as it plays out in a series of smaller, more concrete problems. Every one of these problems is discussed over and over at Compassionate Friends' meetings. Every one was an important problem in the early years of the child's death, and has since become less important. None of the problems seems to disappear, however, and years later, the parents still want to talk about them. In fact, the very persistence of these problems is a measure of the pervasiveness of a child's presence in a parent's life.

For example: Do you give the child's belongings away as useless now, or do you keep the belongings as a remembrance? Do you keep pictures of the child private, in an album, or do you hang them on the wall where you and everyone else can see them? (Compassionate Friends' attitude toward these questions is, of course, do whatever you want to do.)

Betty Jones gave away some of Bruce's things, and packed away the rest for her grandson. "As my daughter's child grows up, he will get to know his uncle through his uncle's belongings." Elaine Levin gave away a trombone and a bicycle, but not Merrill's books: "I guess they're still part of him I'm holding on to, that's probably it in a nutshell." Marge Ford immediately redecorated David's room. Loretta Marsh's husband kept Mike's room intact for four years. Nickie Copinger did the same: "I didn't change anything in Adam's room. It came through the grapevine that I left Adam's room like that because I was creating a shrine. But the thing was, I really didn't know what to do with it." Mary Norris, like nearly everyone else, kept her son's pictures on the living room wall: "They all said, 'You take the pictures down, you won't think about it.' But I still have those pictures there, all these many years."

Notice that though the parents solve this small problem in different ways, they always solve it. They can't just see the belongings as now-useless and let them go. "I guess I always feel Larry's presence," said Delores Shoda. "I have one of his jackets that just hangs there downstairs in the cupboard. I'll probably always keep it."

Another example: How do you deal with the children's birthdays, the anniversaries of their deaths, and the holidays? The child is gone, so do you ignore these days? The child remains part of you, so do you celebrate them? If so, do you celebrate them as usual? Whatever the solution, the problem has to be faced several times each year, year after year. Moreover, the problem of the anniversary of the child's death is complicated by automatic emotional reactions that researchers call anniversary reactions. Whether or not people remember the anniversary of a traumatic event consciously, they seem to remember it unconsciously, and the emotions that accompanied the original trauma return, usually not at full strength, but disconcertingly strong nevertheless.

I get it all over with at once: T.C.'s birthday and the anniversary of his death coincide with Thanksgiving and the Christmas holidays, and I become impossible to please and so try to go away. Delores Shoda stays busy on those days, calls her daughter, takes roses to the cemetery. Chris Reed's family goes to Mass and has dinner together. Brandt Jones wanted people around: "As long as I had people around, those days went by without my dwelling on Bruce." Brandt's wife, Betty, does better "making them just one more day." Louise Lewis does the same as Betty: "I do whatever is on the schedule. I don't make any kind of to-do." Loretta Marsh and her husband leave town. Julia Marcus puts up Simone's Christmas tree ornaments but can't bake Simone's cinnamon roll: "It's just *so* Simone that now you just can't do it." On Thanksgiving, when Marc traditionally came home, Mitch Dudnikov cleans the basement. On Thanksgiving, Mary Norris's daughter and grandchildren come over: "Right now, she's missing of her father and her brother and I'm missing of a husband and a son. Anniversary of my son's death, it comes and pass. Don't get deep inside it." On Robert's birthday, Anne Perkins does nothing: "I just think about it," she said, and started to cry. "It's March. I remember—this is hard to say—the day he was born, it snowed and so I always think, 'Is it snowing?'"

The last of these small but universal problems with handling an unbroken bond is finding answers to polite social questions about your children, the most frequent being "how many children do you have?" The question is a perennial issue at Compassionate Friends' meetings. Saying you have one child less seems to the parents like lying or disloyalty. But saying you have a child who died always stops a social conversation in its tracks: the context is too casual for such intimate information. Elaine Levin just says, "'Three, or two,' depending on the mood I'm in." Lydia Frasca says, "Tommy's my only living child." Anne says, "'I have a son who died, I have two daughters, one lives in Seattle,' and it works because I've ended with this *fuzz* and not an upsetting thing for everybody. It took me a long time to figure that one out."

An oddity that I noticed during the interviews turns out to be another small continuation. Most of the parents knew, without hesitation or calculation, how old their children would now be. One researcher calls this a "phantom child phenomenon"; another describes it as the parents knowing the child's position on the "empty path." The parents are also endlessly curious about what the child would have been doing. Nickie Copinger: "Adam would have been seventeen on May eighteenth of this year. I guess you grow *with* their memory. You can't grow *for* them. I'm talking about, 'Seventeen, what would he be doing?' And my husband was real light-hearted, he'd say, 'Well, his birthday would have cost you a lot of money, probably a car.' I don't look at it as trying to hold on to him. I call it my *living* memory—'What would Adam, what would he be doing?'"

With notable exceptions, the parents solve these problems as though the child were continuing: keep the belongings, hang the pictures, remember the birthdays and anniversaries of the death, include the child symbolically at the holidays, tell people you had the number of children you once had, know how old they'd be. So on the whole, the answer to how to live with an unbreakable bond appears to be, just continue it.

But "just continue it" is an oversimplification. If the parents' problem is to balance those opposites—do I let the child go or do I continue the child with me?—their solutions are usually inconsistent. They solve one problem by continuing the child, another by letting go. Betty, for instance, keeps most of Bruce's belongings, doesn't celebrate his birthday, but keeps track of his age. The reason for the inconsistency is simply that some reminders are painful, some comforting. When the memory of Simone's cinnamon roll hurts Julia, she lets go of that tradition. When Simone's Christmas ornaments are comforting, Julia continues hanging them.

Why some reminders are painful and some comforting, I don't know. I'd guess the answers are individual to the parent. Maybe reminders that are painful are reminders of the death. The reason I

247

can't put on T.C.'s sweatshirts or read his journal seems to be that those are things I can do only because he's dead; if he were alive, they'd be personal to him and I wouldn't intrude. Painful reminders are left alone: the reminder never becomes emotionally neutral, but it is allowed to rest.

And maybe the reminders that are comforting are all different ways of saying what Anne does when she asks, "Is it snowing?" Maybe these reminders are a highly unreasonable, unarticulated hope: Can they be born all over again? Can they come back? Can they get another chance? No parent holds this hope rationally, but it is difficult to give up emotionally. Or maybe the comforting reminders are a piece of magic; when Delores touches Larry's jacket, she feels a little of his presence. Or maybe they are simply evidence that the child once lived and times were happier.

In any case, all these small decisions—do you continue or let go the various reminders?—are stand-in's for the larger decision: do you continue or let go the child?

But what does "let go" mean anyway? Again, I don't know, though I know I've done it. After my seventy-five-year-old father died, I let go of him. I still love him and think about him and sometimes I am aware of wanting to be a person he would have liked. But I don't mind his being dead. I fit his death into my personal scheme of things, into what I understood about the natural order of the world. He grew old and died; I will too. Does letting go mean accepting that the death is right and proper? Does it mean you feel little longing for the person who died? Does it mean you think about the person with tranquillity—you're sad they died but they were supposed to, and on the whole, better them than you? Does it mean you feel no bitterness about the death? Maybe it means all those things.

Even though the definition of letting go seems uncertain, everyone seems to know whether they've let go or whether they haven't. The only parent who said unequivocally that he let the child go was Tom Ford: "I don't think about Dave all the time. Once in a while. I've essentially let go. I think of him doing kid stuff, playing with the

248

dog, fooling around in the backyard. I still talk to him once in a while when I'm driving the car. Sometimes if you're driving along and see something different—it's like when he was a little guy—and I'll say, 'What do you think of that, Dave?' It doesn't happen very much. Sometimes. I accepted his death a long time ago. I don't know, he's *dead*. He's *gone*. I think about him but I don't—I don't know—I don't feel real bad about it any more. He just happened to die fifty, fifty-five years ahead of time. I'm going to die in another few years."

Tom's reasoning—he still talks to Dave but doesn't feel real bad about his death any more, Dave just died fifty years too soon, and Tom will himself die in another few years—sounds like mine about my father's death.

The other parents who said they'd let go distinguished between the child and the pain caused by the child's death, and seemed to be letting go, not of the child but of the pain. As Ginny Mitchell said, "I don't know that I feel more distant from Joel. You have distanced yourself from the *pain,* I guess. I think it's a learning thing." In other words, the parents learn over time that the pain that now accompanies every reminder of the child is not the same as the child. I'd guess most parents learned to make this distinction, but only two parents other than Ginny seemed explicitly aware of it and talked about letting go in these terms.

Emily Miller, whose daughter committed suicide: "I was afraid I was going to forget her. But I can still close my eyes and see her face and hear her voice. But it's harder to do. She's receding into the past. Which is where she belongs. But I don't want her there. I want her here. It's all part of letting go. I don't want to let her go, but you have to, for your own sake. She will always be part of me. I'm trying to let go of as much grief as I can from her death. I grieve as much for her unhappiness in the last half of her life as I do for her death. She had so much goodness in her, although she couldn't see it. But I'm holding on to the good parts and letting go of the rest. Keeping the good memories with you and trying to put the pain behind you. You can still hold them in the past."

Emily, like Tom, said she was trying to let the child go, but in her case, I'm not quite sure what she meant by it. She went back and forth so many times: she's afraid to forget Sue, she wants Sue in her past, she wants her in the present, she's holding on to her in the past, she's holding on to the good parts, she's letting go of the pain. She seems to be trying to separate Sue into parts to keep and parts to let go. Again, I think she's trying to keep Sue and let go of the grief.

Joan Gresser lost two children, Steven and Teddy. Teddy talked to her in a dream. "Teddy asked me to let him go: 'Mom, I'm fine, let me go, let us go.' That was letting go of the pain. That wasn't letting go of *them*. I don't know how you can hold onto something that you're constantly in pain about. But I can see how you can hold onto something that you treasure and love. Letting go is very hard. It means freeing their spirit up. I believe that in order for my sons to be free, I had to let their spirits go. What I have in me is their memories, what they were to me and still are. I allow their spirits to go, but only because Teddy told me to. If he hadn't told me to, I don't know. But I think people hold on for lots of reasons. I wonder if at each stage of your grief, holding on doesn't change."

I wonder if at the bottom of this confusion about letting go isn't another confusion, odd-sounding but understandable, about where the child now is. No one has any literal doubts, of course; as Walter Farnandis said, "There's no see-him-again." But never seeing someone again is contrary to our everyday experience. People move away and we never see them again, but we could if we tried. We lose things and either find them or don't, but the things are still somewhere reachable. For a person to disappear and be unreachable by any means, and for that person to be so inextricably a part of us, is confusing. So parents have a sense of the child's presence and a disconcerting feeling that the child must be *somewhere*.

But where? The child is dead and cremated or buried. Is the child then in the cemetery? Louise doesn't go to the cemetery much "because to me that's not where Michael is." Delores does go; she knows "it's just a grave," but feels she has to have flowers there. Anne rarely goes because "it's too hard." Chris goes once or twice a month, sometimes "fills up with tears," sometimes doesn't. Elaine says, "I don't have to go to the cemetery; Merrill's in my heart." Loretta goes and talks to Mike: "Do you think I'm nuts?" she asks. "I do."

A few parents—Chris, Mary, Walter Farnandis—believe their children are in heaven. The Fords worry that David is in purgatory. The rest were as confused as I am.

Julia Marcus: "Every now and then, I just feel like we never had Simone. That's a terrible thing. But most of the time I feel very close to Simone, and sometimes I wonder, is this really good? But I think all of us feel close. Do some people really feel very distant from their child?"

Ginny Mitchell: "Joel's still part of our family as far as I'm concerned. Whether that's good or bad, I don't know. Our family's growing because we have a grandchild. You make room for new loves, but that doesn't erase the part of him that he takes up of you."

Estelle Lemaitre: "Robby loved nature. Anything about nature, trees and flowers and seasons. And as a result, we had an epitaph—someone sent this to us in a sympathy card, just this piece of paper."

Estelle showed me the paper, which had on it a poem, Robby's epitaph, that said in part, "I am the rain, the trees, the snow." I asked, "Do you feel that what the poem says is true, that even though he isn't here, he's in all these other things?"

"Absolutely," she said. "Absolutely."

"Do you feel close to Robby or more distant from him?" I asked.

"Sometimes—and it's such a scary feeling—" she said, "I feel as if I can hardly remember what he looked like. I only feel close to Robby when I'm at the cemetery. Many times when I walk out of my house at night, I look up at the sky thinking he's there. Do you feel like that?"

Anne Perkins: "When other people have experiences with your child that you don't have, and when they tell you about that, it fills in the whole person. That's why it's great fun to hear about some of the things Robert did with his friends. It's knowing the whole person, and just making the whole person. *Having* the whole person. It's that quest, of having the whole being."

251

I interrupted: "Do you mean that he's only in your memories now, and you want all of him that you can get?"

Anne got excited: "Yeah, that's it. That's a very good way to put it. Yeah, that's exactly it. It's the experiences that other people have. It's your own experiences. It's trying to get all of what he was."

The parents can't remember what their children looked like, they feel close to their children. The children are in heaven, in the past, in nature, in the sky, in everyone's memories of them. Parents routinely fancy their children in animals and birds; T.C. is sometimes in an orange cat that walks into our house and looks at the pictures. The children are inside and all around these parents. And an occasional parent finds the child in another person altogether.

Mitch Dudnikov: "It's interesting, we were introduced to a young lady. I liked her right away, my wife liked her. To make a long story short, she was almost a reincarnation of my son. She curls her hair around her fingers like Marc did. And she cannot sit still. Same thing, Marc. And I'm going to show you something."

Mitch got a piece of paper and wrote on it, "Marcia Bove." "That's her name," he said. "I want you to see something, this is silly."

He rewrote her name, spacing the letters differently: "Marc I above."

"Marc I above," he said. "Because he had a little sign on his door, Marc I. It's silly, it's silly. But when I looked at that, I said, 'My God. It's just like—.'"

"Do you keep up with her?" I asked.

"Oh *yes,*" he said, "oh yes. She lost her mother, and we've adopted her. She'll come Tuesday at eight, 'I was in the neighborhood, I decided to stop by.' 'Did you eat supper yet?' 'No, I'm going to go home.' 'Well, I'll make you salad and tuna fish.' She has some friends that we like very much also, so we've taken in those friends, semi-adopted."

Joan Gresser: "*My* problem was when my grandson was born. During my daughter Jody's whole pregnancy, I got very obsessive. There wasn't a day I wasn't calling five times, 'How *are* you?' She finally said, "'*Don't* call me.' So I didn't call her. And the baby was born

February the twenty-eighth—on that week when Teddy was missing before they found him, our Michael was born. And then I was very obsessive with *him*. I didn't know it, it was really not on a conscious level. And finally my husband sat me down and said, 'Now listen, you don't know what you're doing.' We talked about it, and I said, 'Boy, here's something that I never thought, that I would look at this little boy and it was just like saying, Is this going to give me a second chance?' It was almost as if I wanted to put him inside me. I had a compulsion with this child. So Jody and I talked about it. And she said, 'Mom, I knew. But part of me said, I owe this to my mother, to have a son, a grandson. The other part of me said, I'm going to kill my mother if she doesn't back off.' So we laughed about it and it worked out fine. I still feel obsessive about Michael, but it's not where he could be affected by it; it's just that he will *always* be special in my heart. Because I know that genetically, he's his uncles. They're living with him."

So if the problem is what to do with a child who's gone and cannot be separate, the parents' solution is to balance pain against small continuations. If the question is where the child now is, the answer is in and around the parents, now and then in other people. If the problem is to hold on or to let go, the parents worry, they go back and forth, they contradict themselves, but they don't let go.

Researchers found the same. One study found parents, seven to nine years after their children had died of cancer, talking not about letting go but about an empty space in their lives. Some of these parents reacted to the emptiness by saying it had no effect on their present lives. Others tried to fill the emptiness with distractions, by working more, or having another child, or getting divorced, or getting involved with organizations. And a third group of parents found ways of keeping connections with their dead children. None of these different reactions, said the researchers, "is suggested as superior to the others."

One researcher who studies Israeli parents whose sons died in the Arab-Israeli wars, says that compared to nonbereaved parents, bereaved parents talked about their sons as less independent, less distinct from themselves. The researcher found that bereaved parents have two tracks in their lives: one is daily functioning; the other is "more covert," an "ongoing relationship to the internal representation of the child."

Dennis Klass agrees and calls this an "interaction with the inner representation of the dead child." Inner representations, he says, are partly the parent's persona with the child, partly the memories of the child, and partly the emotional states connected with the parent's persona and the memories. The interactions include a sense of presence, or dreams and hallucinations, or "conscious incorporation" of the characteristics of the dead child into the parent. "The child lives on," Klass writes, "in the virtues and character of the child that the parent now takes as his/her own."

The child does live on. "Walter started watching teenage movies," said Elaine. "I say, 'Why are you watching this garbage, Walter?' Then all of a sudden it dawned on me—because, of course, Merrill had never gone beyond that. And Walter likes the rock and roll from that era. I never realized it—why is he into this trash? That's exactly where Merrill left off."

Unlike Walter, most parents don't continue their children's lives in the way the children would have done it. The clearest, most obvious way of continuing the child is to set up some memorial that somehow promotes what the child would have done, or to do something that the parents would ordinarily have done for the child. Ginny, whose son died of cancer, volunteers on the pediatric oncology ward where her son died, and established a research fund for pediatric oncology research. The Levins set up a scholarship at Merrill's high school. Mitch, whose son was going to be a doctor, funded aid to medical students: "We're about eight years ahead in our contributions," he said.

Nickie: "My husband took Adam to work one day and they saw a homeless person, and Adam said, 'Can't we give him something?' My husband said to me, 'Nickie, when we were ten, we made fun of people like that.' So I want to continue that charitableness. We established a scholarship in Adam's memory and we've raised a lot of money. Adam's been gone six and a half years and we've raised over $40,000. So it's like an—I don't know—extension."

Octavia's son, Erin, was shot by another young man, who was caught and put in the state penitentiary. Octavia, who has been a special education teacher in an inner-city school, is justifiably frustrated with her job and its future. Recently, she began working on a master's degree to license her to become a school counselor. I asked her if she thought she'd like counseling. "I think so," she said, "because if there's something I can do to keep some kid from ending up in the penitentiary or on drugs, or getting them out of a bad home atmosphere . . . I think with these kids, it's not working. So something else has to work. Because right now, every time I pick up a newspaper and read about another black youth killed, it just discourages me. I think with my son, I can't do anything any more. But maybe, some other child. Maybe that in turn will help me to not miss Erin so much."

Notice that Octavia isn't setting up memorials, she's changing the direction of her life. Loretta's done the same. "Our son, Mike, was nineteen and he was in college—it was his second year—studying criminal justice," Loretta said. "He was on his way home and a car ran a red light—it was estimated at ninety-five miles an hour—and hit our son's car. And the boy that killed Mike never got anything but four hundred hours community service."

When Loretta talked, she jumped around in her logic; she seemed to think I was smart enough that she didn't have to explain every little thing. So because I wasn't quite as smart as she thought I was, some of her story seems disjointed. She had apparently found out that the boy driving the car was legally a juvenile but also had alcohol problems: "That boy who killed my son, at seventeen years old—I got his record pulled, I saw it—he had fifteen things on his record. I did not know that we did not have a law, if a juvenile is convicted—and he got convicted of second-degree vehicular homicide—it wasn't mandatory that he be put in rehabilitation. That, I thought, was bad.

I didn't want to see him go to jail; what good would it do to put him behind bars? No good. I just wanted that boy to get help. I had to see that nobody else could drink to the extent that that boy did."

So Loretta put her case to the family court: "I'm not asking you to put him in jail," she said, "I'm asking you to put him in rehabilitation. I explained to them why I felt that way. But they gave him four hundred hours community service."

So Loretta took her case to the state legislature, and finally to the state's attorney general. "And I told them I wanted to get a bill passed so if this did happen to somebody else, they wouldn't have to go through this with the system like I did. To make a long story short, I did get the bill passed. It took me three years, but if a juvenile is convicted of alcohol or drugs, the court can't let them go."

"They have to go to rehabilitation?" I asked.

"Yes," she said, "that or juvenile school. It took me three years but I was bound and determined. I did it. I still do it."

"Were you an activist before Mike died?" I asked.

"No," she said. "No. No. No. No. I think I did what I did because Mike—from studying criminal justice in college and working with policemen—thought that we had the best justice system. I do it for Mike."

This is what Klass meant by saying the child lives on in the virtues and character the parents now take as their own. When Nickie raises money for charity, and Octavia trains for counseling, and Loretta is politically active, they seem to hear the child's voice inside their heads, or the child seems to look through their eyes and act through their actions. I think the parents insert the children into their lives and continue living, one person now, parent-and-child.

This is difficult to describe. It's as if the child's life was a forward momentum that death interrupted, like a sudden stop in the middle of a song or a dance or a long pass, and the interruption is intolerable. If the parent doesn't let go, the child's trajectory continues via the parent. This trajectory is neither the child's original path nor the parent's; it's somewhere between. A physicist friend who also reads palms told me my life line stopped, then resumed but at a different angle. He said he didn't understand this, and I didn't believe enough in palm-reading to want to explain it to him.

This new, joint trajectory is obvious not only in Loretta, Octavia, and Nickie, but also in the profiles. During the interviews, some parents became terrifically happy talking about something that often seemed peripheral to the subject of the interview. Eventually I learned to look for the connection between whatever they were happy about, and the child.

Leight, for instance, missed doing things with Johnny and talking to him, so Leight volunteers in a hospice program and sits and talks with people who are dying. Chris worried that he hadn't listened enough to Mary; between his other daughter and the Seasons suicide bereavement group, he spends a lot of time listening, especially to people "during their times of difficulty." Anne's son, Robert, loved adventures and was just on the brink of flourishing; Anne has since quit her job, worked in China, came back and got another job, quit that, and is now working in South Africa. All the parents profiled said that these were things they wouldn't otherwise have done; none were aware of the connection.

Here are two last stories.

Walter Farnandis's son, James, was eighteen when he was killed in a motorcycle accident.

"I think the death of your child shows you can be washed out to sea at any moment," said Walter. "That's why, at this point in life, I'm not worried about getting ahead in the world. I've amounted to everything I'm going to amount to. From here on out, it's pleasure."

I interviewed Walter in his tidy and beautiful living room. Next to the couch on which I sat was a table, and on the table was a school picture of James, who, as Walter says, was a good-looking boy. "When James first died," he said, "I put that high school picture of his away. Then I said, 'I don't want to do that. I want that out.'"

Walter sat across from me, in direct line of sight with the picture, in a chair that was obviously his. Walter began, as many parents did, by telling me about raising James, about James's death, and about the next few years. He said he cried a lot: "I always said Jesus wept. There are a lot of tears with this."

"Are there any times that are particularly painful?" I asked.

Not really, he said. "Right now, the only time it's painful is when I sit down and talk about it in detail like I'm doing to you."

Then he reached over to the picture and pulled out of the frame a piece of newspaper with the words to a song on it. "I found this someplace," he said, and read it out loud:

"'Above all the rest, / I'll miss you the most / And I loved you the best. / I thank God I was blest / Just to know you. / But it's all right now. / Keep on singing loud. / It's all right now. / I want you to be proud.'"

He stuck the song back in the frame and said, "I don't know where I found it. I noticed it because of James, found it six months or so after he died."

Then he told me more of his life story. He still practices law. A few years after James died, he remarried, divorced again, and remarried. "When my other wife left me," he said, "I stayed home three months and she didn't come home. So I went out. This first place I went had a piano bar. So I started singing. And then this karaoke thing came along, and man, I'm in that thing with both feet."

Karaoke is an arrangement by which a voice can be edited out of a recording, the backup music left on, and the aspiring singer can then insert his own voice. In fact, people in the audience take turns getting up in front of each other and performing.

"I only knew one song then," Walter continued, "'When Your Old Wedding Ring Was New.' Anyway, this woman who came in there all the time, she wrote me the words to seventy-five songs. So I made photocopies; so then I had the words to seventy-five songs. Then I bought a book of Broadway songs, then a book of Frank Sinatra songs, and after about a year, I thought I would take lessons. I got hold of a teacher who did wonders with me, got me to sing high notes. I'm out singing two nights a week, and I'm good, I'm *good*. I'm seventy-two years old and I'm up there singing 'Taking Care of

Business' and shaking, and I'm *good*. You're going to have to listen to a tape before you leave."

At this point, Walter stood up and showed how he shakes his body, and I did indeed have to listen to a tape before I left. "Two nights a week is about all my constitution will stand," he said.

Walter sat back down and continued. "This would have probably never happened if things had been smooth. And it's been a big help to me. My wife, she fusses at me because I get in at twelve at night. But I have to keep my mind active. If I sit here and talk to her, I'll start looking at that picture of James and then the subject will go back to James and then I'll start feeling bad, you know? So I think the best way to get over something like that is to find something you're interested in that will keep your mind off what happened."

I went on with the questions: "Some people say a part of them has died," I said. "Do you agree?"

"I think that's true," he said. "You try to substitute something to fill that part, that gap. Which fortunately for me, I found. I probably just lucked into this singing."

I thought about that poem, "Keep on singing loud," and I asked, "Any connection between James and the singing?"

"I've never thought of it this way before," he said, "but it may be that the love for him has transcended into singing."

Louise Lewis's son, Michael, died in 1975. Afterward, Louise become one of the early leaders of her local chapter of Compassionate Friends. I asked her whether she thought she was over Michael's death, and what did she think "over it" meant. Louise took off on a roll, telling her story, pausing politely now and then to let me ask other questions, then continuing as though I hadn't asked. The whole interview was her answer to that one question, was she over it?

"Michael had just received his masters degree in land planning and urban development," she said, "and he was in partnership with his father in the construction business. And he was superintendent of a townhouse project in Baltimore County. And he'd been on the job exactly six months."

Then she told how Michael had been shot to death, and later, how she went to the murderer's trial: "Of course I was going to kill this person, but I didn't. I was, I was going into the courtroom with a gun and kill him. Because my life was over and I didn't care." The murderer was sentenced to sixty-seven years, which, Louise said "suited me fine."

And of course her life wasn't over: "You come to some kind of terms and accepting that this is the way your life is going to be, so you function as best you can. I mean I wanted to get back into life, desperately, and I wanted to feel good again, and I tried my best to do that. So now I feel I've recovered about as much as I'll *ever* recover."

Then without missing a beat, she changed the subject: "We do a lot of work with handgun control, in Washington, D.C. So I do have an avenue to direct my anger and I started about three weeks after Michael died. Nobody told me how to do it. My husband and I went to Washington to see why an escaped convict would have a gun and what was being done about that. I'm still doing that. It's bizarre."

I'd heard about this. In 1988, the state of Maryland had banned Saturday night specials, partly through Louise's efforts. In the process, Louise worked on national party platforms, ran for state office, and organized the still-active Marylanders for Handgun Control. I remembered hearing that her gun-control work had won her some awards.

"Yes," she said, "a lot of them all at once. Got some *Newsweek* or *Time* award—think it was *Newsweek*—Volunteer for Maryland, and I got something from the National Council of Jewish Women, the Hannah G. Soloman Award, which was fabulous."

Louise barreled on through the interview, continuing her explanation of being over it.

"I had to go to see about this person," she said, meaning Michael's murderer. "This person was at the Maryland Pen. He's an animal. Did he ever say he's sorry? No. Nothing. I want him to stay in there. And I called maybe every other month, to see if he was still there because they have a lot of escapes. But two summers ago we were moving and I didn't call over the summer. And I think it was in October

260

that I got around to calling, and the answer was that he was no longer there. Where was he? He had earned a lot of points, and he was down at Jessup. Well, Jessup is the place that he'd already escaped from twice, OK?"

Louise called Jessup and made an appointment to go out there. "So I go to meet the counselor and he was very nice but kind of fidgety. And he finally ended up saying, 'I have something to tell you.' And I said, 'Well, tell me already.' And he wanted to tell me that there was a case came up that was called *Lee v. Robertson*."

According to Louise, in the court case *Lee v. Robertson*, the state of Maryland ruled that courts were computing prison sentences incorrectly, and the recomputed sentences applied to Michael's murderer. "Well, he was one of the people, and they reduced his sentence to forty-three years. He'd already been in for fifteen, so guess what, he was up for parole. Well, all of a sudden, I was thrown into this deep—defending my son who is dead and can't talk for himself. I was off the wall. *Fifteen* years later. I worked on it for nine solid months. It interfered with my life. I spent a lot of time writing letters. And I can send you a little article that I wrote."

She did, and several others besides. This particular article reviewed the complicated legal history of the convict's case, then ended: "I am tired of violence. I am tired of misinformation. I am tired of excuses. I am tired of earned points. . . . Victims and their families, by the way, receive no points. Is this truth in sentencing?"

Louise went on with her story: "I finally got a phone call saying that he was coming up for a parole hearing, and there was nothing I could do. I came away from the phone and it was totally fresh—I went all the way back to the moment that I heard Michael died. I got overwhelmed with grief all over again. I was a basket case. I don't know what I did with myself the rest of that day.

"Except they didn't know that I know that Parents of Murdered Children has a truth-in-sentencing plan. They sent out one sheet of paper to me, and I xeroxed it many, many times. It holds about twenty signatures. You get these signed, and you put a little story about what happened. I worked. I worked the stores, I left them everywhere. We got eight thousand signatures. I got four thousand and four thousand came in from around the country. And then my husband, Dick, and I marched ourselves over to the parole board, deposited everything, and we had an article in the *Sun* paper. And he did not get his parole. He will now not be heard for five years."

I asked, "Not just anybody could collect eight thousand signatures, four thousand by themselves and mobilize like that—had you done that before?"

"The only thing I had ever done," she said, "was once when meat prices went up in the market, from sixty-nine cents a pound to a $1.29, and I stood outside the Food Fair and said, 'Don't buy meat.' Otherwise I never did anything."

"What had changed in you?" I asked.

"From the time from the meat?" she said. "I was a follower never a leader. I think I'm still that way, but if I see wrong, I have to get it right. You have to keep tabs on the system, and that burns me up."

Then Louise and I, like old hands, discussed trials and parole procedures and victim impact statements. I told her that I don't feel that strongly about the engineer who was smoking pot and had taped his warning signal shut and so crashed his train into my son's. The engineer served his short sentence—half of it incurred for lying to federal investigators, half for causing the deaths of sixteen people—and is out, and I don't think about it much.

Louise was incredulous: "You don't have the anger toward him, that he should be punished?"

I started to talk about the hopelessness of real justice until it dawned on me that I would as soon kill this man as look at him again. I had the grace to backtrack and agree; I am angry.

"Doesn't that jolt you?" she asked. "How angry do you think your son would be? I think about how angry Michael would be. And his voice is silent. Yet you say, 'Are you over it?' No. You just don't. I don't think 'over it' is the word you want to use."

Robert Weiss once said that he thinks some bereaved parents end up with a mission in life. "The mission comes late," he said, "but with enormous force." I think this mission is what I'm calling the one-person–now trajectory.

This book should properly end with how I continue T.C.'s trajectory. I really don't know. As I said, the parents weren't especially conscious of these trajectories; I noticed them because I was looking for them. The signs were small, for example, the same words used in different contexts: "aware" for Chris Reed, "angry" for Louise and for Janet Wright, "singing" for Walter Farnandis. But whatever I'm doing, if I'm doing anything, it isn't conscious.

T.C. wanted to be an artist, a photographer. I had always wanted to be an artist too, but a novelist. I thought I never had the courage, but I see now that I've never had the interest. I am less interested in stories about an imaginary world and more interested in stories about the real one. True, T.C.'s photographs were also of the real world, but I think that's just a taste we had in common; besides, I started writing about science before he chose photography. In other words, I'd be writing the same articles and books even if T.C. hadn't died.

I wouldn't have written this book, though. And if I had written a book on another subject, I wouldn't have gone about it the way I've gone about this one. T.C. was normally reserved; he once told me coolly that T.C. stood for Total Control. But once he hit art school, he exploded. He was wildly excited and intensely focused. He must have been waiting his whole life to do this. This book, too, was nearly an obsession; working on it, I felt the same hell-for-leather intensity. And finishing it, I didn't feel relieved but frightened. What would I do next? What will I ever care about so much again?

I'll find something, and I hope it's good enough.

Suggestions for Further Reading

∞

Chapter 1, At First

Bowlby, John. "Attachment and Loss: Retrospect and Prospect." *American Journal of Orthopsychiatry* 52 (1982): 664–678.

Braun, Mildred J. "Meaning Reconstruction in the Experience of Parental Bereavement." *Death Studies* 18 (1994): 105–129.

Brice, Charles. "Paradoxes of Maternal Mourning." *Psychiatry* 54 (1991): 1–12.

Brice, Charles. "What Forever Means: An Empirical Existential-Phenomenological Investigation of Maternal Mourning." *Journal of Phenomenological Psychology* 22 (1991): 16–38.

DeVries, Brian; Dalla Lana, Rose; and Falck, Vilma. "Parental Bereavement over the Life Course: A Theoretical Intersection and Empirical Review." *Omega* 29 (1994): 47–69.

Freud, Sigmund. "Mourning and Melancholia." Collected Papers, vol. 4. New York: Basic Books, 1959.

Klass, Dennis. "Bereaved Parents and the Compassionate Friends." *Omega* 15 (1984–85): 353–373.

Klass, Dennis. "John Bowlby's Model of Grief and the Problem of Identification." *Omega* 18 (1987–88): 13–32.

Klass, Dennis. *Parental Grief: Solace and Resolution*. New York: Springer Publishing Company, 1988.

Lindemann, Erich. "Symptomatology and Management of Acute Grief." *American Journal of Psychiatry* 101 (1944): 141–148.

McClowry, S.G.; Davies, E.B.; May, K.A.; Kulenkamp, E.J.; and Martinson, I.M. "The Empty Space Phenomenon: The Process of Grief in the Bereaved Family." *Death Studies* 11 (1987): 361–374.

Osterweis, Morris; Solomon, Fredric; and Green, Morris, eds. *Bereavement: Reactions, Consequences, and Care.* Washington, D.C.: National Academy Press, 1984.

Parkes, Colin Murray. *Bereavement: Studies of Grief in Adult Life.* 2nd American ed. Madison, Connecticut: International Universities Press, 1987.

Raphael, Beverley. *The Anatomy of Bereavement.* New York: Basic Books, 1983.

Rodgers, Beth, and Cowles, Kathleen. "The Concept of Grief: An Analysis of Classical and Contemporary Thought." *Death Studies* 15 (1991): 443–458.

Rubin, Simon S. "Adult-Child Loss and the Two-Track Model of Bereavement." *Omega* 24 (1991–92): 183–203.

Sanders, Catherine. *Grief: The Mourning After.* New York: John Wiley and Sons, 1989.

Stroebe, Margaret; van den Bout, Jan; and Schut, Henk. "Myths and Misconceptions about Bereavement: The Opening of a Debate." *Omega* 29 (1994): 187–203.

Stroebe, Margaret; Stroebe, Wolfgang; and Hansson, Robert, eds. *Handbook of Bereavement.* Cambridge: Cambridge University Press, 1993.

Weiss, Robert. "The attachment bond in childhood and adulthood." *Attachment across the Life Cycle.* Edited by Colin Murray Parkes, Joan Stevenson-Hinde, Peter Marris. London: Tavistock/Routledge, 1991.

Weiss, Robert. "Loss and Recovery." *Journal of Social Issues* 44 (1988): 37–52.

Wortman, Camille, and Silver, Roxane. "The Myths of Coping with Loss." *Journal of Counseling and Clinical Psychology* 57 (1989): 349–355.

Chapter 3, Fathers and Mothers, Husbands and Wives

Bohannon, Judy. "Grief Responses of Spouses Following the Death of a Child: A Longitudinal Study." *Omega* 22 (1990–91): 109–121.

Cook, Judith A. "A Death in the Family: Parental Bereavement in the First Year." *Suicide & Life-Threatening Behavior* 13 (1983): 42–61.

Dyregrov, Atle, and Matthiesen, Stig. "Similarities and Differences in Mothers' and Fathers' Grief Following the Death of an Infant." *Scandinavian Journal of Psychology* 28 (1987): 1–15.

Johnson, Sherry. "Sexual Intimacy and Replacement Children after the Death of a Child." *Omega* 15 (1984–85): 109–118.

Klass, Dennis. "Marriage and Divorce among Bereaved Parents in a Self-Help Group." *Omega* 17 (1986–87): 237–249.

Klass, Dennis. *Parental Grief: Solace and Resolution.* New York: Springer Publishing Company, 1988.

Lehman, Darrin; Lang, Eric; Wortman, Camille; and Sorenson, Susan. "Long-Term Effects of Sudden Bereavement: Marital and Parent-Child Relationships and Children's Reactions." *Journal of Family Psychology* 2 (1989): 344–367.

Osterweis, Morris; Solomon, Fredric; and Green, Morris, eds. *Bereavement: Reactions, Consequences, and Care.* Washington, D.C.: National Academy Press, 1984.

Rando, Therese. "Bereaved Parents: Particular Difficulties, Unique Factors, and Treatment Issues." *Social Work* 19 (1985): 19–23.

Rando, Therese, ed. *Parental Loss of a Child.* Champaign: Research Press Company, 1986.

Raphael, Beverley. *The Anatomy of Bereavement.* New York: Basic Books, 1983.

Roskin, Michael. "Emotional Reactions Among Bereaving Israeli Parents." *Israeli Journal of Psychiatry and Related Sciences* 21 (1984): 73–84.

Rubin, Simon S. "Adult-Child Loss and the Two-Track Model of Bereavement." *Omega* 24 (1991–92): 183–203.

Shanfield, Benjamin; Swain, Barbara; and Benjamin, G. Andrew. "Parents' Responses to the Death of Adult Children from Accidents and Cancer." *Omega* 17 (1986–87): 289–297.

Videka-Sherman, Lynn. "Research on the Effect of Parental Bereavement." *Social Service Review* (March, 1987): 103–116.

Chapter 5, Brothers and Sisters, Sons and Daughters

Applebaum, Debra, and Burns, G. Leonard. "Unexpected Childhood Death: Posttraumatic Stress Disorder in Surviving Siblings, and Parents." *Journal of Clinical Child Psychology* 20 (1991): 114–120.

Johnson, Sherry. "Sexual Intimacy and Replacement Children after the Death of a Child." *Omega* 15 (1984–85): 109–118.

Journal of Adolescent Research. Special Issue: Death and adolescent bereavement. Vol. 6 (1991).

Lehman, Darrin; Lang, Eric; Wortman, Camille; and Sorenson, Susan. "Long-Term Effects of Sudden Bereavement: Marital and Parent-Child

Relationships and Children's Reactions." *Journal of Family Psychology* 2 (1989): 344–367.

Osterweis, Morris; Solomon, Fredric; and Green, Morris, eds. *Bereavement: Reactions, Consequences, and Care.* Washington, D.C.: National Academy Press, 1984.

Pollock, George H. "Childhood sibling loss: A family tragedy." *Psychiatric Annals* 16 (1986): 309–314.

Rando, Therese, ed. *Parental Loss of a Child.* Champaign: Research Press Company, 1986.

Rubin, Simon S. "Death of the Future?: An Outcome Study of Bereaved Parents in Israel." *Omega* 20 (1989–90): 323–339.

Videka-Sherman, Lynn. "Research on the Effect of Parental Bereavement." *Social Service Review* (March, 1987): 103–116.

Wheeler, Inese. "The Role of Meaning and Purpose in Life in Bereaved Parents Associated with a Self-Help Group." *Omega* 28 (1993–94): 261–271.

Chapter 8, Changes Toward Other People

Leahy, Julia. "A Comparison of Depression in Women Bereaved of a Spouse, Child, or a Parent." *Omega* 26 (1992–93): 207–217.

Lehman, Darrin; Wortman, Camille; and Williams, Allan. "Long-Term Effects of Losing a Spouse or Child in a Motor Vehicle Accident." *Journal of Personality and Social Psychology* 52 (1987): 218–231.

Lieberman, Morton, "All Family Losses Are Not Equal." *Journal of Family Psychology* 2 (3), 3/89: 368–372.

Ponzetti, James. "Bereaved Families: A Comparison of Parents' and Grandparents' Reactions to the Death of a Child." *Omega* 25 (1992): 63–71.

Ponzetti, James, and Johnson, Mary. "The Forgotten Grievers: Grandparents' Reactions to the Death of Grandchildren." *Death Studies* 15 (1991): 157–167.

Rando, Therese. "Bereaved Parents: Particular Difficulties, Unique Factors, and Treatment Issues." *Social Work* 19 (1985): 19–23.

Rando, Therese, ed. *Parental Loss of a Child.* Champaign: Research Press Company, 1986.

Sanders, Catherine. "A Comparison of Adult Bereavement in the Death of a Spouse, Child, and Parent." *Omega* 10 (1979–80): 303–322.

Videka-Sherman, Lynn. "Research on the Effect of Parental Bereavement." *Social Service Review* (March, 1987): 103–116.

Zistook, Sidney, and Lyons, Lucy. "Grief and Relationship to the Deceased." *International Journal of Family Psychiatry* 9 (1988): 135–146.

Chapter 10, On Guilt

Bohannon, Judy. "Religiosity Related to Grief Levels of Bereaved Mothers & Fathers." *Omega* 23 (1991): 153–159.

Demi, Alice. "Suicide Bereaved Parents: Emotional Distress and Physical Health Problems." *Death Studies* 12 (1988): 297–307.

DeVries, Brian; Dalla Lana, Rose; and Falck, Vilma. "Parental Bereavement over the Life Course: A Theoretical Intersection and Empirical Review." *Omega* 29 (1994): 47–69.

Downey, Geraldine; Silver, Roxane; and Wortman, Camille. "Reconsidering the Attribution-Adjustment Relation Following a Major Negative Event: Coping with the Loss of a Child." *Journal of Personality and Social Psychology* 59 (1990): 925–940.

Lindemann, Erich. "Symptomatology and Management of Acute Grief." *American Journal of Psychiatry* 101 (1944): 141–148.

Miles, Margaret, and Demi, Alice. "A Comparison of Guilt in Bereaved Parents Whose Children Died by Suicide, Accident, or Chronic Disease." *Omega* 24 (1991–92): 203–215.

Ness, David, and Pfeiffer, Cynthia. "Sequelae of Bereavement Resulting from Suicide." *American Journal of Psychiatry* 146 (1990): 279–285.

Osterweis, Morris; Solomon, Fredric; and Green, Morris, eds. *Bereavement: Reactions, Consequences, and Care.* Washington, D.C.: National Academy Press, 1984.

Parkes, Colin Murray. *Bereavement: Studies of Grief in Adult Life.* 2nd American ed. Madison, Connecticut: International Universities Press, 1987.

Ponzetti, James, and Johnson, Mary. "The Forgotten Grievers: Grandparents' Reactions to the Death of Grandchildren." *Death Studies* 15 (1991): 157–167.

Rando, Therese. "Bereaved Parents: Particular Difficulties, Unique Factors, and Treatment Issues." *Social Work* 19 (1985): 19–23.

Rando, Therese, ed. *Parental Loss of a Child.* Champaign: Research Press Company, 1986.

Raphael, Beverley. *The Anatomy of Bereavement.* New York: Basic Books, 1983.

Sanders, Catherine. *Grief: The Mourning After.* New York: John Wiley and Sons, 1989.

Shanfield, Stephen; Swain, Barbara; and Benjamin, Andrew. "Parents' Responses to the Death of Adult Children from Accidents and Cancer: A Comparison." *Omega* 17 (1986–87): 289–297.

van der Wal, Jan. "The Aftermath of Suicide: A Review of Empirical Evidence." *Omega* 20 (1989–90): 149–171.

Chapter 12, Job's Children

Bloom, Harold, ed. *The Book of Job.* New York: Chelsea House Publishers, 1988.

Bohannon, Judy. "Religiosity Related to Grief Levels of Bereaved Mothers & Fathers." *Omega* 23 (1991): 153–159.

Braun, Mildred J. "Meaning Reconstruction in the Experience of Parental Bereavement." *Death Studies* 19 (1994): 105–129.

Brice, Charles. "What Forever Means: An Empirical Existential-Phenomenological Investigation of Maternal Mourning." *Journal of Phenomenological Psychology* 22 (1991): 16–38.

Gordis, Robert. *The Book of Job: Commentary, New Translation and Special Studies.* New York: The Jewish Theological Seminary of America, 1978.

The Holy Bible. King James Version.

Klass, Dennis. "The Inner Representation of the Dead Child and the Worldviews of Bereaved Parents." *Omega* 26 (1992–93): 255–272.

Klass, Dennis. *Parental Grief: Solace and Resolution.* New York: Springer Publishing Company, 1988.

Lehman, Darrin; Wortman, Camille; and Williams, Allan. "Long-Term Effects of Losing a Spouse or Child in a Motor Vehicle Accident." *Journal of Personality and Social Psychology* 52 (1987): 218–231.

Sanders, Paul, ed. *Twentieth Century Interpretations of the Book of Job.* Englewood Cliffs, N.J.: Prentice-Hall, 1969.

Thearle, M.J.; Vance, J.C.; Najman, J.M.; Embelton, G.; and Foster, W.J. "Church Attendance, Religious Affiliation, and Parental Responses to Sudden Infant Death, Neonatal Death, and Stillbirth." *Omega* 31 (1995): 51–58.

Wheeler, Inese. "The Role of Meaning and Purpose in Life in Bereaved Parents Associated with a Self-Help Group." *Omega* 28 (1993–94): 261–271.

Chapter 14, The Zero Point

Bowlby, John. "Attachment and Loss: Retrospect and Prospect." *American Journal of Orthopsychiatry* 52 (1982): 664–678.

Downey, Geraldine; Silver, Roxane; and Wortman, Camille. "Reconsidering the Attribution-Adjustment Relation Following a Major Negative Event: Coping with the Loss of a Child." *Journal of Personality and Social Psychology* 59 (1990): 925–940.

Klass, Dennis. "The Inner Representation of the Dead Child and the Worldviews of Bereaved Parents." *Omega* 26 (1992–93): 255–272.

Leahy, Julia. "A Comparison of Depression in Women Bereaved of a Spouse, Child, or a Parent." *Omega* 26 (1992–93): 207–217.

Martinson, Ida; Davies, Betty; and McClowry, Sandra. "Parental Depression Following the Death of a Child." *Death Studies* 15 (1991): 259–267.

Purpura, Peter. "The Death of a Child: The Death of an Illusion." *Issues in Ego Psychology* 9 (1986): 20–24.

Rubin, Simon S. "Adult-Child Loss and the Two-Track Model of Bereavement." *Omega* 24 (1991–92): 183–203.

Stroebe, Margaret; van den Bout, Jan; and Schut, Henk. "Myths and Misconceptions about Bereavement: The Opening of a Debate." *Omega* 29 (1994): 187–203.

Wheeler, Inese. "The Role of Meaning and Purpose in Life in Bereaved Parents Associated with a Self-Help Group." *Omega* 28 (1993–94): 261–271.

Wortman, Camille, and Silver, Roxane. "The Myths of Coping with Loss." *Journal of Counseling and Clinical Psychology* 57 (1989): 349–355.

Chapter 16, Surface Ditties and Carpe Diem

Klass, Dennis. *Parental Grief: Solace and Resolution.* New York: Springer Publishing Company, 1988.

Parkes, Colin Murray. *Bereavement: Studies of Grief in Adult Life.* 2nd American ed. Madison, Connecticut: International Universities Press, 1987.

Chapter 18, The Nature of the Bond

Ariès, Phillipe. *The Hour of Our Death.* Translated by Helen Weaver. New York: Oxford University Press, 1981.

Blume, Mary. "A Child's Place in the Middle Ages." *International Herald Tribune,* January 7–8, 1995.

Bowlby, John. "Attachment and Loss: Retrospect and Prospect." *American Journal of Orthopsychiatry* 52 (1982): 664–678.

Dye, Nancy, and Smith, Daniel. "Mother Love and Infant Death, 1750–1920." *Journal of American History* 73 (1986): 329–353.

Egeland, Byron. "Failure of 'bond formation' as a cause of abuse, neglect, and maltreatment." *Annual Progress in Child Psychiatry & Child Development* 1982: 188–198.

Garland, Robert. *The Greek Way of Death*. Ithaca: Cornell University Press, 1985.

Golden, Mark. *Children and Childhood in Classical Athens*. Baltimore: The Johns Hopkins University Press, 1990.

Humphreys, S.C. *The Family, Women, and Death*. London: Routledge & Kegan Paul, 1983.

Kendrick, K.M. "Changes in the sensory processing of olfactory signals induced by birth in sheep." *Science* 256 (1992): 833–836.

Klass, Dennis. "The Inner Representation of the Dead Child and the Worldviews of Bereaved Parents." *Omega* 26 (1992–93): 255–272.

Klass, Dennis. "John Bowlby's Model of Grief and the Problem of Identification." *Omega* 18 (1987–88): 13–32.

Klass, Dennis, and Marwit, Samuel. "Toward a Model of Parental Grief." *Omega* 19 (1988–89): 31–50.

Myers, Barbara J. "Mother-Infant Bonding: The Status of This Critical-Period Hypothesis." *Developmental Review* 4 (1984): 240–274.

Parkes, Colin Murray. *Bereavement: Studies of Grief in Adult Life*. 2nd American ed. Madison, Connecticut: International Universities Press, 1987.

Plutarch. "In Consolation to His Wife," *Moralia*. Translated by Robin Waterfield. New York: Penguin Books, 1992.

Poindron, Pascal. "Genital, olfactory, and endocrine interactions in the development of maternal behaviour in the parturient ewe." *Psychoneuroendocrinology* 13 (1988): 99–125.

Romeyer, A. "Early Maternal Discrimination of Alien Kids by Post-Parturient goats." *Behavioural Processes* 26 (1992): 103–111.

Scheper-Hughes, Nancy. "Culture, Scarcity, and Maternal Thinking: Mother Love and Child Death in Northeast Brazil." In *Child Survival*, edited by Nancy Scheper-Hughes. Dordrecht: D. Reidel Publishing Company, 1978.

Scheper-Hughes, Nancy. *Death Without Weeping*. Berkeley: University of California Press, 1992.

Scheper-Hughes, Nancy. "Death Without Weeping." *Natural History* (October, 1989): 8–16.

Siegel, Harold I. "Effects of Mother-Litter separation on Later Maternal Responsiveness in the hamster." *Physiology & Behavior* 21 (1978): 147–149.

Smart, Laura. "Parental Bereavement in Anglo-American History." *Omega* 28 (1993–94): 49–61.

Sophocles. *Oedipus at Colonus*. Translated by David Grene. Chicago: University of Chicago Press, 1991.

Stone, Lawrence. *The Family, Sex and Marriage, 1500–1800*. Abridged ed. New York: Harper and Row, 1979.

Weiss, Robert. "The Attachment Bond in Childhood and Adulthood." *Attachment across the Life Cycle*. Edited by Colin Murray Parkes, Joan Stevenson-Hinde, Peter Marris. London: Tavistock/Routledge, 1991.

Weiss, Robert. "Loss and Recovery." *Journal of Social Issues* 44 (1988): 37–52.

Chapter 19, One Person Now

Brabant, Sarah. "Old Pain or New Pain." *Omega* 20 (1989–90): 273–279.

Klass, Dennis. "Bereaved Parents and the Compassionate Friends." *Omega* 15 (1984–85): 353–373.

Klass, Dennis. "The Inner Representation of the Dead Child and the Worldviews of Bereaved Parents." *Omega* 26 (1992–93): 255–272.

Klass, Dennis. "Solace and Immortality: Bereaved Parents' Continuing Bond with Their Children." *Death Studies* 17 (1993): 343–368.

Klass, Dennis, and Marwit, Samuel. "Toward a Model of Parental Grief." *Omega* 19 (1988–89): 31–50.

Martinson, Ida; Davies, Betty; and McClowry, Sandra. "Parental Depression Following the Death of a Child." *Death Studies* 15 (1991): 259–267.

McClowry, S.G.; Davies, E.B.; May, K.A.; Kulenkamp, E.J., and Martinson, I.M. "The Empty Space Phenomenon: The Process of Grief in the Bereaved Family." *Death Studies* 11 (1987): 361–374.

Osterweis, Morris; Solomon, Fredric; and Green, Morris, eds. *Bereavement: Reactions, Consequences, and Care*. Washington, D.C.: National Academy Press, 1984.

Rubin, Simon S. "Adult-Child Loss and the Two-Track Model of Bereavement." *Omega* 24 (1991–92): 183–203.

Rubin, Simon S. "Maternal Attachment and Child Death: On Adjustment, Relationship, and Resolution." *Omega* 15 (1984–85): 347–352.